AF709829

It's a proud business

A History of the Shelter Insurance Companies

THE DONNING COMPANY PUBLISHERS

It's a proud business

A History of the Shelter Insurance Companies

The quotation in the book's title is a remark made by former Shelter President Jack Pettit to Jean Madden in a taped interview, February 2, 1994.

Copyright © 1995 by Shelter Mutual Insurance Company

All rights reserved, including the right to reproduce this work in any form whatsoever without permission in writing from the publisher, except for brief passages in connection with a review.

For information write:

The Donning Company/Publishers
184 Business Park Drive, Suite 106
Virginia Beach, Virginia 23462

Steve Mull, General Manager
Nancy Schneiderheinze, Project Director
Mary Elizabeth Downing, Research Coordinator
Betsy Bobbitt, Executive Editor
Chris Decker, Graphic Designer
Dawn Kofroth, Production Manager
Tony Lillis, Director of Marketing

Library of Congress Cataloging-in-Publication Data
Havig, Alan R., 1940-
It's a proud business : a history of the Shelter Mutual Insurance Companies, 1946-1996 / by Alan Havig.
p. cm.
Includes index.
ISBN 0-89865-956-6 (hardcover : alk. paper)
1. Shelter Mutual Insurance Company—History. 2. Insurance, Property—Missouri—History. 3. Missouri Farmers Association—History. I. Title.
HG8540.S47H38 1995
368'.06'5778—dc20 95-39124
CIP

Printed in the United States of America

Table of Contents

introduction & appreciation

This is a business biography, a 50-year profile of the growth of the Shelter Insurance Companies. I use the term biography because, like individual persons, businesses take on lives of their own. The people who lead them, as well as those who perform their daily functions, give businesses personality, as do the geographical locations in which they operate. Beginning as a Missouri mutual casualty insurance company, Shelter has been primarily a Midwestern firm, with strength also in southern states of the lower Mississippi River valley.

Companies, like people, reflect their parentage. Under its original name, the MFA Mutual Insurance Company, Shelter was an outgrowth of the Missouri Farmers Association, or MFA, an economically important farm cooperative whose leaders in 1945 decided to expand its services to members by adding insurance to a list of products like fertilizer, seed, and tires. Although MFA and MFA Mutual (now Shelter Mutual) experienced a legal separation in 1980-1981, the farm co-op's story is at the center of Shelter's story.

Like people, business firms experience good years and poor ones, and over time they grow from youth into maturity and strength. Such has been the case with this company. In spite of unprofitable years, most of them shared with the entire industry, growth to strength has been the hallmark of this half-century-old firm.

Some companies, of course, sicken and die, just as people do. While, at age 50, the Shelter Insurance Companies are healthy and strong, there were points in their history when threats lurking in the external environment or difficulties within threatened that health and undermined the strength. One goal of this historical account is to identify the factors that led to growth, and to analyze the strategies devised by the company's leadership to meet challenges.

Chapters 1 and 5 will detail two significant episodes in the company's life. The first of these events occurred in February, 1964, when the board of directors replaced J. M. Silvey with a new president, A. D. Sappington. The second turning point was a series of interrelated events played out over a nearly two-year period. It began in August, 1979, with the defeat of the MFA Insurance Company's Board Chairman Fred V. Heinkel as head of the parent company, MFA. The events concluded on Shelter Day I, July 1, 1981, as Gustav J. Lehr assumed the presidency of the former MFA Mutual Insurance Company, newly named the Shelter Mutual Insurance Company. So important are the changes of 1964 and 1979-1981 that they divide Shelter's 50-year history into three manageable eras: 1946-1964; 1964-1981; and 1981 to the present.

Every author writes to an audience. The readership of this book will be diverse, including those within and beyond the insurance industry. Readers will include policyholders, agents throughout Shelter's 13-state region, and home office employees. Residents of Columbia, Missouri — the company's home base — as well as of Nebraska City, Nebraska, Alexandria, Louisiana, Springfield, Illinois and other towns will pick the book up and look through it. Executives of other insurance companies may compare their operations with those of Shelter. My job is to write for all these people: specialists in casualty and life insurance as well as laypersons who have nothing more to do with the industry than make an annual premium payment.

This book is the work of an outsider: an outsider to the industry and to the Shelter Insurance Companies. I teach history at Stephens College and write history in Columbia. But though I am Shelter's lone and temporary historian, I have been made to feel a welcome member of the large family of Shelter employees and agents. I have sensed a feeling of belongingness and enjoyment of common purpose all around me as I worked on this book from the spring of 1994 into the autumn of 1995.

Many businesses in recent years have committed resources to preserving company records. Shelter joined this positive trend in 1994. It hired the Winthrop Group, represented by Karen Benedict. Winthrop hired Jeff Patridge to establish a corporate archive. Jean Madden, Shelter's energetic retired vice president of Communications, conducted interviews with retired management personnel and a number of veteran agents from several states. This book owes much to the efforts of both Madden and Patridge. As one who sees daily instances of the neglect and destruction of the evidence we have of past times, I congratulate the far-sightedness of Shelter President Robert W. Maupin, Executive Vice-President Raymond E. Jones, other officers and the board of directors under the leadership of Gustav J. Lehr, in taking these important steps to preserve and record the past.

I must thank others with whom I worked closely for the help and kindness they gave, and also for the freedom they allowed me as I rummaged through records and wrote about what I found. These include President Maupin, whose unique perspective on the insurance industry and Shelter grows out of 21 years' experience working for the Missouri Farmers Association and 15 years at Shelter. Ray Jones gave help and encouragement of many sorts. Lanny Barton, vice president of Communications, first contacted me about writing Shelter's history, and he assisted my work in many tangible and intangible ways. So has Gene Baumann of the Communications Department, who knows so much about the company's history that it seems arrogant for me, not him, to write this book. Gene selected the photographs which appear in this book, many of which he took during more than 30 years at Shelter. Four executive secretaries helped me by locating and copying materials, and answering my questions. They are Roma Wonneman, executive secretary to Bob Maupin; Karen Rohrer, executive secretary to Ray Jones; and Teresa Grissum and Doris Pistel, one who followed the other as executive secretary to Lanny Barton.

I also thank Maggie Wood of Shelter's Communications Department and Tom Apple of Training for help along the way. Maggie deserves special thanks. Her skill as a copy editor and her knowledge of Shelter Insurance made this a much better book than it would have been without her help. I am indebted to other readers of earlier drafts of the book, including Gus Lehr, Howard Lang, and Bob Maupin. All kept errors out of the text.

I appreciate the time and wisdom of those who granted interviews. They include the Chairman of the board of directors Gustav J. Lehr, President and CEO Robert W. Maupin, and former President Howard B. Lang. The following officers willingly granted interviews: Executive Vice Presidents Ray Jones, James Offutt, and John Lenox. Others who shared their recollections were Virginia (Mrs. Ray) Young; Jo Betty (Mrs. R. J.) Rosier; Arthur P. Lang; Paul Keithley; William H. Conboy; and James L. McTurnan. I also interviewed Mr. Jim Silvey, president of the Silvey Insurance Companies and son of former MFA Mutual President J. M. Silvey.

I need to say a few words about three problems of style which came up in the writing of this volume. The first is how to refer to the Missouri Farmers Association, or M.F.A., in brief fashion and in a way that will not confuse some readers about that organization and the MFA Mutual Insurance Company. In this account, for convenience' sake, I will use MFA or the MFA, without periods after each letter, to refer to the Missouri Farmers Association, the insurance company's parent organization.

The second and third stylistic matters regard the insurance company's formal name. It was MFA Mutual Insurance Company until July 1, 1981, and has been Shelter Mutual Insurance Company since then. In either case the mutual company owned subsidiary companies. As a matter of convenience I will follow the practice commonly used on the company's stationery, in minutes of the board, in company publications, and elsewhere, of referring interchangeably to MFA Mutual Insurance Company or companies, and to Shelter Mutual Insurance Company or companies. Finally, until April 6, 1960, at the 15th annual meeting, the M, F, and A in MFA Mutual Insurance had periods behind them, following the practice of the Missouri Farmers Association. In this book MFA will appear without the periods when referring to the insurance company. If these matters seem excessively technical to some, accurate nomenclature is important to those in the company who are aware of the proper names, and ease of expression is significant to this writer who needs to convey information to readers in a convenient form.

A final comment deals with the documentation of sources that I used in constructing this account. Pre-publication drafts of chapters included pages of notes following the text, but I have omitted them from the book for practical reasons. Few readers will be interested in knowing on what letter or set of board minutes a sentence or paragraph draws, preferring instead a more complete text. For those who do care about documentation, printed copies on file in Shelter's Corporate Archive and elsewhere in the Home Office do include the notes. With one exception, this account is based on Shelter Insurance Company's own records, kept in the Home Office. The exception is the collections of papers deposited by Fred V. Heinkel in the Western Historical Manuscripts Collection, University of Missouri-Columbia. I am grateful to the staff of that fine research facility for the opportunity to use the Heinkel papers.

Alan Havig
July 28, 1995

Darris and Terri Ashbrook, right center couple, bought the policies that put Shelter Life over that $6 billion in force mark in 1994. The other couple are Meredith and Pete DeWoody, agent in DeQueen, Arkansas, who sold the policies. Leading ceremonies at the Home Office on Shelter Day were Marketing Vice President Mark Zimmer, left, and President Bob Maupin, right. Maupin wears the commemorative T-shirt given all employees on Shelter Day. Zimmer has headed the Marketing Department through in-force milestones from $2 billion to $6 billion.

Part One:

FOUNDING AND EARLY GROWTH

1946-1964

chapter 1

Overview 1946-1964

The year 1994 was a satisfying one for those who work for Shelter Insurance Company. In January and February, with the past year's financial statements completed, company officers knew that 1993 had been the best year in the 47-year history of the companies. Highlights included an addition to policyholder surplus of $57 million, and a record total surplus of $431 million. The companies boasted a total policy count of 1.44 million. The combined loss-and-expense ratio was 101.5, "the best property/casualty performance since 1987, far exceeding the industry average of 109.2," in the words of CONTACT, Shelter's employee newspaper.

On May 20, 1994, Shelter Life Insurance Company reached a milestone: policies purchased by Terri and Darris Ashbrook and written by agent Pete DeWoody of Prescott, Arkansas were issued, pushing the Life Company past the $6-billion mark in life insurance in force.

While it had taken the company 18 years to reach the first billion of life in force, two years and two months sufficed to add the sixth billion. Impressive numbers! Landmark achievements!

One way to begin this book would be to say that no one in 1946 could have predicted that from quiet and modest beginnings, such a large and successful company could grow in less than 50 years. To begin any new business is to accept a certain amount of risk, and the odds facing a new business in 1945-1946 might have seemed especially formidable. The Great Depression of the 1930s was only six years in the past, still fresh in the memories of Americans. Many pundits feared that the end of massive government spending at the close of World War II would mean the return of hard times.

The men who founded the MFA Mutual Insurance Company left no record of such worries. But if they had qualms about the prospects that their new venture faced, company officials need not have feared. In retrospect it is clear that the immediate post-World War II period was a good time to begin an insurance company. MFA Mutual drew on the strength and support of its parent organization, the Missouri Farmers Association. In addition, perceptive observers could read signs of the economic boom that would begin haltingly in the late 1940s, but then surge through the 1950s and well into the 1960s. For the United States these would be good years economically, and good years, as well, for MFA Insurance to grow to maturity.

Newspapers in Columbia, Missouri — home of the Missouri Farmers Association — carried hints of a reviving civilian economy at war's end. On January 2, 1946, the first active day of business for MFA Mutual, the COLUMBIA DAILY TRIBUNE carried a story about the local housing shortage and also reported that military Quonset huts would provide needed teaching space at the University of Missouri's Columbia campus. In the years to follow, pent-up demand for housing across Missouri and the nation created an unprecedented building boom and created a wonderful opportunity for companies that sold casualty insurance. The G.I. Bill of Rights, which provided educational benefits and affordable mortgage loans to veterans, also helped insurance providers. People with college educations are more likely than those without them to think of insurance, and are better able to afford it over a lifetime. Millions of homes were built following the war with loans provided by the G.I. Bill, homes that needed insurance protection.

The January 2nd TRIBUNE also reported that half of America's auto factories had converted from war production to civilian car production. Although 1946 model automobiles were little different from 1941 models, waiting lists for new cars were long, and buyers, fat with wartime savings, had the money to spend. In fact, nearly 25% of disposable income earned by Americans since Pearl Harbor had been saved — an incredible rate of savings, accounted for mainly by the unavailability of consumer goods. Auto production and sales boomed during the next two decades, peaking in the mid-1950s. But as early as 1948, American manufacturers produced 5,282,000 motor vehicles, a number exceeded only by the output in 1929. More than 41,000,000 motor vehicles were in use at the end of 1948, while at the end of 1949 an 8.6% increase raised the count to over 44,600,000. The U.S. Department of Agriculture estimated that on January 1, 1950, 5.8 million automobiles and 2.2 million trucks were in use on American farms. By that time MFA Mutual, which in its early years was primarily an auto insurer, was a well-established company.

In the postwar years, too, the sheer number of Americans needing homes and automobiles — and therefore insurance — grew as never before. The "baby boom" swelled the population from a figure of 132 million in the 1940 census, to almost 180 million 20 years later. And Americans were a prosperous people in the years that MFA Mutual expanded into its 13-state sales territory. While they spent $120 billion on personal consumption in 1945, that index of economic growth grew to $325 billion by 1960.

Basing a new company's future on the sale of automobile insurance to farmers and small-town folk was a shrewd idea, whether or not company officials were conscious of national statistics. From the beginning of the automobile industry into the 1950s, a greater proportion of rural Americans owned cars than did city dwellers. And in Missouri there were many farmers and small-town residents during the years that the Missouri Farmers Association's new insurance company put down its roots. In 1930, nearly half of the state's population remained "rural" (on farms and small towns), and a safe estimate is that 40% of Missourians were rural in 1945-1946, when MFA Mutual began selling policies. Cars and trucks need good roads before they are very useful. In 1945, 68.4% of the state's farmers lived less than three-tenths of a mile from an all-weather road.

If statistics like these suggest that the post-World War II context favored the growth of a new insurance company — that opportunity was there to be grasped — it is also quite true that companies fail even in the most positive of circumstances. Leadership is crucial. The MFA Insurance Company had the benefit of the proven leadership of those who had built the Missouri Farmers Association into the largest single-state farm organization in the nation, and made its business enterprises into one of America's largest farm cooperatives.

At its founding and for more than three decades, MFA Mutual was only one of several Missouri Farmers Association affiliates which carried on varied economic functions for its members. MFA enterprises refined crude oil and sold petroleum products through retail outlets; operated supply warehouses, feed mills, seed and fertilizer plants, a grain marketing system, and local exchanges (stores); sponsored Department of Agriculture extension agents in more than 20 Missouri counties; organized livestock associations; and lobbied federal and state governments for legislation that benefited the nation's and Missouri's farmers.

Relatives of the seven farmers who met March 10, 1914, to found the MFA gather at the original Newcomer School in Brunswick, Missouri for the 65th anniversary of that first meeting and the unveiling of a painting which depicts the meeting.

Like the insurance company it created, MFA aimed to make a profit each year. But the profit was for its members, not for investors in common stock, for this farm organization was a cooperative, not a corporation. That is an important point, for MFA Mutual Insurance was not a stockholder-owned corporation either. The "Mutual" in MFA Mutual, and in the Shelter Insurance Company name as well, signifies that policyholders own the firm. The profits from a good year for the farm co-op benefited members through lower prices for feed and seed, and through investment in new plant and equipment. The profits generated by MFA Mutual's management returned to policyholders in the form of increased surplus against loss; reasonable rates on policies; investment in tools for conducting business, such as new data processing equipment; and, in the company's early years, dividends paid upon policy renewal.

The large and successful organization that the Missouri Farmers Association had become by the 1960s and 1970s grew from the vision of an inspiring agrarian prophet and skilled organizer, William Andrew Hirth. His German immigrant parents moved from New York state, where Hirth was born on March 28, 1875, to farms in Pike, then Audrain Counties in Missouri, when their son was young. At the age of 16, Hirth joined the Farmers' Alliance, a western and southern farm organization whose program included cooperatives formed to purchase supplies and market crops. After three years of college, and several careers practiced in Columbia, Missouri, Hirth established the MISSOURI FARMER AND BREEDER in 1908, a title soon shortened to the MISSOURI FARMER.

Through its pages, beginning in 1914, Hirth preached his version of the gospel of "cooperation," as 19th century Americans called it. He advocated organization by Missouri farmers of farm clubs through which they could combine to buy what they needed and sell what they produced, at better prices than what profit-driven businesses could offer. Behind the leadership of Aaron Bachtel, a successful farmer in the Newcomer school district of Chariton County, the first farm club organized in 1914. During the annual Farmers Week sponsored by the University's College of Agriculture in Columbia, in meetings held on January 2-5, 1917, Hirth gathered delegates from farm clubs to form the Missouri Farmers Association. MFA's first annual convention met in Sedalia on August 17 of that year.

Fred V. Heinkel, who became president of the Missouri Farmers Association following William Hirth's death on October 24, 1940, led the farm co-op to a membership size and economic impact that Hirth could only have dreamed about. The organization grew under Hirth's leadership even during the Depression of the 1930s. In

The MFA Headquarters, located between Columbia's business district and the MU campus at 201 South Seventh Street, was the first Home Office of MFA Mutual. The building now belongs to the University and has been named The Heinkel Building, in honor of Fred. V. Heinkel, longtime MFA president.

1933 it claimed approximately 18,000 members, and enrolled over 25,000 in 1936. In 1940, the year of its founder's death, MFA counted 32,000 members. In the first year of operations for the insurance company, 1946, MFA's membership topped 100,000 for the first time. The cooperative's economic impact grew with its membership. In 1944, for example, the combined sales of local exchanges and co-ops were $144,678,000, with resulting savings for member farmers of $3,976,000. During the early years of the MFA Mutual Insurance Company, the farm co-op continued enrolling members who were potential buyers of insurance: a total of nearly 120,000 in 1947, over 126,000 in 1949, and 142,000 by 1952. It was this vital farm organization that created a new insurance company in 1945, as World War II drew to a close and Americans focused their hopes on the postwar era.

Like most of us, the MFA Mutual Insurance Company came into the world unaccompanied by fanfare. A brief article in a Columbia newspaper on January 4, 1946 announced that both the Missouri Farmers Association and the Missouri Farm Bureau Federation planned to begin selling insurance in the new year. The MISSOURI FARMER, of course, carried advertisements and articles about the insurance company's initial coverages. No known records exist to tell us what MFA officials thought and said outside of formal meetings during the busy days of late 1945. But we do have the record of those meetings, as reported in the businesslike minutes of Secretary-Treasurer Russell J. Rosier, that give us insight into the beginnings of the present-day Shelter Insurance Company.

Fred V. Heinkel, shown here about 1950, saw the insurance company he helped form grow into Missouri's largest writer in a few short years.

On July 6, 1945, 24 members of MFA's board of directors met together with several of the cooperative's officers at the Daniel Boone Hotel in downtown Columbia. At the meeting were several men who would serve MFA Mutual as directors or officers during the company's early years. MFA President Fred V. Heinkel, L. O. Wallis of Springfield, Arthur Neuenschwander of Deepwater, Roy D. Hatcher of Shelbyville, John L. Meisner of Clarence, D. E. Ellis of Crane, and C. C. Collins would constitute the insurance company's initial board of directors. Among others present were Missouri Farmers Association Secretary R. J. Rosier, editor of the MISSOURI FARMER, H. E. Klinefelter, legal counsel A. D. Sappington, head of several MFA divisions, J. M. Silvey, and MFA's Director of Research, Herman Haag. This group of "founding fathers" included the first three presidents of MFA Insurance — Heinkel, Silvey, and Sappington — who would lead the company through the first 33 years of its history.

After the MFA board had attended to other agenda items, "Mr. Heinkel placed before the directors the advisability of the M.F.A. organizing its own Casualty Insurance Company and gave reasons why it should be given consideration." Silvey reviewed for the board the experience of MFA's Insurance Department, established in 1939 to obtain policies from insurers for local co-ops and exchanges. Haag reported on several matters, including the experience of other farm organizations which had sponsored casualty

Everett Van Ness, longtime fleet administrator, and his successor Doreen Nichols, with the company's 1942 Hudson, an identical vehicle to the one Fred Heinkel insured with MFA Mutual policy No. 1. The trophies are the result of car show entries of the authentically restored vehicle. The Hudson has been used in parades, displays, shows, and appeared in two corporate TV commercials.

companies. Attorney Sappington then outlined the legal procedures required to establish an insurance company. After a discussion of "some length," Secretary Rosier recorded, J. C. Breshears moved that the farm cooperative "proceed to organize and incorporate an M.F.A. Casualty Insurance Company. Motion carried unanimously."

The MFA board elected the insurance company's board of directors, and only then took up the question of whether the new company's policies should be assessable or non-assessable. As an early company publication explained non-assessable policies: "premiums shown on policies are all that can be collected — no other assessments can be made." Missouri insurance regulations required that any company issuing only nonassessable policies, which was the board's choice, deposit $100,000 in securities as a guarantee with the State Insurance Department. The MFA board authorized a timely delivery of securities in that amount to Jefferson City.

At its first meeting on September 26, 1945, in MFA's building on South Seventh Street in Columbia, the insurance company's board organized, and then concluded important items of business. It elected Fred V. Heinkel as board and company president, Roy D. Hatcher as board vice-president, and R. J. Rosier as the board's secretary-treasurer. J. M. "Jack" Silvey was selected as executive vice-president. It was he who would serve as MFA Mutual's chief executive officer until February, 1964: until September 30, 1949, as executive vice-president, and after that date as company president. The board authorized company officers to establish treaties with reinsurance companies, authorized the writing of policies for MFA members and local cooperatives, and agreed that the $100,000 in securities deposited with the state of Missouri be considered a loan from MFA to be repaid at an interest rate of 4% annually.

In its second meeting, the last before the company began doing business, the new board approved reinsurance agreements with the Employers Mutual Liability Insurance Company of Wisconsin and Employers Reinsurance Corporation of Kansas City, Missouri. It also determined the company's initial lines of coverage: automobile, general liability, and standard workmen's compensation and employers liability insurance. Chairman Heinkel's comments included a suggestion that was prophetic of the company's aggressive expansion into states beyond Missouri during the 1950s, 1960s, and early 1970s: since MFA Oil's refinery was located in Kansas, he said, the insurance company should seek permission to write policies in that state. Mr. Silvey reported that Wilbert Stone had been employed as agent supervisor, to recruit and oversee the activities of agents. The board concluded its business by authorizing a salary of $200 per month for J. M. Silvey as executive vice-president, to supplement the salary he would continue to receive as an officer in MFA.

Thus were plans carefully laid in the second half of 1945 for the founding of the MFA Mutual Insurance Company. Biographical sketches of the key individuals responsible for the new company will reveal not only their origins and the business experience they brought to the venture, but also the reasons they moved beyond the farm association's established supply and marketing enterprises into insurance.

At the time of MFA Mutual's founding, Fred V. Heinkel had been president of the Missouri Farmers Association for nearly five years, having succeeded William Hirth in 1940. Heinkel was born on September 22, 1897, and raised in the German farming community of Franklin County in eastern Missouri. Elected secretary-treasurer of the local farm club and livestock shipping association, Heinkel attended his first state MFA convention in 1924. The convention of 1936 elected him vice-president of the Missouri Farmers Association. Heinkel's career with MFA Mutual differs from those of other company presidents: he was not a lawyer, as five of them have been, nor was he a college graduate. Heinkel was a farmer himself, a shrewd practitioner of national farm politics, and an agribusinessman who never became so powerful or citified that he forgot the needs of the state's farmers. Witnesses ranging from MFA Oil President Raymond Young to then University of Missouri President C. Brice Ratchford have testified to Heinkel's influence in the decision to locate the university's medical school in Columbia, when powerful pressures mounted for placing it in Kansas City. Heinkel believed that an urban-based medical school would ignore rural Missouri's need for doctors. Likewise,

Heinkel's personal experience demonstrated the need for insurance. Returning to Franklin County from an MFA meeting in Polk County in the late 1930s, Heinkel stopped in Rolla for gasoline. As he resumed his trip, he nearly hit a boy who had fallen off his bicycle onto the pavement. Shaken, Heinkel called MFA headquarters in Columbia the next day to ask the co-op's Insurance Department about automobile insurance. Like most Missourians before World War II, he had none. "I want an insurance policy as quickly as possible," he recalled saying, "that will cover my car and me, too." When MFA Mutual began doing business in 1946, Heinkel took out policy NO. 1, which he retained until his death in 1990.

Mr. Heinkel's closest associate in the founding of MFA Mutual was Russell J. Rosier, secretary of the Missouri Farmers Association from 1929 until his retirement in 1973. Rosier, a "very quiet man" but a highly effective one within MFA, worked with William Hirth for more than a decade, then with F. V. Heinkel for more than three decades. Born on May 6, 1899, in Passiac, Missouri, Rosier became bookkeeper at the Adrian MFA Elevator and Supply Company in September, 1920, and later manager of that facility. The Missouri Farmers' Association was already a Rosier family tradition in 1920, as Russell's father, A. C. Rosier, was a founder of the first farm club, in Bates County and served as a member of the first MFA board of directors. In 1922 R. J. Rosier became a traveling auditor for MFA, examining the books of exchanges across the state. In November, 1928, at age 29, he became the organization's secretary-treasurer.

MFA Official Ray Young stated that the farm cooperative "got to be a big business largely due to Mr. Rosier's influence." He explained that during Hirth's presidency and the early part of Heinkel's, the secretary was the co-op's chief business officer. Only after the organization became "big business" did Mr. Heinkel play a more active management role. It was these two, Heinkel and Rosier, who came up with the $100,000 bond required of MFA Mutual by the state in 1945. Only they truly knew how immense a sum that was. As Gustav Lehr, then the MFA Insurance Company's executive vice president, commented at the time of Heinkel's retirement as board chairman in 1981: it was an act of courage to pledge "virtually all the assets then owned by M.F.A., Inc. to go into a business none of them had much experience in."

The MFA official who had the greatest amount of experience was J. M. "Jack" Silvey. It was he who was most responsible for establishing MFA's Insurance Department, the agency that was MFA Mutual's direct predecessor. MFA created its Insurance Department in 1939 to meet a critical need. Local exchanges and co-ops had to insure their real property and vehicles against loss and liability, but some of the insurers with which they individually negotiated policies were difficult to deal with. Increasingly in the 1930s, local MFA enterprises and members called for an MFA insurance company. An intermediate step was the Insurance Department, a licensed agency which obtained policies for local and statewide MFA enterprises from sound insurance companies. From its start, the Insurance Department seems to have had a long-term goal. A 1947 article in the insurance company's newsletter, for example, asserted that one purpose of the 1939 agency was "to gain experience and to plan for the formation of an M.F.A. Insurance Company."

In 1928, when R. J. Rosier came to Columbia as secretary-treasurer of MFA, Silvey began working as bookkeeper for the Gifford, Missouri, MFA exchange. Like Rosier, Silvey was born into an MFA family. His father, J. M. Silvey, Sr., retired from the railroad to become traffic manager for the MFA Grain and Feed Division in St. Joseph. The younger Silvey was raised near Gifford in Macon County, and, while a senior in high school, he began keeping books for the Gifford exchange. He familiarized himself with MFA's business operations while holding several out-state jobs. In 1938, Silvey came to Columbia as assistant secretary of the Missouri Farmers Association with three assignments: to manage a group of local co-ops that he organized as MFA Central Cooperative; to organize a Farm Supply Division for MFA; and to develop the MFA Insurance Department.

To help build the case for an insurance company, Silvey and Heinkel used the reports of Dr. Herman Haag, who came to MFA in 1945 from the University of Missouri's College of Agriculture. Raised on a farm near Poplar Bluff and fortified with a Ph.D. in agricultural economics from Cornell University, Haag headed MFA's Research Department. His "Report No. 4," probably issued in mid-1945, was entitled: "Expected Savings and Benefits of an M.F.A. Mutual Automobile Casualty Company." The anticipated savings were substantial, and together with other advantages, no doubt presented forcefully by Mr. Silvey, they persuaded MFA to launch its new insurance company. J. M. Silvey did not cut his ties with the farm co-op. He remained general manager of MFA's Farm Supply Division even after he became MFA Mutual's president in 1949.

The fourth key founder of MFA Mutual — the man who drew up the papers of incorporation and drafted the original policy forms — was A. D. Sappington, MFA general counsel. Legal expertise, which Heinkel, Rosier, and Silvey could not provide, was essential to a new firm entering the closely-regulated insurance industry, an industry in which lawsuits were part of the normal conduct of business. Unlike the other founders, Sappington was a native of Columbia. His father, Dot, founded the Central Dairy and Ice Cream Company in 1920, eight years after A. D.'s birth on October 20, 1912. The Sappingtons came to be known as civic-minded as well as successful in business. A. D.'s brother Roy, for example, served as Columbia's mayor from 1949 to 1953. In 1936, A. D. Sappington graduated from the law school of the University of Missouri, and joined Rubey M. Hulen, the MFA's attorney, in general law practice. Columbia's voters elected Sappington to three consecutive terms as City Attorney, the first in 1939, and, while holding that part-time office, A. D. formed a partnership with

The seven original employees of MFA Mutual in 1946: back row left to right are Glenn Denham, Arthur Lang, J. M. Silvey, A. D. Sappington; in front row are Jane Edwards, Louise Meyer, and Merry Clatanoff.

Hulen in 1940. When Hulen became a federal judge in August, 1943, Sappington became MFA's attorney. Beginning in April, 1945, he left private practice to become general counsel for the farm organization, for MFA Oil Company, and, after its formation, for MFA Mutual as well. It would be in 1957, as the latter was moving into its new Home Office building, that Sappington left his positions with MFA and MFA Oil to serve as full-time general counsel and vice president of the insurance company.

Financially, how did the company that these men founded fare in the years 1946-1964? The answer is: very well, very quickly. MFA Mutual defied the predictions of "experts" who assured company officers that several years of losses would precede the first profitable year. The record of these years, read 30 to 50 years later, is filled with signs of success that surpassed the best hopes of 1945. The following pages will chart the company's growth as measured by indicators familiar to those who work in the insurance industry and meaningful as well to those who do not. The growth in some years was slow, of course, as was true of the industry as a whole. But in most individual years and over the entire span of this era, MFA Mutual's financial record represented a company gaining in importance in Missouri and nationally. Between January, 1946 and

December, 1963, MFA Mutual grew to become the 27th largest mutual casualty company in the United States, as measured by premium income.

The authors of the company's "First Annual Report" (early 1947) reflected on a demanding year. Although "we gained a great deal of knowledge and experience . . . the actual operations of our company brought many new problems. Some of them were pretty 'knotty'." The personnel who had to untie the knotty problems worked in the headquarters of MFA, at 201 South Seventh Street at the edge of downtown Columbia, adjacent to the University of Missouri campus. The insurance company's seven original employees were: Glenn Denham, Arthur P. Lang, J. M. Silvey, A. D. Sappington, Jane Ridgeway Edwards, Louise Meyer (Mr. Silvey's secretary until he left the company in

Arthur Lang, MFA Mutual's first full-time employee, works at his claims desk in the office at 201 South Seventh.

1964), and Merry Clatanoff. Art Lang was the first full-time insurance company employee, while the others worked both for it and for MFA. Late in 1945, the fledgling company began recruiting its initial group of agents, who started soliciting business after the New Year holiday. Most, if not all, had connections with the Missouri Farmers Association: as exchange managers, as officials in local farm clubs, or simply as dedicated MFA members. Most agents sold insurance part-time and learned the business as they wrote policies. As untrained novices, many knew little about insurance and made errors ranging from poor risk selection to improperly-submitted forms. The company's earliest correspondence with new policyholders was typed on stationery of the MFA Insurance Department. A form letter, probably prepared in 1946, thanked the newly-insured for doing business with MFA Mutual and added: "We need your help, too." Word-of-mouth endorsements to friends would build a larger, and stronger, company.

MFA Mutual began business in 1946 with a contributed surplus of $100,000 provided by the Missouri Farmers Association. In September, 1947, the board of directors authorized payment to MFA of the $4,000 interest on the loan for 1946, and on April 6, 1948, the company repaid the loan itself, plus the interest for 1947. The

Table 1.1 MFA Key Indicators of Growth, 1946-1963

	1946	**1947**	**1948**	**1949**
Net Premium	$555,094	$1,274,636	$1,976,061	______
Earned Premium	347,818	1,040,131	1,717,661	$2,420,068
Net Underwriting Gain (Loss)	36,481	______	491,781	772,440
Earned Surplus for Year	5,193	147,409	272,042	347,3[illegible]4
Total Policy - holder Surplus	105,193	252,602	424,644	771,959
	1950	**1951**	**1952**	**1953**
Net Premium	$3,852,219	$5,349,302	$6,877,395	$9,813,086
Earned Premium	3,276,341	4,761,193	6,232,834	8,561,079
Net Underwriting Gain (Loss)	636,314	934,632	1,081,530	114,879
Earned Surplus for Year	335,781	341,274	261,594	378,086
Total Policy-holder Surplus	1,089,939	1,381,929	1,643,523	2,021,609
	1954	**1955**	**1956**	**1957**
Net Premium	$12,779,923	$16,194,586	$18,292,245	$19,010,397
Earned Premium	11,913,215	14,908,889	17,509,770	19,010,397
Net Under-writing Gain (Loss)	12,153	(601,756)	(1,260,842)	(353,179)
Earned Surplus for year	492,962	88,747	(397,289)	425,140
Total Policy holder surplus	$2,514,571	2,603,319	2,206,030	2,631,169

rapid settlement of the debt which made MFA Mutual possible reflected the company's early success. Rather than lose money during its first years of operation, the company increased policyholder surplus in each of its first ten years. Only once during the 18 Silvey years did it suffer a reduction of total surplus. By 1948 the Investment Committee was not only making regular purchases of U.S. Government securities and municipal bonds in $100,000 amounts, but also making loans to sister company MFA Oil. At the end of the company's fifth year, 1950, total surplus was over $1 million, and Dunne's Insurance Report for that year, as that rating service and later the A. M. Best Company usually did, gave MFA Mutual an A+ (Excellent) rating.

In 1951 the company became the largest mutual casualty company in Missouri, as measured by premium volume. By September 30, 1954, total surplus exceeded $2.5 million; and, after several years of slow growth, it passed the $3 million mark as of September 30, 1958. The surplus surpassed $4 million half-way through 1959 and was almost $5.9 million at the end of that very good year. Forty-four percent of the total surplus on December 31, 1959, had been earned in that year! By March 31, 1960, surplus surpassed $6 million, and in the first seven months of that year it grew by over $1

	1958	**1959**	**1960**	**1961**	**1962**	**1963**
Net Premium	$20,622,888	$22,524,712	$24,146,353	$26,274,145	$30,203,318	$34,393,704
Earned Premium	19,708,557	22,000,729	23,912,678	25,960,063	29,299,022	33,452,963
Net Under-writing Gain (Loss)	(322,058)	1,450,685	588,914	(573,768)	(1,004,861)	(1,369,004)
Earned Surplus for Year	673,809	2,574,100	1,875,338	1,051,585	611,329	587,434
Total Policy-holder Surplus	3,304,978	5,879,078	7,754,416	8,806,001	9,417,330	10,004,765

In March of 1948, the first branch office was opened in Springfield, Missouri, with Dwight Darby as manager. A second branch was opened in St. Joseph in June, with F. B. McCurry becoming manager.

right: Unlike the Springfield stand-alone office, the St. Joseph branch occupied space in a downtown office building.

million. Increasing sales volume and investment income pushed accumulated surplus past $8.8 million in 1961 and past $10 million in 1963.

As impressive as these figures are, two special features of MFA Mutual's operating statements explain why its surplus was not even larger. Over the entire period 1946-1963, the company paid $14,819,594.24 in dividends to policyholders, and $2,101,947.75 to the parent company, MFA. "MFA Mutual belongs to its policyholders, therefore excessive profits are returned to policyholders in the form of dividends" — so a 1947 company publication explained dividends. Paid to those who renewed their policies, the bulk of dividends went to auto policyholders during the company's first 11 years, although for some years renewed policies in all lines of coverage earned dividends. In 1957 the auto renewal dividend fell from 20% to 10%, and in subsequent years it disappeared altogether, while dividends continued on some other lines. Though reduced from earlier years, the company's total of paid dividends as late as 1961 exceeded one-half million dollars. The annual payments to MFA were in exchange for key considerations rendered by the farm cooperative, including access to its membership lists. The first agreement between the two organizations, signed in October, 1949, called for the insurance company to pay MFA seventy-five cents annually for each of its members. In 1952 the per capita payment rose to one dollar, and there it remained until the two organizations dissolved their ties in 1980. The total of dividends and payments to MFA, from 1946 through 1963, exceeded MFA Mutual's total surplus in the latter year by 59%. Had these payments been added to surplus, the total would have been $26,926,306 in 1963. On the other hand, of course, the company's actual surplus in 1963 of $10,004,746.51 existed in part because of customers attracted and retained by the dividend, and by the tie to MFA.

A few summary statistics further illustrate the impressive growth of the company to the year 1964. In its first nine years, 1946-1954, the company wrote $45,076,000 in premiums, paid $4,728,000 in commissions and $2,481,000 in salaries, and returned $6,375,486.75 in dividends to policyholders. By 1954 it had paid $688,335.75 to MFA and received $1,406,000 in investment income.

For the life of the company through the end of 1958, the MFA Insurance Company had paid $1,117,553.42 in federal income taxes, $2,121,606.87 in state premium taxes, and $321,364.32 in other taxes: a total of $3,560,524.61. As of the close of business on December 31, 1963, for the life of the company over eighteen years, net premium amounted to $257,120,866.11, and earned premium $246,063,251.77. For all five MFA Insurance Companies, on December 31, 1963, total assets were $47,270,000.

Yes, there were poor years during the middle 1950s and the early 1960s, and to some extent these resulted from problems shared with the entire casualty and property insurance industry. In part, the company's decline in surplus in 1956 and its slow growth in other years resulted from added expenses incurred in expanding operations beyond

COMMERCE BUILDING
M-F-A
MUTUAL INSURANCE
COMMERCE LOAN
COMMERCE
MONEY WHEN YOU NEED
COMMERCE LOAN & INV. CO.
CHRISTIE SCHOOL OF DANCING
AUTO PERSONAL LOANS
NO PARKING
RAINBO

The 1947 Missouri Sales Team: John Baumgartner, southeast district; Mike Spelman, northwest; R. E. Hoefert, sales manager; J. O. Creasy, southwest; W. L Stone, northeast.

Missouri, and also from less-than-careful underwriting. A comparative loss ratio statement prepared for the 1958 annual meeting suggests both the acceptance of poor risk and the increasing costs of auto repair. For all types of auto policies over the period 1946-1954, the loss ratio was 50.49; for 1955 it was 61.48, for 1956, 70.34, and for 1957, 72.38. The totals for all of the company's casualty lines were 50.19 for 1946-1954, 59.77 for 1955, 67.32 for 1956, and 68.91 for 1957.

In 1962 and 1963, the company again experienced soaring loss ratios, particularly in automobile policies. For the months January through August, 1962, for example, it was 75.0 on these policies. For January and February, 1963, auto loss ratios climbed to 87.56, while workmen's compensation was 116.24. For all of 1963, the loss ratios on auto policies was 78.88; in 1962 it had been 75.88. Perhaps the most telling statement J. M. Silvey ever made as chief executive officer of MFA Mutual occurred at the Annual Meeting in April, 1962. Reviewing the company's entire history, 1946 through 1961, he revealed that "there was only an under-writing gain of $64,890.26; and that of the $8,806,001.27 in Surplus, $8,741,111.01 was income from investments." The company's failure to record an underwriting gain over the long term was a concern to some company leaders.

The causes of the early and sustained success of the MFA Mutual Insurance Company are no mystery, but they deserve explanation. Some were external, including the United States' growth economy following 1945. Other critical external factors include the assistance rendered by the insurance company's parent, MFA, and Missouri's financial responsibility laws of 1946 and 1953. Other causes of growth were internal. The most important of these was the leadership provided by J. M. Silvey and the team he assembled.

The MFA-MFA Mutual relationship was multi-faceted and complex, and can only be suggested here through a few examples. The ties that were formalized in five legal agreements between 1949 and 1970 were expressed in many ways. For example, each August insurance company people served picnic lunches to delegates attending the annual MFA convention. First given in 1950 and expanded to two meals in 1961, the massive picnics were expensive to produce. On August 9, 1954, for example, 3,500 MFA delegates consumed 400 pounds of beef, 600 pounds of ham, 225 loaves of bread, 1,500 half-pints of milk, and other products of Missouri farms. The 1961 picnics cost MFA Mutual $5,253.58, but President Silvey believed the expenditure was fully justified and of benefit to the company. He regarded the food as a "thank you" for past business and access to future policyholders.

Although January 1, 1946 was a legal holiday, the new MFA Mutual Insurance

Company received considerable business that day. MFA's Insurance Department, under Mr. Silvey's direction, arranged for all of the cooperative's truck, general liability, and workmen's compensation policies with various insurers to expire on December 31, 1945. At 12:01 a.m. January 1, MFA Mutual picked up all of them. Another early boost to the insurance company was MFA's provision, without charge, of office space, equipment, and personnel during 1946. In 1948, MFA Mutual began writing hospitalization insurance because Missouri Farmers Association members were asking for it, and the MFA board of directors recommended that the company offer it. For years thereafter, MFA Mutual Hospital and Surgical Benefits group policies were sold through the farm co-op. In 1964, to help celebrate MFA's 50th anniversary, the MFA Life Insurance Company designed an MFA 50 Life Policy for MFA employees and members. Even after MFA Mutual's formation, MFA operated its Insurance Department, and that agency continued to generate business for the insurance company. Russell Rouse, the department's manager, appeared at MFA Mutual's annual meeting in April, 1962 to report that his agency had "developed approximately $640,000 in annual premiums for

The 1947 Claims Team: Claims attorneys J. L Parks, left, Ken Slankard, and Claims Manager Arthur Lang.

the MFA Insurance Companies." "Our success," MFA Mutual's First Annual Report stated, "would have been greatly limited without the help of the Missouri Farmers Association." The statement was valid at any point during the years 1946-1964.

To earn the business provided by the MFA and Missouri farmers, the company, in the early years, urged its agents to appear at the farm cooperative's activities and learn about the issues important to farmers. The first agents' bulletin, for example, advised agents to "make yourselves well known to the MFA exchanges in your territory and attend the Farm Club, meetings and other MFA functions." As late as 1961, all agents still received free copies of the MISSOURI FARMER, so that they would be well-informed about the parent organization and prepared "to answer the question so often heard from prospects: 'What does "MFA" stand for?'" Agents outside of Missouri may have found the publication useful for that purpose. Agent Wayne Skinner of Coffeyville, Kansas gave away 50 copies of each issue in 1959 and found that it helped his business to grow.

For some agents the MFA connection created problems. Outside of Missouri, the MFA and MFA Mutual names caused confusion. Within the state, non-farmer prospects wondered if they were eligible to buy policies. In 1949 agents representing other companies spread the falsehood that MFA Mutual paid claims only on automobile accidents that happened in Missouri. In fact, by that year the company had paid claims on accidents in 28 states, the District of Columbia, and the territory of Alaska, and stood by its policyholders wherever their mishaps occurred. MFA Mutual management found that negative attitudes and misinformation about cooperatives affected their operations. One instance of "false and harmful propaganda" was that co-ops and mutual insurance companies did not pay taxes.

Another controversy arose in 1954 which the insurance company would just as soon have avoided. Traditionally, farm organizations like the Missouri Farmers Association and the Missouri Farm Bureau Federation "sponsored" county agents, though they were public employees paid with tax dollars who worked out of the university's College of Agriculture. When the Franklin County MFA fired that county's extension agent in the spring of 1954, a statewide controversy erupted over the power of the farm groups, especially that of the MFA. With its political power symbolized by Fred Heinkel's membership on the university's board of curators, allegations flew about the co-op's tax-free status (untrue) and its use of county agents to promote its commercial ventures, including the sale of insurance (probably untrue, but unverifiable). True or false, charges like these had the potential to harm MFA Mutual. All things considered, however, there can be no question that the MFA affiliation aided a great deal more than it could have harmed MFA Mutual during its first 18 years.

Another external factor which promoted the company's early growth was state legislation, specifically the Missouri financial responsibility laws of 1946 and 1953. To a degree that seems irresponsible from a later perspective, many motorists did not carry insurance prior to 1945. Missouri's first Motor Vehicle Safety Responsibility Act took effect on October 6, 1946, requiring drivers to pay for damage to property or injury resulting from a vehicular accident. General Counsel A. D. Sappington, in the August 15, 1946 MISSOURI FARMER, generated a great deal of business for MFA Mutual with this statement: "The one sure way in which every M.F.A. member can protect himself is to secure automobile insurance before the accident in your MFA Insurance Company. If you wait until after the accident, it may be too late."

The law and the company's advertising worked. "During the months of September, October, and November, about all the agent had to do was take orders," a publication recalled in 1947. To this day, Shelter Insurance Company lore includes stories about agents like George Pearson in Columbia and Harold Remley in Jefferson City writing policies on the hoods of their cars in farmyards, and about the long lines of applicants stretching down the street from agents' offices. The company's first annual report (spring, 1947) expressed concern that some of these panic policies would not be renewed, but, in fact, most of the business became permanent. A second and more effective financial responsibility law took effect in Missouri on August 29, 1953, and other states in the company's growing sales territory passed similar laws in the 1950s. To

The MFA Mutual board of directors in the late '40s. Left to right are John L. Meisner, Roy D. Hatcher, B. M. Seaman, R. J. Rosier, secretary, F. V. Heinkel, J. M. Silvey (not on the board at this time), L. O. Wallis, D. E. Ellis, and Arthur Neuenschwander. All except Seaman and Silvey were members of the founding board in 1945. Seaman replaced founding member C. C. Collins on April 2, 1947.

take advantage of these laws, the board of directors authorized an "advertising and publicity campaign" in June, 1953.

In addition to external factors that explain the company's growth, there is an essential internal one. It is the people who were MFA Mutual: from top management people and members of the board of directors to agents in the field and employees working in the Home Office and across the sales territory. It is impossible to evaluate the quality of employee performance during the 18 years being considered here — except by inference and in broad generalizations. Never in the records of the board of directors or of policyholders' annual meetings was there even a slight hint that employees were exerting anything short of maximum effort to advance the company's best interests. In fact, J. M. Silvey and Fred V. Heinkel often closed annual meetings with words of high praise for all who had contributed to the financial results of a particular year. Of course, in years that saw underwriting losses, company officers expressed concern over poor risk selection made by some agents, a responsibility shared by underwriting personnel in branch offices and the Home Office. But, as revealed in 18 years of minutes and memos, MFA Mutual's executives regarded the agent force as the backbone of the company and a major reason for its impressive success. This attitude continues to this day.

The company's officers and directors in April 1952 were, left to right, Chester Meals, L. O. Wallis, Arthur Neuenschwander, A. D. Sappington, R. J. Rosier, F. V. Heinkel, J. M. Silvey, Paul Keithley, John Meisner, B. M. Seaman, and Sam Murrell. Seaman and Murrell retain emeritus member status to this date.

Many employees and officers who would be instrumental in MFA Mutual's growth in the 1960s, 1970s, and 1980s joined the company during these years. In late 1946, Paul Keithley began his long years of service, and three years later J. M. Silvey appointed him secretary-treasurer of the company. Also in 1949, Howard B. Lang, Jr. and Jack Pettit joined the claims department; each would later become president of the company. Arthur Lang, the company's first full-time employee, supervised the handling of claims for the entire state of Missouri in 1949. In 1952 Henry Kilburn was not only chief underwriter, but also in charge of training agents and employees. The company's roster of supervisors and department heads in 1953 and 1954 included these: Jack Huddleston headed liability underwriting in 1953 and joined Claims in 1954; John Pelot was chief underwriter; Henry Kilburn was production manager; and W. Judd Wyatt had become director of Advertising by 1953. Phil Dysart headed Endorsements;

Lloyd Krofft directed Statistics, Curtis Aufranc supervised IBM equipment, Kenneth Backues was in charge of Farm Liability; and Russ Shaw of Fire Policies in 1953.

A spot check of MFA Mutual's top personnel in 1959-1961 reveals this profile of leadership. Jim McTurnan, who began 1959 as chief underwriter, gave up that position to Jim Silvey in July, as he became vice president of Sales. Judd Wyatt's title in that year was publicity director. In April, 1959 William Toler became director of sales for the new MFA Life Insurance Company. William L. Redmon was personnel director, a position he would hold until 1981. In addition to President J. M. Silvey, the company's officers in 1961 were A. D. Sappington, Howard B. Lang, Jr., James L. McTurnan, and Paul Keithley. These listings of persons and positions demonstrate the quality people who filled important posts in the company.

The members of the board of directors also served the company well in its initial years. At a typical board meeting company officers presented reports on current

W. L. Redmon was MFA Mutual's first personnel director, a position he held until retirement in 1981.

above: John Pelot, chief underwriter in 1953-54.

left: Jim McTurnan held many jobs with MFA/Shelter Mutual from 1953 to 1982. He headed the sales, underwriting, and claims departments, but his longest tenure was as vice president of underwriting. He also served on the board of directors from 1982 to his retirement in 1985.

operations and recommendations for action. Reports included the company's current operating statement — for the immediate past month, for the year to date, and, presented in February, for the entire year. Directors took a more active role than simply vote to approve reports and proposals. Toward the end of each meeting directors and officers held an open discussion of the company's business. These men did more than attend regular board meetings. In October, 1955, for example, the company held six district agents' meetings. President Silvey urged the directors to attend, both to meet agents and to "become better informed to help direct the Company's business."

Early in 1962, five board members spent a week at the Home Office "studying operations to put them in a position to better assume their responsibility as directors." These training sessions became a regular feature of board membership.

Who were the directors of the MFA Mutual Insurance Company? Until October, 1958, the company's by-laws required that they also be members of the board of the Missouri Farmers Association. When the company applied to do business in Iowa, that state's insurance department objected to this requirement, and the by-laws were amended to require only that board members be policyholders with MFA Mutual. Besides having ties to MFA, all directors were from Missouri, most from rural communities or farms. In April, 1960, when the board expanded from seven to nine members, J. M. Silvey and A. D. Sappington became board members. Table 1.2 lists the directors during the years 1946 to early 1964.

The board room was a busy place during the week of January 9-13, 1961. The directors had come for "Directors Evaluation Week," to appraise the intricate workings of the companies. The five-day program included discussions with department managers and tours of those departments. In this photo, Henry Kilburn, director of agent training, answers questions from the directors. Seated in the background is Jim McTurnan, vice president, sales.

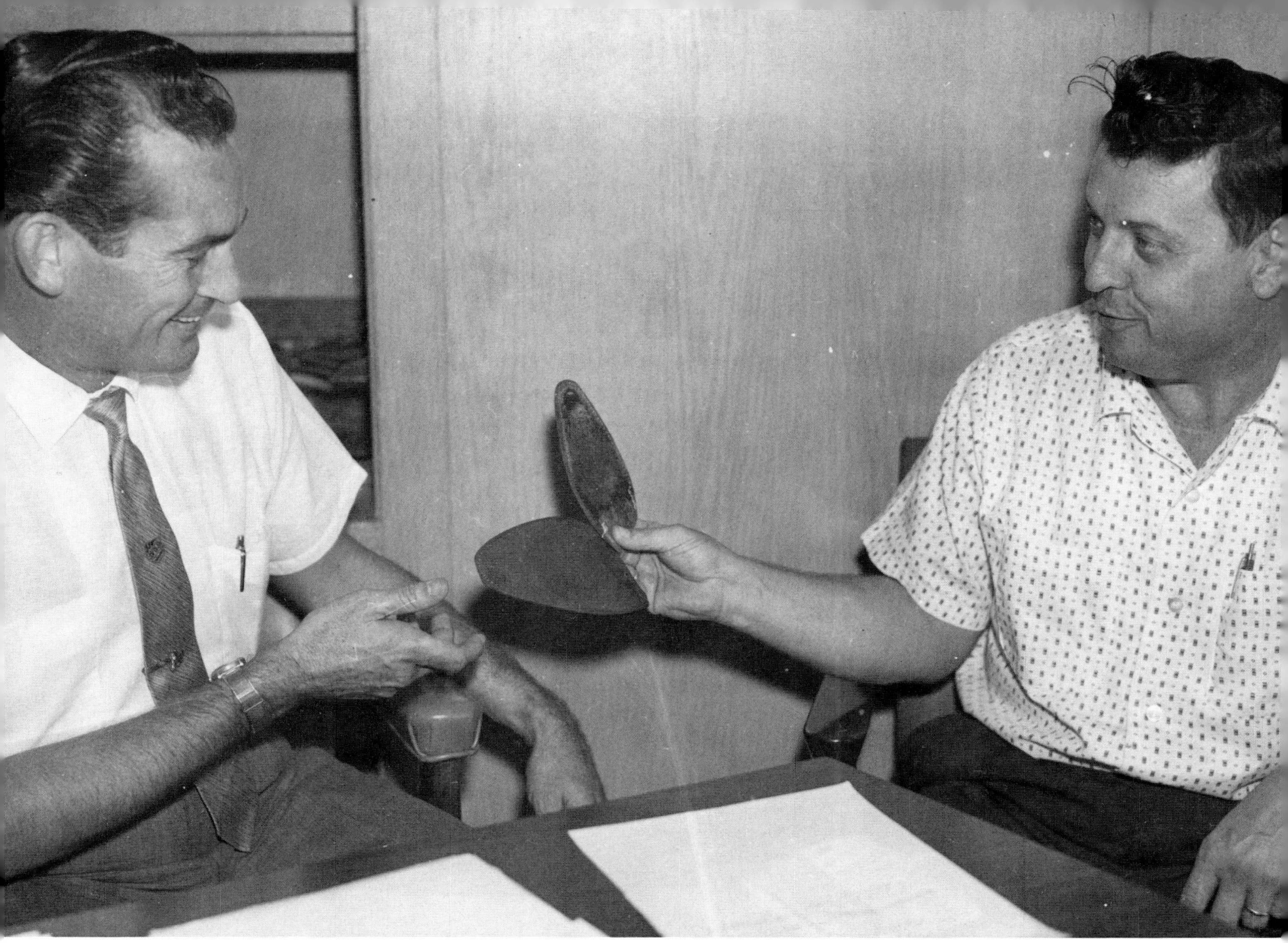

Marketing and underwriting working together in 1960 — Fire underwriter Fred Walden right, presents a pair of shoe soles to Missouri sales manager Tex Graham. The soles were sent to Walden by an agent who claimed to have worn them out while selling so many fire policies. Walden suggested there were a few more apps in them and they should be returned to the agent.

Enjoying the 1964 Charlotte Peters Show in Columbia's Hall Theatre are, left to right, Ron Wright, Ken Sanford, Larry Renfro, Don Northway, and Jim Royer.

Table 1.2 MFA Mutual's Board of Directors, 1946-1964

Member	Residence	Years of Service
Fred V. Heinkel, Chair	Columbia	1945 to 1964
Roy D. Hatcher, Vice-Chair	Shelbyville	1945 to 1952
L. O. Wallis, Vice-Chair	Springfield	1945 to 1964
D.E. Ellis	Crane	1945 to 1954
John L. Meisner	Clarence	1945 to 1957
Arthur Neuenschwander	Deepwater	1945 to 1964
C. C. Collins	(unknown)	1945 to 1947
Bernice M. Seaman	Ethel/New Boston	1947 to 1964 (succeeded Collins)
Sam Murrell	Lancaster	1952 to 1964 (succeeded Hatcher)
Chester Meals	Moberly	1952 to 1963
Miller Hern	Rocheport	1957 to 1964 (succeeded Meisner)
J. M. Silvey	Columbia	1960 to 1964
A. D. Sappington	Columbia	1960 to 1964
R. J. Rosier	Columbia	
Secretary of Board		1945 to 1964
Board Member (succeeded Meals)		1963 to 1964

Of all the company's leaders, no one was more central to MFA Mutual's success or shortcomings than James Madison (J. M. or "Jack") Silvey, the company's chief executive officer. Silvey was a strong leader. At a time when college training was becoming almost a necessity for management success, Silvey epitomized the self-taught, self-made man whose formal education ended with receipt of his high school diploma. Silvey won and held the personal loyalty of many employees and agents. His personal leadership is reflected in a comment by Bill Conboy that many employees and agents could have echoed: "We feel that your success is our success. . . . Jack, you've won respect and loyalty that is rare. . . . your well-being is the company's greatest asset."

J. M. Silvey adhered to high standards of personal morality and business ethics. Religion was important to him, especially after a close confrontation with death in a January, 1949 automobile accident. (He was insured.) An active member of the Christian Church (Disciples of Christ), Silvey persuaded MFA Mutual's board to make annual contributions to the Missouri Bible College, later called the Missouri School of Religion, located on the university campus in Columbia. Silvey scheduled the pastor of his own church, C. E. Lemmon, as an inspirational speaker at agent and employee meetings. Although he came from the Missouri Farmers Association, Silvey applied a principle that others at times forgot: MFA did not own the company; the insurance company's policyholders did.

James Madison (J. M. or Jack) Silvey served as chief executive officer of MFA Mutual from 1946 to February of 1964. He served as executive vice president until September 30, 1949, when be succeeded Fred Heinkel as president.

J. M. Silvey was not afraid of aggressive expansion: addition of new lines of coverage, creation of subsidiary companies, and expansion into states beyond Missouri. Silvey had a good investment sense, and most of the decisions about where to place the company's accumulating gains were his, by authority granted by the board. Silvey also designed the company's efforts to counter underwriting losses. His strategies — imposing more stringent underwriting standards, canceling policyholders with poor accident records, reviewing the performance of agents with high loss ratios, and adjusting rates on some lines — were conventional and perhaps too lightly applied. Concentrated in the late 1950s and early 1960s, these measures failed to solve the persistent problem of underwriting losses. Therefore, Silvey's investment skills had to be good.

J. M. Silvey: a man who led a new company to success between 1946 and the last full year of his presidency, 1963. What, then, explains his sudden release by the board of directors on February 20, 1964? A complicated, interwoven set of factors led to Silvey's firing.

It seems clear that Fred V. Heinkel and J. M. Silvey did not get along. Some sources maintain that their troubled relationship was of long-standing, others that it developed only toward the end of their association. Whenever it began, the problems between the two had several causes. Heinkel and Silvey were strong men who wanted to control the organizations they led. Unfortunately, they shared leadership of the same organization. In a defense of his record as MFA Mutual's president, issued a month after his firing,

As president of the Missouri Farmers Association from 1940 to 1979, Heinkel took a keen interest in the insurance company. He was chairman of the board of MFA Insurance from 1945 to 1981. This photo is from the mid-1970s.

Silvey mentioned jealousy of his salary as one element in the mix of factors that led to his dismissal. If Mr. Heinkel resented Silvey's pay is not and probably never can be known. It is true that Silvey's salary was double that received by Heinkel as board chairman — a not unusual ratio in corporate affairs. It should be noted that Mr. Heinkel was present at every meeting but one when the board approved raises for Executive Vice President and President Silvey and never openly objected to them.

Newspaper accounts of the February 20, 1964, meeting at which J. M. Silvey was relieved of his duties mentioned, in some cases vaguely, several other causes of the board's action. One was a "precipitate action" that Silvey took on February 17, the Monday prior to the change in management on Thursday. He fired Bill Toler as head of sales for the MFA Life Insurance Company, an act which Heinkel and the board reversed the same day that they released Silvey. Toler was a close friend of Heinkel, chosen by him to head the Life Company. Several persons who were with the company in 1964 have described the Toler incident as a "trigger" or catalyst of Silvey's removal as head of the MFA Insurance Companies. Also mentioned in public accounts of these events is the "Silvey dynasty" that the president was supposedly building within MFA Mutual. The reference was to Jim Silvey who had, indeed, risen rapidly within the company to the position of chief underwriter. No record exists to show who believed that nepotism was overriding merit in Jim Silvey's promotions. Former president Silvey's defense of his actions in both matters was simple: Jim had earned his job, and even if he had not, a dynasty was not possible in a policyholder-owned company. And Bill Toler was not performing his job up to expectations and deserved h is fate.

Another possible cause of a Heinkel-Silvey rift was politics. His long leadership of the Missouri Farmers Association made Fred Heinkel the prominent national spokesman on farm policy, one with predominantly Democratic party ties. The team which shaped the John F. Kennedy administration following the 1960 election interviewed Heinkel as the possible Secretary of Agriculture. During these weeks of late 1960 and early 1961, when it seemed that the top position in MFA might become vacant, Heinkel came to believe that J. M. Silvey was maneuvering for the job. That, at least, is what the Silvey family believes, although corroborating evidence has not surfaced. Suspicion created in 1960-1961, justified or not, could have found an outlet early in 1964 when triggered by an event like the Toler firing.

Or, when triggered by a remarkable meeting of the board of directors held on November 6, 1963, three and one-half months prior to Silvey's discharge. As he had done many times in the past, President Silvey brought a proposal for the company's expansion to the board for approval. Earlier, on October 29, 1958, the board had approved Silvey's recommendation that the company create a mutual fund whose shares agents would sell to policyholders. But only now, more than five years later, did the president propose implementing the board's endorsement in principle of the mutual fund idea. A mutual fund management company in St. Louis could be acquired, Silvey reported, and he recommended that the board purchase a controlling interest in it for approximately $400,000. He recited the ways in which the MFA Insurance Companies would benefit from entry into a non-insurance field. In the discussion which followed, the other company officers present argued in favor of diversification into mutual funds. They included Howard Lang, Paul Kiethley, James L. McTurnan, Jim Silvey, William Redmon, and Judd Wyatt. But, for the first time, a Silvey proposal met firm opposition. A. D. Sappington argued, among other points, that "the sale of mutual funds is contrary to the whole theory of life insurance." Board Chairman Heinkel opposed the purchase of the fund. R. J. Rosier, a member of the board for only one month, also rejected Silvey's recommendation. A director as well as company president, Mr. Silvey moved that the mutual fund's management company be purchased. No one seconded the motion, so it died. Quickly, the meeting adjourned. Never before had a Silvey initiative been openly opposed, much less defeated, during a board meeting. If behind the incident lay the failure of personalities to co-exist or dissatisfaction with persistent underwriting losses is not known. And it is hard to draw a precise connection between the November 6, 1963 meeting and Silvey's firing on February 20, 1964.

At a special meeting held in the afternoon of February 20, 1964, the board met "to consider the problems of the management of the company." Chairman Heinkel, who had called the meeting, cited low morale among employees "both in and out of the Home Office" as cause for making a change in the company's management. Heinkel said that he had spoken with President Silvey "some time ago" about the problem, but with no result forthcoming, it was time to act. Earlier in the day and during this meeting, Silvey was offered the chance to resign, but he refused. He now stated his belief that the morale problem did not exist, and asserted that the companies were well-managed and in "sound financial condition." With A. D. Sappington abstaining and director B. M. Seaman joining Silvey in opposition, a motion to relieve President Silvey of his duties as of February 20 carried. Mr. Silvey then announced that his son Jim had resigned as chief underwriter. Chairman Heinkel recommended Vice President and General Counsel A. D. Sappington as Silvey's replacement, an appointment which the board approved. Sappington and Silvey refrained from voting. Mr. Silvey then resigned as a member of the board. And so suddenly and, to most, unexpectedly, the first period of the company's development closed.

IN APPRECIATION OF YOUR SUPPORT
M·F·A MUTUAL INSURANCE CO.
DRINK
Coca-Cola
M·F·A
INSURANCE
CREAM
cane sugar
HOMOGENIZED MILK
VITAMIN D
MILK

Chapters 2, 3, and 4 will continue with the years from 1946 to early 1964, to explore in greater detail what chapter 1 could only suggest. The main theme of chapter 2 is the expansion and diversification of the company. Aggressively pursuing admission to neighboring states from a secure base in Missouri, the company operated in 11 states by the end of 1963 and planned for an even larger territory. During these years the company also expanded its casualty lines and successfully entered the life insurance field in 1959. To improve its service to present policyholders and to reach new ones, MFA Mutual under Mr. Heinkel's and Mr. Silvey's leadership also created three new companies and purchased a fourth, KMMO radio. MFA Mutual became an innovative corporate advertiser during these years and a nationally-honored promoter of highway and farm safety. As advertising, product diversification, and sales territory grew, so, too, did the need for office space and the technology to handle an increasing flow of paper. This chapter will discuss how the Home Office moved from the South Seventh Street headquarters of MFA to West Broadway in Columbia.

Remarkably, these forms of expansion all occurred at the same time. As company officers applied to do business in a dozen new states, they also devised — and trained agents and employees to handle — new lines of coverage. While they formed companies subsidiary to MFA Mutual and discussed possible diversification into non-insurance financial functions, they also adopted plans to build a new home office. To keep up with a growing volume of business, every function carried on in the home and branch offices had to expand: from marketing to underwriting, from advertising to claims. Little wonder, then, that J. M. Silvey and A. D. Sappington gave up the jobs they had continued to perform for MFA. The insurance business commanded their full attention!

Between 1951 and 1958, MFA Mutual acquired four subsidiary companies. In 1951 it purchased KMMO, a radio station located in Marshall. On November 15 of that year, the Federal Communications Commission in Washington approved the purchase. On December 14, 1956, the State of Missouri chartered the Securities Service Company (later changed to the Security Service Company), and three days later the board of directors first met. On November 11, 1957, the Missouri Secretary of State issued the charter of Countryside Casualty Company, and on December 12 it began marketing insurance policies. Finally, MFA Mutual founded the MFA Life Insurance Company: the Secretary of State's office issued the charter on November 13, 1958; and the company began selling insurance in early March, 1959.

Two of the new companies joined MFA Mutual in the sale of insurance: Countryside Casualty and MFA Life. Security Service Company and KMMO supported their sister companies in the sale of insurance. All four of the new firms were capital stock companies wholly owned by MFA Mutual Insurance Company. By 1959, a full family of companies existed.

chapter 2

Our Progress 1946-1964

left: An annual tradition at Missouri Farmers Association conventions was the MFA Mutual picnic, at which more than a thousand delegates were fed two meals by insurance employees.

William R. Toler headed the MFA Life Insurance Company's operations from its founding in 1959 until his retirement in 1983.

Why this burst of organizational expansion? Company management and agents saw several good reasons, and time has confirmed their wisdom. One argument was the fundamental conviction that business firms, like people, either grow or stagnate. As Jim McTurnan, vice president of sales, said in 1960: "Either you advance aggressively or you are lost in the other fellow's dust." A second important reason for adding new companies offering new lines of coverage was that "multiple-line selling" strengthened the position of the agents on whom the company's success depended. Oklahoma agent Jim Ethington said in 1963: "People tell me they'd like to have everything with one agent. They get tired of having to call one agent for one type [of policy] and another for something else."

In the financially difficult year 1957, company officers heard a similar appeal from agents — and they responded. The directors' meeting of July 11 that year was important for the future of the company. Seeking ways to reverse current losses — surplus had declined $165,579 during the first five months of 1957 — the board heard President Silvey report on agents' meetings that he, A. D. Sappington, and Jim McTurnan had attended. Agents, Silvey said, had suggested ways "to improve the operations and future of the Company. From the information obtained it appeared that it is advisable to have another Casualty Insurance Company through which insurance might be written that is not now being written by, or acceptable to, this Company." The reference to unacceptable business included car drivers with poor accident records and other bad risks. Following discussion, the board instructed company officers "to organize a capital stock miscellaneous casualty insurance company."

Silvey also reported that "a substantial number" of MFA agents wrote life insurance for various other companies "in order to have a complete insurance program available." The board authorized the officers to investigate the "feasibility" of creating an MFA life insurance company. From the belief that diversification would help to counter hard times and strengthen the competitive position of agents came subsidiary companies that have bolstered MFA/Shelter Insurance since the 1950s.

As A. D. Sappington explained in April, 1958, the purpose of Countryside Casualty "was to supplement the lines of coverage being written by this Company and to provide new coverage not available through MFA Mutual." The company would "also serve those who prefer a stock company" rather than a mutual insurance company. Working through the same agents, Home Office staff and officers as MFA Mutual, Countryside Casualty wrote policies with rates that averaged 35% greater than MFA Mutual's in September 1961 for its higher risk insureds. In that year, the company offered the following lines of coverage:

Accident and Health
Aircraft
Automobile full coverage
Boiler, Steam
Burglary and Theft
Credit
Employers Liability
Fidelity
Fire and Allied Lines
Liability, Property Damage, and Collision other than automobile
Livestock, full coverage
Machinery
Marine
Plate Glass
Surety and Workmen's Compensation

Countryside Casualty's business grew rapidly, though when increases of surplus began in 1960, they came from investment income rather than from underwriting. The company's earned premium in 1959 was $681,565, and in 1963, $2,757,959. For the life of the company to the end of 1963, earned premium was $7,512,221. The underwriting loss was $715,828, investment income $575,879, and decrease in contributed surplus $139,949. As early as the first quarter of 1959, agent Troy Hightower of Springdale became the first top-selling Countryside agent in the entire agency force to outpace the top-selling MFA Mutual agent — a milestone of growth for the new company.

As was the case with Countryside Casualty, the Life Company shared the directors, officers, agents, and Home Office staff of MFA Mutual. William R. Toler became director of sales for the company on February 16, 1959, while Tex Graham continued as sales manager for MFA Mutual and Countryside Casualty. Toler, a Columbia native, obtained a business degree from the University of Missouri in 1948, following Navy service in World War II. He came to MFA Life from the Prudential Life Insurance Company's Kansas City region. Early in 1959, regional meetings occurred throughout Missouri to acquaint agents with the new company and what it could do for their business. They cut their teeth on the Charter Policy, the company's initial product. By

Harold Douglas at the KMMO microphone in 1954, three years after the company bought the station and made Douglas its manager. Douglas had done a program, "Man at the Exchange," on KFRU in Columbia, sponsored by Missouri Farmers Association and MFA Mutual, and was picked to manage the newly owned KMMO. He retired from that position in 1980, ending a 47-year career in radio. He is shown at his retirement (next page) with President Howard Lang.

the end of 1961, MFA Life offered 16 different policies together with seven riders containing additional benefits. After losses in the first three years of operations, the Life Company experienced underwriting gains of $18,000 in 1962 and $26,000 in 1963. By the end of 1960, the company's policy count was 6,347, and total insurance in force exceeded $32,700,000. On December 31, 1963 the policy count was 13,900, while insurance in force exceeded $76,227,000.

Security Service Company, which became MFA Security Service Company on February 2, 1959, did not sell insurance. Instead, it was a financial-services company with several actual functions — and others that J. M. Silvey and the board considered adding — designed to help agents attract and retain business. Until January, 1959 the company financed insurance premiums for policyholders of its sister companies. Beginning in 1959, as Security Service phased out its premium financing plan, its purpose was to finance consumer purchase of automobiles and other personal property through MFA insurance agents. Although underwritten and owned by MFA Mutual, Security Service was not in competition with local banks; it obtained loan funds from them (and from the sale of debentures), which it then made available to policyholders. From January, 1959 until November, 1961, Lee Appleman was vice president and manager of Security Service Company. He was succeeded in January, 1962 by Ferd Lightner. Bob Settlage, who assumed his duties in February, 1959, was the first auto-finance manager. Late in 1958, when the companies' directors changed Security Service's primary function to financing automobile purchases, President Silvey proposed that the MFA insurance companies offer additional financial services. These included the sale of mutual funds through MFA Life, and a savings and loan company to offer home mortgage money. Neither proposal was implemented.

The fifth member of the family of MFA Insurance Companies was KMMO radio. Fred Heinkel's desire to serve rural Missourians lay behind the acquisition. A member of its board of curators, Heinkel wanted the University of Missouri to establish a television station which would reach the farm population of the central part of the state, but at the time the University declined to do so. MFA's Heinkel then decided that the farm co-op would take the lead, and as a first step MFA Mutual purchased KMMO. With an FCC license and broadcasting experience, the thinking was, MFA or its affiliated insurance company could more easily obtain permission to operate a TV station. That never happened, as the University began operating KOMU-TV in 1954. Over the years one value of KMMO was that it became a sort of laboratory, in which various advertising approaches could be tried.

MFA Insurance also expanded its operations by offering new lines of coverage. From its earliest years the company took pride in the fact that it made available to policyholders multiple lines of sound, often innovative policies at competitive rates, supported by helpful and friendly advice and service from the agency and Home Office personnel. From a company that sold only automobile insurance in 1946, to three separate companies each of which wrote a spectrum of policies by 1959, MFA Insurance offered insurance buyers a rich choice of options.

In a deliberate but steady procession, new policies flowed from the careful research of company officers, with General Counsel A. D. Sappington playing the key role. In March, 1949, for example, the board endorsed his recommendation that the company amend its charter to allow the writing of fire insurance and other lines. By mid-1949, MFA Mutual wrote school bus insurance, and in April, 1950 it offered a Hospital and Surgical Benefits Policy. At the start of 1952, the Marketing Department began promoting business-interruption coverage. In 1954 the company sold inland-marine insurance for the first time. The Missouri Insurance Examiners Report of December 31, 1958 reported that the company offered these lines:

Accident and Health
Livestock, full coverage
Automobile full coverage
Machinery
Boiler, steam
Marine
Burglary and Theft
Plate Glass
Employers Liability
Surety
Fidelity
Workmen's Compensation
Fire and Allied Lines
Liability, Property, Damage, and Collision other than automobile

Some of the policies innovated during these years deserve special mention. In 1948 this company, which still largely served a rural clientele, made available to townspeople a comprehensive personal-liability policy. "Everything is included," agents were instructed, " — Bodily Injury Liability, Property Damage Liability, Employees Liability and Medical Payments on and off the premises."

Also in 1948, Congressman Clarence Cannon, a charter member of MFA and farm owner in Lincoln County, gave a ringing endorsement of MFA Mutual's Farm Liability Policy. Farmers' cherished independence, Cannon noted, was threatened in this modern age by liability "to lawsuits based on minor accidents and events which in times past were overlooked by a sympathetic public." "The blessings of insurance" protected farmers from this "sinister threat." Cannon concluded: "I am glad that the progressive MFA Mutual Insurance Company has seen fit to tailor-make such protection for the benefit of farmers of Missouri, and I am happy to be listed among those Missouri farmers who are taking advantage of this fine protection."

U.S. Congressman Clarence Cannon at his farm near Elsberry, Missouri, listens as Mike Spelman explains the coverages of Cannon's farm liability policy.

MFA Mutual entered the health insurance field in 1950. Appropriately, as an affiliate of MFA, the company promoted "prepaid insurance for hospital and surgical expenses [as] the best way to improve rural health." Reflecting issues still current in the 1990s, the company's Hospital and Surgical Benefits plan avoided prescribing the services of specified doctors or hospitals. "It believes that the patient-physician relationship should be maintained at all times and that the patient should have a free choice of physician and hospital." Interesting in light of later experience were the hospital room allowances: a choice of $4, $5, or $7 daily hospital room and board payments. A Family Protection Policy marketed in 1962 offered a choice of $6 to $25 daily room allowance.

In 1954 MFA Mutual pioneered in its sales territory Unsatisfied Judgment automobile insurance. In spite of Missouri's and Arkansas's financial-responsibility laws, MFA Mutual's policyholders still could be involved in an injury accident with drivers who did not carry insurance or have the ability to pay for damages awarded in a lawsuit. "Unsatisfied Judgment insurance will now pay for court judgments that the irresponsible driver can't pay." Company officials were so excited about the new coverage that they urged agents to place ads in local newspapers to educate potential policyholders about it, and they informed lawyers about "this startling new type of automobile insurance protection offered by MFA Mutual." Innovation was not limited to casualty policies. In 1962 MFA Life Insurance Company created a policy that awarded double death benefits to insureds who wore properly installed automobile seat belts at the time of a fatal accident.

Bev Crouch, agent in Kansas City, was one of the pioneers of the move into metropolitan markets. She became an agent in 1960 and remains active today.

Perhaps the most obvious form of expansion to those who observed MFA Mutual's growth during the 1950s and early 1960s was the spread of its sales territory, first within, and then beyond, Missouri. If the company's leaders seemed ambitious when they contemplated marketing financial services like mutual funds and mortgage loans, they appeared positively imperial when they projected a sales territory stretching from the Appalachian Mountains to the Pacific Coast. That dream fell short of realization by 1963, as will be explained below. Whether the failure to fulfill the exciting, expansive plans of the late 1950s-early 1960s was a cause of Mr. Silvey's dismissal is not known. What is clear is that MFA/Shelter Insurance never again looked as far beyond Missouri for business as it did in the early 1960s.

First, a look at growth within the company's home state. By the end of 1946, MFA Mutual sold auto insurance in all but three of Missouri's 114 counties. By the autumn of 1947, President Silvey divided the state into four districts with a sales manager heading each. Both Springfield and St. Joseph were in lucrative sales territory for MFA Mutual, and there were located the company's first branch offices in March and June, 1948. By January, 1950, the company created two new Missouri sales districts, for a total of six. While MFA Mutual early in its history decided "not to write insurance for persons living

in the St. Louis and Kansas City territories," a small-town bias could not last in a company that, by the mid-1950s, actively sought expansion. By December, 1958 Sales Manager Tex Graham wrote to Missouri and Kansas agents about writing business, in early 1959, in the Kansas City area. By mid-1960, George Baker, formerly an underwriter in the Home Office, became supervisor of the new St. Louis sales district, where he oversaw the work of agents like Ben McIntosh. A small-town boy from St. James, Missouri, Ben came from a long-time MFA family, but his non-metropolitan roots proved no handicap to selling insurance in an urban-suburban complex. Continued expansion in the Show-Me State supported eleven sales districts in early 1959. By early 1962, the company had established twelve claims offices in Missouri. At least one, that in Springfield, had a drive-in claims facility since 1958.

As business grew in the metropolitan areas, the need for offices became evident. This building on Lindbergh Boulevard in St. Louis was a single-story structure when purchased on April 30, 1968. The second level was added in 1971 as growth continued, and the building has since been sold and replaced with a new East Missouri State Office.

"Someday, perhaps, the company may go after business in other states . . . but right now there's still a big job to do here in Missouri." Less than a year after that statement appeared in 1948, MFA Mutual had begun the process of expanding beyond Missouri. By mid-1961 the company had established an 11-state sales territory. Besides Missouri, it solicited business in Arkansas, Kansas, Nebraska, Illinois, Iowa, Kentucky, Tennessee, Minnesota, Oklahoma, and Indiana. What follows is a brief account of the company's expansion into the 10 states, representing the spirit of expansion that animated the MFA Insurance Company during these years.

Company officials selected Arkansas and Kansas as the first expansion states. Kansas attracted the earliest attention, but Arkansas, by 1953-1954, emerged as MFA Mutual's second state in terms of sales. In December, 1945, at the second meeting of the board of directors, Fred Heinkel suggested that Kansas was a likely state in which to write insurance, since MFA's oil refinery was located there. It took several years, but by May, 1949 application had been made, and in the following month Kansas insurance regulators admitted the company to do business. Apparently some lines were being written as early as 1950 on a very limited basis, but it was not until 1954 that Bob Lasley was named the first Kansas state supervisor and that the initial agents' training school was held in the state. By late December, 1954, MFA Mutual had signed contracts with 30 Kansas agents. In June, 1955, the company established a state office in Topeka.

Operations in Arkansas also seem to have begun on a small scale in 1950, the year in which MFA Mutual was approved to do business in the state. At the company's eighth annual policyholders' meeting in April, 1953, President Silvey announced that Arkansas was the only state beside Missouri "in which any effort had been made to write any substantial volume" of insurance. In June of that year, the first state office outside of Missouri was established in Little Rock. In the first four months of 1954, earned premium in Arkansas surpassed $148,000, and, as of September 30 that year four of the company's top ten agents in the sale of new business were from Arkansas. They were the Ben Whitaker-Troy Hightower Agency of Rogers and Springdale, Paul Benham of Marianna, Charles Pattillo of DeWitt, and Harrell Brawner of Wynne. By 1960, Arkansas could boast of six sales districts, 170 agents, and over $2 million in sales through September 30. From January through September, 1960, to return to Kansas, 201 state agents accounted for nearly $600,000 in premium. In July, 1961, Kansas became the fifth state in which Countryside Casualty did business, and in February, 1963 MFA Life Insurance Company made the state the third in its sales territory.

In no other "new" state was progress as rapid as in Arkansas and Kansas. Illinois was the fourth state to approve MFA Mutual's application to write insurance (December, 1952), but the fifth one in which the company began operations. Nebraska was the fifth state to admit the company (1953), but the fourth in which it wrote policies. In July, 1954, James L. McTurnan and family moved from Columbia, where Jim had worked in underwriting and briefly served as Missouri District 4 supervisor, to Lincoln, where by December he had signed up 20 agents. By the end of 1957, the company established a Nebraska state office in Lincoln. Through the first three quarters of 1960, 103 Nebraska agents had sold nearly $250,000 of casualty insurance. By 1960, 1961, and 1962 each issue of CONTACT was crowded with news of new states entered, state and district supervisors (sales managers) appointed, and agents recruited. In a "report from

Nebraska" published in August, 1961, Roscoe Creed discussed his visit with Richard Kratz in Falls City. The first MFA insurance agent in Nebraska, licensed in August, 1954, Dick Kratz still ran his agency in 1994, when he received a 40-year service award at the Home Office. Creed also reported on the experiences of agents Mark Wurtele of Nebraska City, Bob Hall of Lincoln, and T. I. Chambers of North Platte — all of them pioneers in introducing MFA Mutual and its coverages to citizens of the Cornhusker State.

The company's move into Illinois in 1956 was led by John Baumgartner, who had joined MFA Mutual in August, 1947, spending most of his years as the district supervisor in southeast Missouri. He set up the initial agencies in the Quincy area. With his car serving as his office, Johnny roamed northwestern Illinois seeking good agent prospects. One man he interviewed, outdoors in front of a store, was in retail sales. His employer threatened to call the police if Baumgartner did not pay $2 for his clerk's time. "The man didn't get the $2 and I didn't get an agent," Johnny reported. By September 30, the 1960 sales for 147 Illinois agents was close to a quarter million dollars, and early in 1961 MFA insurance was available in all parts of the state but the Chicago area. In April, 1961, Illinois became the fourth state in Countryside Casualty's sales territory.

The approval of Iowa's insurance regulators proved especially difficult to obtain. Let former President Howard B. Lang, Jr. tell the story:

A. D.'s office applied by mail to be admitted to Iowa, with no result. Alfred J. Hoffman . . then went to Iowa in person where he met with Commissioner Fisher. During the discussion Fisher said he knew of Mr. Hirth. Our application was again rejected. . . . Jack [Silvey] decided that he and I should meet with Fisher. After removing the requirement that the insurance board had to come from the MFA board [to meet Iowa Insurance regulations], Jack decided to put a scrapbook together on Mr. Hirth and present it to the Commissioner. Jack and I got along fine with him, and Jack, at the end of our successful visit, presented the scrapbook. The commissioner in some very uncomplimentary language told us that in early days as a young man he was a salesman and called on Mr. Hirth who treated him very shabbily.

MFA Mutual gained admission to Iowa in the summer of 1959. In 1960, 37 agents solicited business in Iowa.

The last five states to join the MFA Insurance sales area during this era were Kentucky, Tennessee, Minnesota, Oklahoma, and Indiana. The state insurance departments of the first two granted the company permission to do business by 1955. The company gained admission to the last three in 1960.

MFA Mutual opened Kentucky and Tennessee during the summer of 1960 by sending to each a complete team consisting of a state manager and district supervisors. The state manager in the Volunteer State was Jim Jose, with the company since 1956 and a district supervisor in Arkansas before his move eastward. In Kentucky a Missouri agent with eight years' experience, Lloyd Snodgrass, became the first state manager. By 1962 roving CONTACT reporter Roscoe Creed found a "fired-up" and enthusiastic sales force at work in the Bluegrass State. Among the agents he featured in an article were William "Sonnie" Buckman of Mayfield, Bill Tidwell of Paducah, Luton Tatum of Hopkinsville, Delbert Lawson of Nicholasville, and Jim and Kathryn Brantley of Lexington. The enthusiasm that Creed found in Kentucky, he thought, "is rapidly building MFA Insurance into one of the top companies in the state."

MFA Mutual began operations in Minnesota, Oklahoma, and Indiana in 1961. The volume of business in all three remained small through 1963 as state managers Jim May, Felix Hendrickson, and Jim Bradley, and their district supervisors, recruited agents and made known the MFA Insurance name and trademark. By the summer of 1961, therefore, 15 years after its founding, the company's sales territory had spread into ten states outside of Missouri, an area which stretched from the Appalachian Mountains of eastern Tennessee and Kentucky to the High Plains of western Nebraska, Kansas, and Oklahoma. But the officers and directors, several years earlier, had projected a much larger territory even than this, one that they hoped would be a reality by 1964.

At least $50 million in premium sales by 1964 was the goal set by J. M. Silvey in 1959.

On September 28 and 29, 1959, President Silvey and his officers unveiled "an extensive five-year program" before a meeting of company employees. The slogan "50

or More by 64" pointed the way: $50 million in annual premium sold by 1964. To accomplish that more than doubling of the 1959 premium amount, company officials projected over 5,000 MFA Insurance agents by 1964, working a territory that reached from the eastern boundaries of Michigan, Ohio, Kentucky, and Tennessee all the way to the West Coast. "I'm sure that 5,000 agents will produce $50 million in premium by 1964," Jim McTurnan, by now vice president in charge of sales, told the meeting. "I believe — I have not a single doubt that we will write more than $50 million before '64!" affirmed J. M. Silvey. There were sound reasons for further expansion. One that A. D. Sappington reiterated was that by increasing the geographical territory in which it did business, a casualty company spread the risk — increased the odds that natural disasters would not devastate it. To reach their goal, company officers, with Sappington as general counsel taking the lead, applied for admission to a number of states. In its meeting of September 24, 1959, the board authorized applications in the following states not already mentioned:

Wisconsin
Idaho
South Dakota
Utah
North Dakota
Oregon
Arizona
Nevada
Colorado
Texas
Wyoming
California
Montana
New Mexico
Washington

Vice President of Sales Jim McTurnan addresses the agents meeting in 1960, promoting expansion plans.

The first move from the downtown office was into this building just behind the site of the Home Office, which was under construction. This building now is encased within the Training Center.

By late 1962 MFA Insurance had gained admission to Arizona, Idaho, Michigan, Nevada, North Dakota, Texas, Utah and Washington, but soon actual — and even paper — expansion slowed. At the 1963 Annual Meeting McTurnan reported to policyholders that the existing 11-state region was the company's focus: "our efforts were devoted largely toward upgrading personnel in those states and increasing our volume in them during 1962." The cost of expanding into the full 11-state territory, continued underwriting losses in two of the insurance companies, and disappointing progress in moving toward the goals set for 1964 no doubt all contributed to a temporary step backward from the "50 or More in 64" program. As early as 1961, Paul Keithley, the company's secretary-treasurer, pointed out that the 7.1% increase in 1960's sales over 1959's was not good enough. At that rate of growth, 1964 would see $31 million, not $50 million in sales.

It is clear from company statistics that MFA Mutual and its sister companies had much growing still to do within the existing sales territory. It was active in 11 states by 1961, but the home state of Missouri held a dominant position by any measurement. A couple of examples will suffice. In the first nine months of 1960, for example, sales in the then eight-state sales territory totaled $18,181,659. Sales in Missouri alone were $14,981,057, or 82% of the total. The count of active policies by states is another way to compare their relative importance. Of the total of 366,777 MFA Mutual policies in force on July 12, 1963 in the 11 state sales territory, 238,636 of them, or 65%, were held by Missouri policyholders. The proportion had been higher on July 24, 1962 — 69.5% — and it would continue to decline after 1963.

The point is that the companies could fully employ their resources for years in the mid-continent region. Fred Heinkel recalled in 1970 the expansive late 1950s, early 1960s. "We haven't gone into any additional states in the last few years because we expanded a little too fast at one time and we had some catching up to do. We had to [be]come firmly entrenched and successful in those states where we were operating." Company officers would continue to pursue far-flung expansion plans after J. M. Silvey's release on February 20, 1964. A. D. Sappington, company president after that date, was no less committed to optimum geographic growth than his predecessor and former boss. Under neither Silvey nor Sappington were the ambitious plans for a sales territory covering most of the nation realized.

Not surprisingly, this expanding company soon outgrew its Home Office space. For more than a decade, MFA Insurance shared space with MFA in the latter's Columbia headquarters. But even when the farm cooperative reorganized and added to its facilities, the insurance operation outgrew the space allotted to it. Until the mid-1950s, Heinkel, Silvey and the board planned to keep MFA Mutual in a central Columbia location, either in a new building adjacent to MFA's headquarters or nearby. For a time in the spring of 1954, the company held an option to buy the nine-story Tiger Hotel as a home office, but by late July of that year, its leaders had found a different solution to the need for more spacious quarters. They purchased a 56-acre tract of farmland on what would become an extension of West Broadway, the city's main east-west street, and on this suburban site approximately one and one-half miles from the downtown business district they planned a building that would be "low and spread out."

The planning and construction of two buildings on the West Broadway site occurred from the fall of 1954 to the late summer of 1957. Working with the Chicago architectural firm of Childs and Smith, specialists in the design of facilities for insurance companies, the company first erected an Annex Building behind what would be the Home Office structure. This 50x120 foot brick facility was to provide immediate relief from the overcrowding of departments at several downtown locations, and, after its occupants moved to the completed headquarters building, provide storage space. In November, 1955 the underwriting and claims departments moved into the Annex. Meanwhile, with Personnel Director Bill Redmon serving as chief liaison between the company, the architects, and the general contractor, M. W. Watson of Topeka, Kansas,

This photo is a 1954 look toward southwest Columbia. The Fairgrounds are nearest the bottom. The lighter patch of grass is now the Home Office grounds. Broadway crosses about midway in the photo, but there is no Stadium Boulevard, and Ash Street stops at the Fairgrounds. The drive-in theater is now Gerbes and the Broadway Shopping Center. This same view today will reveal residential and commercial development throughout the area.

The original Home Office building, before additions doubled its size in the 1960s, stood in a rural setting at the western edge of Columbia.

This flag-raising ceremony on August 26, 1957 marked the first day that all employees were moved into the new Home Office building.

work on the Home Office proceeded. Officials and guests broke ground for the 265x110 foot, two-story plus full basement structure on February 10, 1956. The cornerstone, filled with company memorabilia, was ceremonially set in place on November 8, 1956. Employees moved into the new building during the second half of August, 1957, and in November a large crowd took advantage of a gala open house. The company was now at home at 1505 — later changed to 1817 — West Broadway.

As later events proved, there were interesting implications in the insurance company's physical separation from MFA. In 1980-1981 the two organizations, finding that their interests had sharply diverged, broke all formal ties, and the MFA Insurance Company became the Shelter Insurance Company. The separate Columbia locations of the two businesses both symbolized and helped ease the legal divorce of the two. But that physical separation might not have occurred. In the spring of 1955 the MFA Mutual board, headed by Fred V. Heinkel, president of MFA, endorsed the concept that the farm cooperative would also build a new headquarters on the insurance company's land. The two home offices would "be joined by tunnel or corridor." For reason or

These three panels of the mural, "The Golden Link," painted by Columbia artist Sidney Larson, are on display in the Home Office cafeteria and tell the history of insurance, from its earliest beginnings to modern times.

reasons unknown, the second construction project never proceeded.

The embellishment and expansion of the new Home Office continued after 1957. A year after the company occupied the building, it commissioned Sid Larson, director of art at Christian (now Columbia) College, to create a 54-foot mural depicting the history and social significance of insurance. From the fall of 1958 through the spring of 1959, Larson painted the mural on the north wall of the cafeteria, dividing its message among three panels. The first depicts the development of the insurance idea in ancient civilizations such as the Egyptian; the second shows the beginnings of mutual insurance in the United States and the central role played by Benjamin Franklin in that development; while the third panel illustrates the benefits that insurance has bestowed upon America throughout its history. Entitled "The Golden Link," the mural received a proper dedication on September 27, 1959 when a 30-minute ceremony was "kinescoped" (filmed) for later showing on television stations.

This group constituted a small but important unit in the company in 1961. At the table is Bill Griffin, manager of loss prevention, with members of the loss prevention department.

Adjacent to where Professor Larson had worked in the lower level of the Home Office, the company constructed a 22,610-square-foot addition to the north of the original building. Ready for occupancy in August, 1962, the new work space was on the ground floor only, but it was designed so that other floors could be added later.

While the new office space was utilitarian, the mural was not. As attractive and interesting today as when Sid Larson finished it, the mural clearly is a "touch of class" that did not have to be done. Through it MFA/Shelter Insurance added sparkle to its fine office building, and has continued to make a statement about its commitments: not to a profitable business operation alone, but also to the ideal of service to policyholders and to society.

The remainder of this chapter will focus on two aspects of the daily work-life of the company that affected every department in the organization: the company's utilization of innovative office technology, and its advertising efforts. In its advertising, especially in its promotion of safety among the general public, the MFA Insurance Company combined a public service with sales promotion so successfully that it became a nationally-recognized, frequently-honored corporate citizen.

In MFA Mutual's early days, much of the office work was done by traditional, often slow and laborious methods. Typists handled each policy and renewal notice individually, and file clerks carefully placed each piece of paper in its proper folder. But soon new equipment made operations both more cost-effective and accurate. For example, by 1950 claims adjusters used the Audograph Electronic Soundwriter, or "electronic secretary," as they visited accident scenes and interviewed claimants. The machine was a dictaphone through which the adjuster recorded information on an 8.5-inch disk which was mailed to the claims department in the Home Office for use and storage. Disks proved valuable as sources of evidence in court proceedings and in other ways. By 1954 the Home Office employed teletype machines to keep in touch with

First use of magnetic tape drives came with the installation in 1961 of the IBM 7070 and 1401 systems.

left: The 1957 installation of the IBM 650 gave the company information storage on a magnetic drum, with input from punched cards. Wyman Heath sits at the console in this 1961 photo.

claims and branch offices. In the same year a letter "stuffing" machine was in use in the mail room; it could fill 3,000 envelopes an hour with premium notices and other communications.

The greatest relievers of routine human labor were the business machines which MFA mutual began leasing from IBM as early as 1946. During most of the period under review, the company employed a collection of sorters, tabulators, and punchers that manipulated what the world then knew as IBM cards. The machines not only stored data on each policyholder, but also prepared premium and dividend notices, compiled the data that appeared on the company's monthly reports, and performed other tasks.

In the early 1960s, when the IBM 7070 Computer came on the scene, MFA Insurance began to store data on magnetic tape rather than machine-readable punch cards. Personnel in the Data Processing Division began training to use the 7070 in the fall of 1960, but the machine did not arrive until a year later, and was put to work processing auto policies during 1963. The new equipment was capable of updating all of the company's more than 300,000 auto policies in less than three hours, and could print over 130 premium notices per minute. If MFA Insurance's roots lay partly in 19th century rural co-ops, a part of its ability to meet the future depended on the most recent technology.

A small group of energetic, talented people devised and implemented MFA Mutual's advertising program. A native of Spickard and graduate of the University of Missouri College of Agriculture, W. Judd Wyatt was advertising director. He went to work for MFA in October, 1945 after doing wartime publicity duty for the U.S. Department of Agriculture, and soon found himself working for the insurance company as well. Wyatt's assistants included Dottie Strickler, Dick Ferguson, and, beginning in 1955, artist Bill Hume. A University of Missouri School of Journalism graduate, Hume drew cartoon ads which appeared in many company publicity efforts, from full-page spreads in the MISSOURI FARMER to animated television commercials and safety films. These publicists executed a three-pronged strategy: developing company

In late 1994 the last of the key punch equipment was ceremonially discarded by those who had worked with it over a 30-40 year span. Terry Pauley, Norman Wilson, Jim Kunze and Bob Sappington carry a key punch machine, while Pauley, Mel Wilson, Jim Again, Kunze, and Sappingotn move an interpreter off the dock.

Sponsor, broadcaster and coaches look forward to the 1953 Missouri Tiger football season. MFA Mutual helped create the Missouri Sports Network in 1949. In photo are Advertising Director Judd Wyatt, KFRU Radio Manager Mahlon Aldridge, and Tiger coaches Don Faurot and Sparky Stalcup.

advertising that would reach a broad audience; encouraging agents to do their own advertising; and devising a line of MFA Insurance trademark items that carried the company's emblem and message to actual and potential policyholders.

The company advertised in both print and broadcast media, but it increasingly recognized the effectiveness of radio and television. One popular program sponsored together with MFA appeared on KWTO, Springfield, Missouri in the late 1940s. Country singers the Carter Family, before they left for Nashville's Grand Ole Opry, helped sell insurance on a 15-minute show. In 1950, MFA Mutual and other MFA divisions and affiliates began sponsoring the radio play-by-play broadcasts of Missouri Tiger football games on an 18-station network. By 1959, company messages appeared on 106 radio and 17 television stations.

A major thrust of the company's product promotion was to convince agents that appropriate local advertising was one key dimension of salesmanship. Probably because

of both Home Office prompting and their own good business sense, many agents reported success with their own advertising. A few examples will illustrate. Ronald McConnell of Greenfield assessed the results of his advertising in 1951: "You never really know the exact amount of good you receive from advertising. You receive its benefit over a long period of time, and I'm for it 100%." In 1953, Earl Doerrie of St. Charles had five spot announcements and a 10-minute interview program on a Warrenton station each week. In the same year, Ben Whitaker in Benton County, Arkansas advertised MFA Insurance on one radio station, in two newspapers, at a drive-in theater, in five telephone directories, and by handing out matches, pencils, and balloons. In 1954, Bob Bushmeyer of Boonville advertised on station KWRT; in 1955,

Advertising took many forms other than radio. Here Fulton Agent Harvey Chirnside shows off his new road sign in 1957, and Beulah Dawson of Policy Service (next page) has equipped her daughter, Debbie, with a popular 1955 advertising novelty, plastic baby pants.

left: In the late 1940s, MFA Mutual sponsored the Carter Family, Mother Maybelle and daughters Anita, Helen and June, on a 15-minute show on KWTO Radio in Springfield, Missouri. The Carters left Springfield for the Grand Old Opry and legendary status in country music.

M-F-A
INSURED

Mel Cunningham of Leavenworth, Kansas distributed 1,500 handbills that he had printed; and in 1962, Vernon M. Wolff of Gillespie, Illinois sponsored an MFA Mutual bowling team. There were many ways to get the word out.

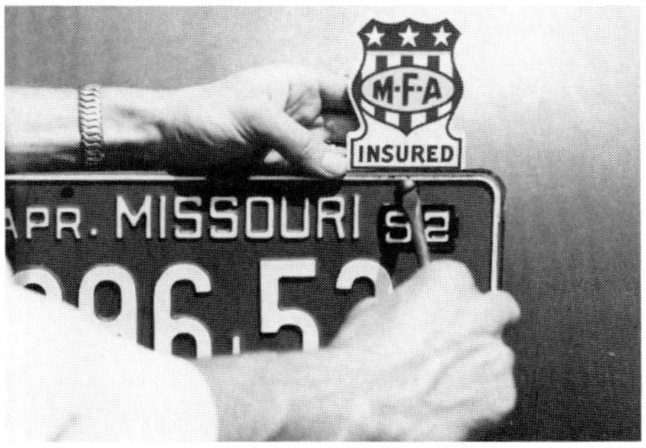

Metal emblems attached to license plates of insureds, the predecessor to today's bumper sticker.

MFA Insurance give-away items became effective ways for customers to identify, and identify with, the company and its policies. One trademark object was the cardboard fan with a wood handle, distributed by agents at summer events such as county fairs, well-attended by overheated people during July and August across the sales territory. Although they may have first appeared during the 1940s, the fans were very popular during the 1950s. One well-used survivor, on the back side of the MFA Shield, reads: "Protect yourself from the heat with this fan. Protect yourself and others with MFA Mutual Insurance. . . . See or write Otis J. Browning, Leonard, MO." Many agents set up booths at fairs and offered passers-by cold water, a place to sit, an insurance pamphlet, and a fan. More famous — and enduring — than the fan is the MFA/Shelter Almanac, first assembled in 1950 by Judd Wyatt and still issued today. Mentioned on company radio ads, the Almanac was requested by listeners and distributed, free of charge, by

In this 1953 photo, a Missouri State Highway Patrol officer commends a farmer for his use of an MFA Mutual red flag to warn of his slow moving farm equipment. The flags, many of which were manufactured by housewife seamstresses, were given away free to anyone who asked throughout the 1950s and '60s.

agents. In its first year the company gave away 15,000 copies of the MFA Mutual Farm Almanac, and by the mid-1970s, 300,000 per year.

It is no mystery why insurance companies promote safety, and MFA Mutual did so from the beginning. One promotion unique to the company was the red flag program, initiated in 1954. Agents paid a small fee (four cents each in 1959) for red flags to place on tractors and other slow-moving, hazardous vehicles — to be given free on request. From 1954 through 1966 the company gave away 335,000 red flags, enough "to reach more than 50 miles into the sky if laced to one pole." The company was also proud of its role in cooperating with the Missouri State Highway Patrol to organize the Missouri Safety Council, and in sponsoring youth safety meetings in Nebraska, Kansas, and Missouri.

The best-known and perhaps most effective of the safety-promotions was a series of films produced by Wyatt and the Advertising Department between 1950 and 1965. The staff turned out the first five films in the summer and fall of 1950. The use of free talent, including Jim Silvey in several films, and of sports celebrities — including the St. Louis Cardinals in "Safe at Home" and Don Faurot's Missouri University football Tigers in "Fifty-Yard Line" — kept the production costs of each twenty-minute film below $2,000 each. The Highway Patrol contributed technical assistance in making the films. In the late 1950s, with Bill Hume's talents available, the films began using animation to deliver their safety messages. An amazing number of people saw the films over at least a 20-year period. To cite just one example, in 1952 the Missouri Highway Patrol showed the five existing titles a total of 365 times to audiences totaling 34,253 persons.

Jim Silvey, chief underwriter in the early 1960s, had played leading roles in several of the company's safety films in the early 1950s. His co-star, Billie Hopper (seen below), later became his wife.

St. Louis Cardinal great, Stan "The Man" Musial at bat during filming of the 1950 MFA Mutual safety movie, "Safe At Home."

In New York City on May 6, 1958, Judd Wyatt, left, receives the company's first Alfred P. Sloan Award for the promotion of traffic safety. Presenting the plaque is Mr. Sloan, former president and board chairman of General Motors. Seated is Charles E. Wilson, former GM president and Secretary of Defense in the Eisenhower administration. The company went on to win six Sloan Awards for its traffic safety work.

The films helped MFA Insurance win important awards in impressive fashion — impressive because of the unprecedented number of the awards won by a relatively small company. Beginning with the award year 1954 (presented in April, 1955), the company won 10 consecutive Public Interest Awards from the National Safety Council. It was the only company in the United States to compile that record. And MFA Insurance won the first of six Alfred P. Sloan Radio-TV Awards for Distinguished Service in Highway Safety in the award year 1957 (presented in May, 1958 in New York City). An informed well-wisher wrote to Judd Wyatt about the 1958 Sloan Award: "Do you know that you nosed out Standard Oil Company (Indiana), Esso Standard, and Standard of California? When you can beat that kind of competition, you've really got it!"

It is true that industry awards are only one indicator of MFA Insurance's exemplary record. For policyholders and company officers, indeed, the ratings given the companies by A. M. Best — indicating financial soundness — were of more practical significance than plaques on a wall. Yet, the NSC and Sloan Awards deserve an honored place in the company's history.

Members of the MFA Insurance family — directors and officers, employees and agents, and also quite a number of policyholders — would have agreed at the start of 1964 that "you've really got it." The company really had what it took to develop from birth to impressive size and success in 17 years of business. Although a leadership change would take place early in 1964, the fundamental soundness of the company remained — remained most of all in its people. Chapter 3 will consider some of them.

left & above: The animated safety film "Fair Game" won the nation's highest honors for companies art director Bill Hume. Here Hume presents a copy of the film to Lt. Shadwell of the Highway Patrol, whose officers used many company films in their appearances around the state. Also shown is a scene from the film.

This training class from 1956 included many who went on to claims management and then retirement from the companies.

chapter 3

Our People 1946-1964

What MFA Mutual's employees and agents contributed to their company is obvious. They, with the company's leadership, created the record of success described in the first two chapters. Company officers and directors have always praised the employees' and agents' roles in building MFA/Shelter Mutual. At the same time, the company contributed much to employees' and agents' well-being. It created hundreds of jobs; provided fine professional training for those who held these positions; paid salaries, commissions, and bonuses; and supplemented paychecks with a growing list of benefits. Through these, communities as well as families prospered, and governments at all levels benefited from taxes paid by the company and its employees and agents. The rewards realized by MFA people will be one focus of this chapter.

Table 3.1 Reported Numbers of Employees for Selected Years

Year	Total Employees	Employees working in Home Office versus other locations
1946, January	7	
1951, April	126	(not available)
1953, December	271	(not available)
1957, December	491	380 in Home Office In field: 76 Missouri 35 other states
1960, March	578	412 in Home Office In field: 114 Missouri 52 other states
1963, January	687	466 in Home Office In field: 122 Missouri 99 other states
1963, November	759	481 in Home Office In field: 147 Missouri 131 other states

Source: various MFA Mutual board of directors minutes and company publications.

Table 3.1 suggests the growth of employee numbers — and why a new Home Office building was necessary by the mid-1950s. A CONTACT article in 1959 marveled at the growth in Home Office staff during the company's first 13 years. "In 1946 the MFA Mutual Insurance Company employed 3 women and 4 men selling only auto insurance." In 1959, 405 people, "138 men and 267 women, are employed in the Home Office." A 1953 document listed a wide variety of job titles held by

The cafeteria, looking toward the single food line, showing blank panels left for mural. Today the cafeteria has three line choices, full plate dinners, deli, and salad bar.

personnel: from mail clerk to claims attorney; from underwriter, statistician, and actuary to fire inspector, cashier, and advertising specialist.

A roster of 24 professionals in the Claims Department dated 1953 revealed that 15 were Missouri natives and that a large proportion had received at least part of their education in Columbia: six at Hickman High School and 13 at the University of Missouri School of Law.

The Columbia community provided other employees too, as Bill Conboy, future head of marketing, noted: MFA Mutual had made "wise utilization . . . of competent female help who are predominantly wives of students at the University of Missouri." Male students themselves became part-time employees, and some remained with the company after graduation. An example is Gustav J. Lehr, who began on a part-time basis in 1953. Conboy also reported that MFA Mutual employed many "who have long family ties with the Missouri Farmers Association. The company's origin has caused the personnel department to favor persons of rural background."

Long-term employees gave continuity to the company's operations. In 1959, MFA Mutual honored six employees who had served the company since 1946, four since 1947, and nine since 1948. Employees not only handled the company's day-

MFA Mutual's human resource needs ranged from mail clerks, to department heads, and to those whose job was crucial to all the others — cooks. Part of the kitchen staff prepares lunch in the "new" home office cafeteria kitchen, shortly after the office was occupied in 1957. At left is Odelia Buckner who continued as pastry chef until she retired in 1990.

to-day business, but also served picnic lunches at Missouri Farmers Association conventions and contributed in other ways not covered in job descriptions.

In 1959, company payroll totaled $2,018,869.47, and fringe benefits amounted to an additional $113,950.80. The benefits package was a full one by the end of 1963, although the company did not inaugurate it until 1951. Beginning on July 1 of that year, MFA Insurance employees became eligible for MFA's retirement plan. Initially employees contributed 5% of their salary up to $5,000 annually, and the company matched that amount. The plan also provided disability, death, and severance benefits. In 1955, MFA Mutual began providing moving expenses "where we request employees to move from one location to another," and added a group life insurance plan. As the Home Office moved to West Broadway, employees enjoyed other benefits, including a nearby MFA service station for convenient gasoline purchases. In 1956, company management developed sick leave and vacation plans.

The new Home Office housed both an employee cafeteria, operated initially by the management firm Crotty Brothers, but, by 1962, by the company itself, and an employee credit union. Douglas (Scotty) Garrett directed cafeteria operations. After its formation in May, 1958, the credit union grew rapidly, as both agents and

Vern and Ottie Golden in front of Golden's MFA Service Station, 1956. Golden became an agent in 1958, and was named Agent of the Year at the 1976 Conference of Champions in Los Angeles. The MFA presence in Arkansas facilitated the recruiting of excellent agents when the company moved into Arkansas after being admitted in October 1949.

employees took advantage of its savings and loan services. With elected officers and a board of directors — Jack Pettit was chosen president in 1959 and Henry Kilburn in 1960 — the credit union's assets surpassed $250,000 in September, 1961. President Silvey calculated that employee benefits cost the company $534,708 in 1960, and $626,457 in 1961. He included cafeteria operations, influenza vaccine, Christmas gifts, and two daily breaks among the benefits offered by the company.

Table 3.2 Reported Numbers of Agents for Selected Years

Year	Total Agents	Agents by States (or Sales Districts)
1946, June	"about 155"	
1947, September	440	By Missouri sales districts
		158, District 1: Southwest
		98, District 2: Northwest
		116, District 3: Northeast
		68, District 4: Southeast
1950, December	537	535 Missouri
		1 Arkansas
		1 Kansas
1953, April	434	413 Missouri
		19 Arkansas
		2 Kansas
1957, September	716	376 Missouri
		119 Arkansas
		121 Kansas
		72 Nebraska
		28 Illinois
1960, April	885	395 Missouri
		159 Arkansas
		154 Kansas
		104 Illinois
		73 Nebraska
1961, June	1596	496 Missouri
		252 Kansas
		214 Arkansas
		210 Illinois
		153 Nebraska
		102 Iowa
		74 Tennessee
		58 Kentucky
		14 Indiana
		23 Minnesota
1963, December	1862	483 Missouri
		200 Kansas
		187 Arkansas
		190 Illinois
		144 Nebraska
		131 Tennessee
		125 Indiana
		114 Iowa
		112 Oklahoma
		104 Kentucky
		72 Minnesota

Source: various MFA Mutual board of directors minutes and company publications

Table 3.2 indicates the growing company agency force, in an expanding sales territory, which marketed MFA Mutual's coverages. Silvey's large number of agents included many part-timers who worked out of their homes, who did not actively solicit business, and who sold few policies. These agents mixed insurance with farming, operating or working for an MFA exchange, or — in the case of an Arkansas agent in 1954 — co-managing the Flintrock Strawberry Growers Association. Bill Conboy estimated that, of approximately 750 agents contracted by the company in the spring of 1959, 400 were part-time. Conboy's educated guess was that "average agent compensation" was $3,000 per year, although "numerous" agents in small towns earned "from $10,000 to $15,000 annually." An important part of A. D. Sappington's transformation of MFA Mutual was the move to full-time agents who actively solicited business.

Unlike employees on salary, agents are independent contractors: in business for themselves and owners of their agencies, but affiliated with the company in a joint enterprise. While they are independent, it is the company's job carefully to select and train them, and to motivate their sales efforts. In these and other functions, effective communication between the Home Office and agents is essential.

One very effective method of communication with agents has been the MFA/Shelter Insurance Company's newsletters and magazines. To read these publications today is to see a company come to life and grow, and to observe the human beings who gave it direction. The first newsletter, a mimeographed "Agent's Bulletin," appeared in January, 1947; it was succeeded in the spring by a thin monthly magazine entitled "MFA Mutual Beam." On August 6, 1949, Judd Wyatt and Dick Ferguson put out the first issue of CONTACT, the title of the weekly newsletter still in use today. Ferguson's call to active duty in Korea created a staff shortage, and a return to a mimeographed newsletter, "MFA Mutual's Once-Over Lightly" ("providing an occasional contact with MFA Mutual Agents"). With the issue of April 8, 1952, CONTACT, printed on glossy paper in magazine format, returned.

The company's publications provided occasional humor:

Orator: "All that I am I owe to my mother."

Heckler: "Send her two bits and make it square."

They printed compliments from satisfied policyholders. Agent Glenn O'Connell of Cape Girardeau, shared a letter with CONTACT in 1953: "Glenn, it certainly is a pleasure to do business with such a wonderful insurance company and agent." The publications offered advice to agents: urging an orderly filing system for their records, explaining the company's underwriting rules, discussing effective sales techniques, and setting forth the advantages of moving their business from homes to offices in commercial areas of town.

These 1949 photos by Dick Ferguson show Mike Spelman (below) in a quandary over which piece of birthday cake to eat, and Russ Shaw playing tricks with the tape measure. Shaw, known for his lack of height, reaches the 7-foot mark here.

CONTACT and other publications introduced new Home Office personnel and agent supervisors, and new policies. They reported on training classes, employee meetings, and agent get-togethers, from sales meetings in the field to "Visitation Days" on which agents and spouses toured the Home Office. Through its publications the company urged better performance: for example, filling out accurately and fully all policy applications and claim reports, which some agents failed repeatedly to do, and cutting high loss ratios which harmed both company and agent. And in interesting articles, agents learned what their fellows in other locations were doing. In the early 1950s, for example, agents Gloria and Lawrence Brukerhoff of Hermann gave an annual thank-you "party for policyholders." More than 450 people attended the fourth event in 1954.

In addition to communicating with agents through publications, district and company-wide agent meetings were an effective way for the company to instruct, encourage, and motivate agents. MFA Mutual held its first district meetings in November, 1946. Attendance at meetings held throughout Missouri in the spring of 1947 was important, a writer in the Home Office stated. "It is your duty as a good agent to support these meetings. . . . a lot of agents are still not very well acquainted with what they are selling," so they needed what the get-togethers offered: an exchange of ideas among those attending and sound instruction by Home Office personnel.

In October, 1949, CONTACT's assistant editor Dick Ferguson observed speakers in action at a Sedalia district meeting. Underwriters Troy Hightower and Bob Buschmeyer discussed the auto and farm liability policies. Russell Shaw, head of the company's new fire insurance division, explained that line of coverage, while Judd Wyatt stressed the key role of advertising in spurring sales. Following lunch, a cast of actors whose humor surpassed their talent presented a skit on how to sell, and not to sell, insurance. Mike Spelman, production manager, Bill Conboy, District Two supervisor, A. D. Sappington, and Wyatt "brought out much hilarious laughter from the audience." In October, 1955, district meetings occurred in six locations, at sites that included the Elks Club in Macon, St. Rita's Catholic School in Cameron, and the First Methodist Church in Poplar Bluff.

The first annual agents' convention met in Columbia on April 12 and 13, 1948, and into the 1960s this annual meeting was a central event on the company's calendar. Intended for as many agents as could come, the agents' meeting virtually took over downtown Columbia, as hotels, theaters, and churches at one time or another housed speeches, discussions, and banquets. President Silvey saw the event as an opportunity "to present a constructive and informative schooling that would not be possible in a district meeting." At the June, 1949 meeting, 150 agents gathered at the Daniel Boone Hotel to hear Paul Keithley, Office Manager, and Byron Beavers, Chief Examiner of the Missouri State Insurance Department, among others. Dale Carnegie, Missouri native and nationally-known speaker and writer, addressed 650 agents and employees on "getting along with people" at the 1950 gathering. The 1960 convention featured television humorist Herb Shriner.

Essential to the creation of a successful agency force were the company's training programs. From its first year, MFA Mutual offered instruction for new and veteran agents. As training programs grew they involved employees as well as agents. And as they grew in number and complexity, training courses required increased leadership from the Home Office. When Henry Kilburn retired in 1975, he was the only director of training the MFA Insurance Companies had ever known. Trained himself as a professional educator — he earned a graduate degree in education, served as a superintendent of schools in Dixon, Missouri, and was a training officer for the Veterans Administration before coming to MFA Mutual in 1948 — Kilburn was a natural choice to head training. He wore several hats during his career: an agent supervisor, the company's production manager, and chief underwriter. In January, 1950 he set to work on a part-time basis developing and scheduling courses, and in 1957 Kilburn became full-time director of training.

Inspirational speaker and author Dale Carnegie, here in 1950, was among guest speakers at early agent meetings.

J. M. Silvey liked to bring agents to Columbia for meetings, such as this 1960 event at Stephens College.

Famed entertainer Herb Shriner performed for the 1960 agents meeting.

Henry Kilburn, director of training beginning in 1957, was one of several MFA Mutual managers who had enjoyed earlier careers as teachers.

Mention of some courses offered and some students who attended tells us more about the company's early training program. While some sessions were designed for agents alone, others included supervisors and employees. Some courses featured Home Office instructors exclusively, and others made room for agents to relate "How I Sell Farm Liability Insurance" and other proven techniques drawn from experience. In August, 1953 the first state-wide training school to meet outside of Missouri was held in Little Rock, as seven speakers from the Home Office traveled to Arkansas to conduct the meetings. And in August, 1954 the first Kansas training school was judged a success.

From an early date these classes were coeducational. The lists of students and photos of participants reveal a number of women, most of whom were the spouses of agents or secretaries who worked in agency or state offices. As the business became more complex, the training classes became more specialized: a physical damage school for claims adjusters in 1956, for example, and IIA (Insurance Institute of America) classes in the early 1960s. Graduates of one IIA course included Jim Offutt and Vic Ohman of the Home Office. Jim Silvey, Bill Redmon, Gus Lehr, and Cletus Baurichter, all of the Home Office, joined agents in a 1953 class.

Gus Lehr, front row closest to camera, was a student in this 1960 claims school.

M·F·A INSURED
M·F·A INSURED
M·F·A INSURED
M·F·A INSURED
M·F·A INSURED
M·F·A INSURED
M·F·A INSURED

President Silvey celebrated his birthday and sales promotion called Silvey Month during August. This 1961 cake's candles each represents a policy sold during the promotion.

Glenn Pratt, manager of auto underwriting, and Jim McDonnell, claims adjuster, led the nation in Insurance Institute of America test scores in 1960, and were honored at the Institute's annual luncheon in New York.

If company schooling provided knowledge and technique for agents' success, company sales promotions and contests created motivation for exceptional sales effort. It was not until 1960 that J. M. Silvey created the President's Conference (later called the Conference of Champions) to honor and showcase the company's top agents. But agents had many earlier opportunities to compete for prizes and recognition in interesting sales contests. As early as 1949, agents who earned merit sales points earned prizes from a catalog. Four agents in Missouri and Arkansas won television sets for gaining $4,000 in new business in the contest month of March, 1953. Wall clocks and rings, each with the MFA Mutual shield on them, were won by 135 and 130 agents, respectively, in 1954 contests.

The most prominent sales promotion during the Silvey years was the August

facing page: C. W. "Chub" Watkins shows what the well-dressed sales supervisor was wearing in 1958.

The six leading producers in May 1948 explain their pace-setting methods. Left to right, Sam Still, Kirksville; George Pearson, Columbia; Ralph Ross, Chillicothe; Roy Kilmer, Dexter; R.V. Smith, Springfield; and Otto Young, Union.

"Silvey Month" campaign. Production Manager Mike Spelman and Judd Wyatt began the event in 1949, and annually through 1963, Silvey's birthday month became the company's most dependable one for increased sales. In 1952, Silvey received 5,103 kernels of MFA seed corn, one for each new application in August. Silvey received a huge birthday cake adorned with 1,783 candles — one for each ten policies submitted by agents — in August, 1961. That Silvey Month was the biggest month yet in company history.

Beginning in 1947, the company publicized the names of each year's top-selling agents. S. N. Still of Kirksville was 1946's Top Agent with over $12,600 in premium written. Sales leaders during the 1950s included agents whose names appeared year after year: Lloyd Rush of Carthage, Harold Remley of Jefferson City, Ralph Ross of Chillicothe, George Pearson of Columbia — and in Arkansas, Ben Whitaker of Rogers and Bill Holmes of Paragould. By 1958, two Kansas agents, Earl S. Smith of Wichita and Forest Richardson of Chanute, produced more than $10,000 in business.

The four President's Conferences to occur during the Silvey years (1960-1963)

Sam Still, Kirksville, perennial leader in the companies early years, was the 1946 production leader.

Gayle Helterbrand, Cabool, Missouri, with his agency car, which even in the late 1940s was a classic.

One of the most successful agents from the 1950s through the '80s is Earl Doerrie, shown here with wife and agency partner, Edith, accepting the 1962 Agent of the Year award from Silvey at the New York President's Conference. The Doerries have retired from their St. Charles, Missouri, agency.

were held in St. Louis, New Orleans, New York, and Colorado Springs. During this period the company did not give a separate award for Life Company sales, so award winners, including Agent of the Year, were the top sellers in all lines of coverage. Agents of the Year were Harold Remley (1960), George Pearson (1961), Earle Doerrie (1962), and Troy Hightower of Springdale, Arkansas (1963). Thirty-three agents qualified for the first conference, headquartered at the Chase Hotel in St. Louis in June, 1960. Missouri sent 28 agents, while Arkansas sent four and Kansas one. In 1961, 63 agents qualified for the President's Conference. As "the highest honor an MFA Insurance agent can achieve," conference established a valued goal for all agents.

The final portion of this chapter will provide more information about the key management people who directed the work of employees and agents. First hired by MFA Mutual in the 1940s or early 1950s, members of this team began their careers under J. M. Silvey and continued to serve during A. D. Sappington's presidency. Most did not retire until after Mr. Sappington's death in 1979. Thus they bridged three eras. From them the company received stability and continuity through the rush of expansion from the mid-1950s to the mid-1960s, and the potentially disruptive change of leadership in 1964.

Chapter 1 discussed the origins and early careers of MFA Mutual's founders: Heinkel, Rosier, Silvey, and Sappington. Patterns they established continued in the careers of other company officers and department managers who joined MFA Mutual in the late 1940s or early 1950s. Like J. M. Silvey and veteran director B. M. Seaman, Paul Keithley and Bill Redmon, director of personnel beginning in 1953, came from the Gifford-LaPlata area of Macon County in north-central Missouri. In adjacent Shelby County, in Shelbyville, William Conboy grew up. Brothers Arthur and Howard B. Lang Jr. came to Columbia in 1929 from their hometown of Fulton. Jack Pettit, Will L. Nelson, and William Toler, grew up in Columbia and attended its public schools. Only James L. McTurnan, born in Fairmont, Indiana, and Gustav J. Lehr, from Chicago, were raised outside of Missouri.

While McTurnan received degrees from Butler University in Indianapolis, Conboy, both Langs, Lehr, Pettit, and Nelson — as well as A. D. Sappington — graduated from the University of Missouri. The last six listed were alumni of that University's law school. Conboy, Art Lang, Keithley, and Redmon worked briefly for

Troy Hightower, an early employee-turned-agent in Springdale, Arkansas, earned two consecutive Agent-of-the-Year Awards, this one at Colorado Springs in 1963 and the following year in Quebec.

Harold Remley, Jefferson City, Missouri, was a consistently top producer from the 1940s into the '60s, and was the first to win the Agent of the Year award, in 1960. His son, Harold Jr., continues to operate the agency today.

Panels of award winning agents shared their techniques with others at the conferences. Here, Ralph Ross, Chillicothe, takes his turn, while Harold Riekhof, Higginsville, Missouri and Jewell Roberts, Arkadelphia, Arkansas listen.

Jim Sawyer, Jonesboro, Arkansas, also a former employee, outdid his fellow Razorback, winning the top award three times, in 1965, '66 and '67. The rules were changed beginning in 1968, allowing only one chance to win the award.

As Paul Keithley's retirement approached in 1978, he could look back on many years and several roles with MFA Mutual, including that of secretary of the board of directors, and one of the investors of company funds.

MFA before joining the insurance company. Those old enough to do so served in their nation's armed forces during World War II, and Bill Conboy also saw duty in Korea. Their individual biographies reveal the talents these leaders contributed to the company.

Paul Keithley, who knew Jack Silvey at Gifford High School, graduated from Chillicothe Business College and went to work as a cost accountant for a Kansas City steel firm from 1937 to 1942. In 1942, he joined MFA's auditing department and, like Silvey before him, examined the books of local exchanges. Keithley joined MFA Mutual as a bookkeeper in November, 1946 after military service and additional experience with the farm cooperative. While serving as secretary-treasurer of the company beginning in 1948, and secretary of the board of directors starting in 1973, Keithley shared responsibility for investing the company's surplus and drew up monthly and annual financial statements. His early duties with the company included the details of office management.

The office Keithley managed had been the workplace of Arthur Lang since before the insurance company's official first day of business. A graduate of the University of Missouri's College of Agriculture in 1938 and its law school in 1941, Lang then served four years in the Army. He was wounded in France in 1944, spent months in military hospitals, and returned to Columbia in the fall of 1945 sharing a need with millions of veterans: a job. Lang's brother Howard was a good friend and law school classmate of A. D. Sappington, and Arthur himself had worked briefly in Sappington's office before the war. In October, A. D., in the midst of plans for launching the insurance company, hired Art Lang as a claims adjuster, and before the year ended he spent a month in the St. Louis offices of Employers Mutual Insurance Company learning the business. Lang spent his early years on the road investigating claims, returning on weekends to write his reports in the Home Office, located in the southwest corner, first floor, of the MFA headquarters building. Arthur Lang would devote his entire career to the Claims Department: he became claims manager in 1947 and retired in 1981 as vice president of claims.

When J. M. and Jim Silvey left the companies in 1964, two veteran employees stepped into vice presidencies. As James L. McTurnan vacated the position vice president of sales for his new post as vice president, underwriting, William H. Conboy took over as head of marketing. Both men made influential contributions to MFA Insurance's continued growth until their retirement in the 1980s.

After his military discharge in 1945, Conboy worked part- time for MFA and for MFA Mutual while he pursued a degree in finance — completed in 28 months — at the University of Missouri. After graduation in 1948, he served as district sales manager in northwest Missouri. When he left for a job with the Allstate Insurance Company in 1958, Conboy had managed MFA's Health Insurance Division for five years. President Sappington called Conboy "home" in March, 1964 to join his management team.

After completing his education, Jim McTurnan worked as an accountant and auditor for General Motors from 1940 to 1949, a job interrupted by military service in World War II. In 1949, he came to central Missouri as general manager of an insulation company, from which position he joined MFA Mutual in early 1953. McTurnan knew the company's operations from first-hand experience, for he held an impressive number of jobs: with the fire division in 1953-1954, as Missouri District 4 supervisor in 1954, as Nebraska and Arkansas state supervisors from 1954 to 1956, as chief underwriter from 1956 to 1959, and as vice president in charge of sales from 1959 to 1964. When he became vice president for underwriting in 1964, it was a new position.

Howard B. Lang, Jr., who would become the company's fourth president in 1979, became manager of the claims department and chief claims attorney 30 years earlier. After earning his law degree in 1936, Lang worked for the U. S. Department of Agriculture, conducted a private law practice in Columbia, and served as the elected Boone County Prosecuting Attorney from 1947 to 1949. He saw 30 months of duty in the Navy during the Second World War. Joining MFA Mutual in 1949,

Bill Conboy, marketing vice president, was a familiar figure at the speaker's rostrum.

Will L. Nelson, longtime friend and associate of both A. D. Sappington and Howard Lang, was MFA Mutual's general counsel from 1964 to 1981.

Lang became vice president in charge of claims in 1954. Ten years later, as A. D. Sappington became companies' president, the board named Lang senior vice president, the second-ranking officer in the company.

When Howard Lang became vice president of claims, he hired Will L. Nelson as an assistant claims attorney. Also a 1936 graduate of the law school in Columbia, Nelson established a practice in his home town and succeeded Sappington as the city attorney. The son of a veteran member of Congress, Nelson ran unsuccessfully for the U. S. House in 1946. When Sappington became president in 1964, Nelson became vice president and general counsel, a position he held until his retirement in 1981.

Two younger managers — men rising to prominence in the company during the Silvey and early Sappington years — were Gustav J. Lehr and Jack Pettit. Pettit joined MFA Mutual first, in April, 1949, hired by A. D. Sappington as a claims attorney. A graduate of Columbia's Hickman High School where he was student body president in 1940-41, Pettit served in Burma and China during WWII, and during law school worked in Howard Lang's prosecutor's office. Like Bill Conboy, Pettit worked briefly in Chicago for Allstate Insurance, as associate general counsel, in the early 1960s. He was assistant general counsel under Sappington beginning in 1956, A. D.'s administrative assistant in 1964, and administrative vice president in 1966. Jack Pettit's knowledge of the insurance business and his broad learning are the stuff of company legend even today.

In the seventh year of the company's existence, 1953, Gus Lehr came to work for MFA Mutual. In 1995, this former president remains chairman of the board of directors. It is doubtful if anyone in the 50-year history of the MFA/Shelter Insurance Companies — except Director Emeritus Bernice Seaman and a few policyholders and agents — has had a longer association with the firm. A claims adjuster before his graduation from the University of Missouri School of Law in 1959, and a claims attorney after that date, Lehr was hired by Howard Lang. Gus Lehr rose to become assistant general counsel in 1961 and vice president for public affairs in 1966.

Later chapters, of course, will have much more to say about Lehr and others whose careers this narrative have brought into the 1960s.

facing page: This early sign over the Lloyd Rush agency in Carthage, Missouri, boasted of the many benefits for insuring with MFA Mutual.

LEE'S
WALKER
INSURANCE
SPEEDY
MFA INSURANCE
AGENCY
M·F·A
INSURED
•LOW RATES
•RENEWAL DIVIDENDS
•QUICK CLAIM SERVICE
•NO MEMBERSHIP FEES
•NO ASSESSMENTS
LLOYD H. RUSH Agent
PROTECTION-SAVINGS AND SERVICE THROUGH THE CENTURIES
M·F·A
INSURED
MFA MUTUAL
Cancer strikes one in five
Strike back
Give to conquer cancer
McCORMICK'S

While still a young company, MFA Mutual became well known in the industry, and company leaders made a point to get to know other insurance leaders. Here President Silvey hosts a 1958 visit by Murray Lincoln, president of Nationwide Insurance.

chapter 4

Our Widening Ties 1946-1964

The first three chapters have discussed the internal history of MFA Mutual from 1946 to 1964. "Our Widening Ties" intends to cover the company's relations with insurance trade organizations; some of its legislative activities; and examples of its contributions to community betterment in the towns and cities where it did business during these same years.

Through the willingness of MFA Mutual people to accept responsibilities beyond those assigned by their employer, the company has assumed a leading role in the trade associations to which it belongs. Trade associations are organizations of like firms created to facilitate the exchange of ideas and information, and to allow united action in the pursuit of common interests before lawmakers and public opinion. The company's earliest active affiliation was with the National Association of Mutual Insurance Companies. NAMIC, organized in 1895, has been most closely identified with smaller mutual insurance companies. It enlisted more than 1,200 company-members as it began its second century. The National Association of Independent Insurers was organized when MFA Mutual was, in 1945. In the mid-1990s, it represented over 550 companies, both mutual and stock, which tended to be the larger firms. Beginning in the 1950s, but especially under President A. D. Sappington's leadership in the 1960s and 1970s, MFA Mutual became quite active in the NAII's affairs. A few examples will illustrate the company's involvement with both groups.

As early as 1951, J. O. Creasy, MFA Mutual's safety engineer, was named to the five-man safety committee of NAMIC. The committee's goal was to promote highway safety through school driver-training programs and local safety committees. In November, 1952 Chief Claims Attorney Howard B. Lang, Jr. was named a member of the arbitration committee of NAMIC. A year old at the time, the committee was formed to mediate claims between the 51 mutual casualty carriers whose primary business was auto insurance. By the summer of 1953, Lang became chairman of the arbitration committee. In April, 1954 this key five-man group met in Columbia to conduct its business.

Other MFA Mutual people obtained NAMIC committee appointments. They included Ken Backues to the general liability underwriting committee, W. Judd Wyatt to the public relations committee, and Vic Ohman to the safety and loss prevention committee — all in 1954. In the following year, seven MFA Mutual professionals served on the National Association's committees, including John Pelot, chief underwriter, Henry Kilburn, production manager, and Lloyd Krofft, manager of the statistical department.

With other National Association of Mutual Insurance Companies members, MFA Mutual celebrated the bicentennial of mutual insurance in the United States in 1952. On March 25, 1752 Benjamin Franklin established The Philadelphia

MFA/Shelter Mutual has always promoted the concept of mutuality, and this panel of agents and employees helped celebrate the 200th anniversary of mutual insurance in 1952, also the company's sixth anniversary.

Through its Conference of Mutual Casualty Companies membership, the company participated in the organization's claims arbitration committee. Here Will L. Nelson, second from left, hosts the committee during a 1963 meeting in Columbia. Nelson chaired the industry-wide committee which negotiated claims for 60 companies.

Contributionship For The Insurance of Houses From Loss by Fire, America's first mutual insurance company. On that date in 1952, Jack Silvey, A. D. Sappington, Howard B. Lang, Jr. and Henry Kilburn attended a banquet in Franklin's home city to commemorate the event, while other company officers participated in a similar ceremony in Jefferson City. A week earlier in Columbia, MFA Mutual held its own 200th birthday dinner, complete with a large cake, and in October a group of company personnel returned to Philadelphia for the "Mutual Insurance Advertising Exhibit," held in the Benjamin Franklin Hotel.

In the late 1950s and early 1960s, the company assumed an active role in the National Association of Independent Insurers. Nationally respected in the field of claims, Howard B. Lang, Jr. was chairman of the group's Claim Study Committee in 1958-1959, after which he continued as a member. President J. M. Silvey was elected a vice president of NAII at the 1959 annual meeting. In 1963, Will L. Nelson was chairman of the Claims Arbitration Committee, which he hosted in Columbia in August. In 1961, five MFA Mutual managers were members of NAII committees, a number which grew to eight two years later.

CONTACT editor Gene Baumann, in 1963, became editor of "The Mutual Piper," the monthly newsletter of MICE (Mutual Insurance Council of Editors). As Gene said: "I thought it would be good experience and a chance to spread the name of MFA Insurance around the country." That, in fact, was one by-product of participation in national insurance organizations, participation whose main goal

was a better industry. Other professional organizations in which MFA Mutual people were active included the American Institute of Cooperation and the American Institute of Management. In 1953, Silvey was elected to the President's Council of the latter group. MFA Mutual's advertising and publications regularly won commendations by NAMIC, NAII, and other professional organizations. And its emergence as a leader in the mutual insurance business nationwide made MFA Mutual a model for those seeking to establish insurance protection in other nations. In December, 1953 two Indonesian government representatives visited the Home Office to learn more about mutual insurance companies which offered non-assessable policies.

Earl and Mary Smith, Wichita

From an early date, MFA Mutual took advantage of its right to convey to legislators its positions on proposed federal and state legislation. Mindful of the boost Missouri's 1946 financial-responsibility law had given to auto insurance sales, the company's leaders were as ready to support bills that would promote the policyholders' interests as to discourage passage of harmful ones. "America's highway system is in a mess," the newsletter commented in 1952. MFA Mutual helped to generate, through its agents, support for federal spending on better, safer highways during the 1950s. It advocated a stronger financial-responsibility law before one was enacted to take effect in 1953, state motor vehicle inspection years before it became law, and a larger highway patrol — all in Missouri. In 1957, the board of directors approved the company's taking advantage of a federal flood insurance program, should it become available. Under consideration was a plan to provide citizens with flood insurance through private insurers.

Fred Heinkel, standing next to then Senator Hubert Humphrey, watches President John F. Kennedy sign legislation in September of 1962. Also at the signing were Vice President Lyndon Johnson, center of back row, and Secretary of Agriculture Orville Freeman, to Johnson's right. Heinkel had unquestioned influence on the shaping of farm bills in Congress, and was mentioned as a possible candidate for Secretary of Agriculture in the Kennedy Administration.

Four years later, A. D. Sappington reported to the board an example of harmful federal action. Before Congress was a bill to increase the taxes on mutual insurance companies. And MFA Mutual joined the industry in stating "the case against compulsory auto insurance." What sounded too good to be true, was. Compulsory insurance systems in the three states that had them in 1963 could not compel, were costly to administer, did not protect the responsibly-insured driver, and increased the cost of car insurance.

Some of MFA Mutual's legislative positions mirrored the views of the parent MFA. In 1948, the farm co-op gave strong support to the Curry Bill in the Missouri General Assembly. The measure proposed to raise the gas tax to improve county roads and city streets. A competing measure would have increased the money available for state highways, but not rural county roads. J. M. Silvey urged the company's agents to work for passage of the Curry Bill by contacting their legislators.

In September, 1953, wishing to influence the shape of the next farm bill in Washington, Fred Heinkel called six "mass meetings" of MFA members at which Missouri farmers could express their views. A. D. Sappington contacted all MFA Mutual agents, urging them to attend the nearest meeting and "see to it that a carload or more of farmers from your area go[es] with you . . ." The insurance company owed this support to MFA, for it "has time and again protected the principle of mutual insurance and has defended MFA Mutual against its enemies."

As a company and through the actions of individuals who were a part of it, MFA Mutual resoundingly succeeded in being a good business citizen of the communities where it operated. This fact was most evident in its hometown of Columbia during this early period. But in numerous other places as well, agents' and employees' civic spirit and volunteer work made "MFA Insurance" stand for more than sound insurance protection.

In its financial support of the Missouri School of Religion, MFA Mutual showed again that it was a reflection of its second president, and expressed its continuing interest in the betterment of rural communities. Founded in 1895 as the Bible College of Missouri and renamed the School of Religion in 1958, the school was located on the University of Missouri campus. It had a special affiliation with J. M. Silvey's own denomination, though its coursework was non-denominational Protestant. In 1948, Executive Vice-President Silvey became a member of the Advisory Committee of the Bible College, as it was about to embark on a pioneer effort in the training of rural ministers. Silvey, with

Dick Ferguson, left, and Bill Conboy, following their recall into active duty for the Korean War. Both had served during World War II, and were representative of a number of employees who took leave from the company to serve in the military.

President A. D. Sappington was honored by the Missouri State Highway Department for his significant role in the development of Missouri's highways, including the interstate system.

his MFA background, had "a keen insight into the needs of rural Missouri." Beginning that fall, the company made cash donations to the school, and that support continued during Silvey's tenure with the company. In 1961, MFA Mutual agents established the J. M. Silvey Endowment Fund, for agents' contributions to the School of Religion in Silvey's name. It is fair to say that MFA Mutual's support was largely responsible for the institution's survival. By 1964, Silvey was chair of the board of trustees of the school, and a member of the board of Christian College.

The company made donations to both Christian and Stephens College fund-raising drives, and supported special University of Missouri programs. In 1956, as the university replaced its two-year medical program with a full medical school curriculum, MFA Mutual contributed to a revolving student loan fund for students heading for practices in rural Missouri. Four years later the company agreed to partially underwrite the salary of a professional who would promote farm safety. The board of directors approved a three-year contract. Fred Heinkel became a university curator in 1953, while Howard Lang served for many years on the Stephens College Board of Curators.

In its home city MFA Mutual gave financial support to the Chamber of

Walter Baird was a longtime underwriting manager, and was instrumental in the development of the resident underwriting program.

Fred Heinkel's reputation as a farm leader helped bring President Jimmy Carter to Columbia to address the 1978 MFA Convention.

Dwight Darby, after managing the first branch office outside Columbia, finished his career as an agent in Springfield, Missouri.

Commerce and to the expansion of the county hospital. Although their departure disrupted office routine, the company proudly saw some of its male employees depart for the Korean War. One, Lt. Burl Baker, gave his life for his country in Korea. CARE, an organization through which Americans helped feed the free world's hungry during the Cold War years, received the wholehearted support of MFA Mutual agents and employees. In 1959, for example, company personnel and those of MFA made contributions that paid for 180,000 meals.

J. M. Silvey's public service reached far beyond his religious commitments. With other civic leaders like Mayor Roy Sappington, Martin Faust, and Marjorie Carpenter, he served on the Columbia Charter Commission in 1949, a group whose work brought the city manager form of government to the town. In the same year Silvey co-chaired a Committee on Rural and Forestry Fire Problems in Missouri. Established by Governor Forrest Smith, the committee presented its report at an all-day conference in Jefferson City on September 12. Silvey took advantage of his contact with the governor to point out an "even more serious safety problem in this state," the auto accident rates of drivers under age 26. In 1954-1955, Silvey was one of 29 state leaders appointed to an educational commission charged with preparing recommendations on such matters as school financing and teacher training.

Other MFA Mutual personnel served state and local governments during these years. In the spring of 1955, claims attorney Will L. Nelson was chosen president of the Columbia School Board. Paul Keithley served on the same body from 1954 to 1957. In the wake of the Supreme Court's desegregation decision in 1954, these were crucial years in public education, and MFA Mutual people were on the front lines. Vice President A. D. Sappington, in April, 1954, joined the Missouri State Highway Commission upon appointment by Governor Phil M. Donnelly. Sappington remained on the commission until 1963, a period during which Missouri became the first state to begin building the interstate system. In 1968 the commission named Sappington one of "The Builders" (six in number) of Missouri's modern highway system.

To list Howard B. Lang, Jr.'s civic contributions is to fill a large sheet of paper. Among his responsibilities not already mentioned was service as Columbia's mayor from 1953 to 1957, during which time major road expansion, urban renewal, and municipal utilities growth occurred. At his last city council meeting in April, 1957, the group recognized Lang's accomplishment: "When history is written your administration will be known as one of the greatest." One account of the company's history says that Howard Lang and A. D. Sappington, friends since law school, "brought MFA Insurance in closer contact" with the Columbia community than it had been in its earliest years. "Together these two lawyers brought the insurance company, and to a lesser extent, the MFA, Inc., into the main stream of responsible corporate citizenship."

Agents, too, volunteered time and talents to community betterment. Gene Taylor of Sarcoxie — later a member of the House of Representatives from his district — attended the 1960 Republican nominating convention as a delegate. The February 22, 1953 issue of CONTACT reported the sponsorship of school safety programs by four agencies in Missouri. John Eisenbeis in Ste. Genevieve, Ambrose Maasen in Lynn, and 14 other agents headed their county Heart Fund drives in 1954. MFA agents in numerous towns combined business and civic responsibility as they led "clean-up week" campaigns in their communities during the mid-1950s. Cleaning out trash promoted loss-prevention and made for more pleasant living environments. "We encourage agents to be active in community affairs," was the introduction CONTACT gave to a busy agent, John A. Frazier of Van Buren late in 1955. Frazier was Carter County treasurer, mayor of Van Buren, operator of the automobile license bureau, a notary public, president of the Rotary Club, and a member of the county draft board. In May, 1961, MFA Mutual employees Cleo Ross and Randall Earnest became key figures in an emergency flood rescue effort. After a flash flood inundated Harrison, Arkansas, the two men, each in his own boat, rescued victims — as many as 50 people between them. In the aftermath of the disaster, which killed four people and destroyed 80% of the town's business district and many homes, the safety representative and claims adjuster helped a wounded community to recover.

NAII committee service and charity organization leadership are the stuff of which American business and American communities are made. Both are essential to understanding the full life of MFA Mutual during this or any other era in its history.

In Chapter 5 a very important period in the company's history comes under review. The following four chapters will deal with the period from J. M. Silvey's release in 1964, through the successful administration of A. D. Sappington until his premature death in 1979, to the series of events which caused MFA Mutual and MFA to go their separate ways by 1981. In that landmark year, a seasoned company took a new name: Shelter Insurance.

F. B. Manion (above) and Gene Smith (below), Salisbury, Missouri

A uniform sign program was introduced in 1967, to create a consistent image at agent offices throughout the operating territory. Here Columbia's Orian Smith watches the installation of his new sign.

Of the many aspects of the president's job, Sappington's favorite was getting out among the people. Here he greets office staff at Agent Earl Doerrie's open house in 1969.

Part Two:

A TIME OF CHALLENGE AND TRANSFORMATION, 1964-1981

chapter 5

Overview 1964-1981

The title of Part 2 — "a time of challenge and transformation" — accurately characterizes the middle period of the MFA Mutual Insurance Company's development. With continued growth to financial strength and quality service to policyholders, formidable challenges did confront the company, led during these years by Presidents A. D. Sappington and Howard B. Lang, Jr., and Board Chairman Fred V. Heinkel. A major goal, for example, was most elusive for this and for other casualty companies: earning an underwriting profit. The company did not meet that challenge every year between 1964 and 1980, but, with the notable exception of 1974, the company added to surplus each year during this period.

Other major challenges included a consolidation of the sales territory in 1975, and a second unplanned leadership transition following the death of President A. D. Sappington in early 1979 — topics covered in chapters 5 and 6. Chapter 8 will call attention to several ways in which the political climate in Jefferson City and Washington became a growing factor in the company's operations. A persisting dispute with the Internal Revenue Service over the taxable status of its agents, the rise of "no-fault" insurance plans and other governmental intrusions into an already tightly-regulated industry, and a Missouri gubernatorial administration that was conspicuously unfriendly to insurance companies absorbed the time and taxed the other resources of MFA Mutual's management and employees.

The major transformation, as those even slightly familiar with the company's history well know, grew out of a dispute with the parent organization, the Missouri Farmers Association. The conflict began in August, 1979 with the defeat of Fred V. Heinkel for a 40th annual term as MFA president by a challenger who soon made unacceptable demands of the insurance company. It ended with a legal agreement formalized in 1980 under which the two entities separated, and with the renaming of MFA Mutual as Shelter Mutual in July, 1981, now under the presidential leadership of Gustav J. Lehr. This fascinating story will occupy the latter pages of the chapter.

Of course, most days in the life of a business are not dominated by electrifying, newsworthy events. MFA/Shelter employees, and historians too, realize that the important work of the company is routine: agents meeting with policyholders in homes and offices across a 13-state region; underwriters evaluating applications and issuing policies; training instructors meeting with classes of new agents or veteran claims adjusters, and so on. The day-in, day-out activity of several thousand people in the years 1964-1981 also will permeate the pages of this and the three chapters which follow.

A. D. Sappington wrote the incorporation papers for the new company in 1945, and served as president from 1964 to 1979. He served on the board of directors from 1960 to 1979.

The company that A. D. Sappington began to lead in February, 1964 possessed many strengths. So did he, and that was important. Quickly forming a team of capable officers and shaping a plan of action to deal with such conditions as persistent underwriting losses, A. D. set out to make a fundamentally sound company even stronger.

What sort of man was A. D. Sappington? What sort of leadership style did he exhibit during the 15 years from February, 1964 to February, 1979? Although A. D., as he asked everyone in the company to call him, had to issue orders and directives, he characteristically led by force of intellect, a thorough knowledge of the insurance business, and an intimate familiarity with his own company from the days when it was only an idea. He was a respected leader in the casualty insurance industry nationwide (see chapter 8), and one of the most influential private citizens in Columbia and Missouri. A 1977 journalists' study of influentials who worked quietly behind the scenes to get things done in Columbia prominently featured both Sappington and Fred Heinkel. Whereas J. M. Silvey gave close attention to detail — perhaps too close attention to what today would be called "micro-management" — A. D. was an "idea man," to use the phrase of Howard Lang. He could envision the company's role and future consistent with its past, and could place its year-to-year experience within the context of the industry experience and the nation's economy. And he often did just those things in articulate, easy-to-understand addresses to company personnel at Conferences of Champions or employees' meetings, or before gatherings of industry leaders. A. D. Sappington showed an uncommon ability clearly to articulate MFA Mutual's and the casualty industry's best interests in the face of supposedly beneficial "reforms" of insurance practice in this country.

A. D. was such a towering figure that, without knowing it or desiring it, he intimidated some younger associates, at least early in their relationships. The same people found Sappington to be very gracious. He is still fondly recalled as an agents' and employees' president. Many of A. D.'s letters to individual agents are preserved, letters offering encouragement, explaining company decisions, and responding to concerns. Sappington also routinely scrawled messages across the bottom of form letters sent to the agency force: hope you had a good Christmas; hope to see you at the Conference of Champions.

In the Home Office, A. D. made it a practice to stroll through the departments, often in casual dress on a Friday, to visit with employees, most of whom he knew by name. Howard Lang, Sappington's closest associate for 30 years in MFA Mutual and the one whom he made second in command in 1964, recalls that A. D. was uncomfortable delivering bad news. He sent Lang and Bill Conboy, for example, to tell Texas and Minnesota agents that the company was pulling out of their states in 1975. Above all else, A. D. was a decent man. As Howard Lang recalls: "I never heard him say an unkind word about anyone."

President Sappington, in the months following his election by the board, instituted changes of tactics and strategy. Some of these were subtle differences of emphasis, some were visible parts of the company's daily routine but detectable only by the expert perception of insurance insiders, and others clear and explicit, for all to see. By April, 1964 a newly configured team of veteran managers was in place. Its most important players were Howard Lang, as senior vice president, James L.

Three special guests at the dedication of the Home Office fountain were Scottie Garrett, grounds manager, with two contractors who supervised construction of the fountain, Charlie Bugg and Jim Moore.

James L. McTurnan, vice president of underwriting, in 1980.

Jim Offutt was named vice president of actuarial in April 1972.

McTurnan as vice president of Underwriting, William H. Conboy as vice president of Marketing, Will L. Nelson as vice president and general counsel, and Arthur P. Lang as vice president of Claims. A. D. also mentored talented younger managers: Jack L. Pettit, who in 1964 became administrative assistant to the president, Gustav J. Lehr, who in 1966 became vice president for Public Affairs, and Jean Madden, brought into the company in 1971 as vice president of Communications. Only a few MFA Mutual personnel followed J. M. Silvey into the new insurance company which he led until his death in 1988.

During the next few years, under Conboy's leadership, the company purposefully reduced and professionalized its agency force, phasing out part-time agents and those with chronic high loss ratios. (See chapter 7) Underwriters in the Home Office tightened standards, so that all applications did not earn MFA insurance policies. Training assumed a new importance, and Henry Kilburn soon devoted full time to it.

Of genuine importance was more detailed and comprehensive data collection. First in a department of research and development under Glenn Pratt, and then in an actuarial department headed by James A. Offutt, an able staff calculated the need for rate increases for various lines in the states, and filed the applications for

below: Chairman Heinkel, left, and President Lang, right, flank three newly reelected board members in 1979 — Sam Murrell, Fred Brehe, and Miller Hern.

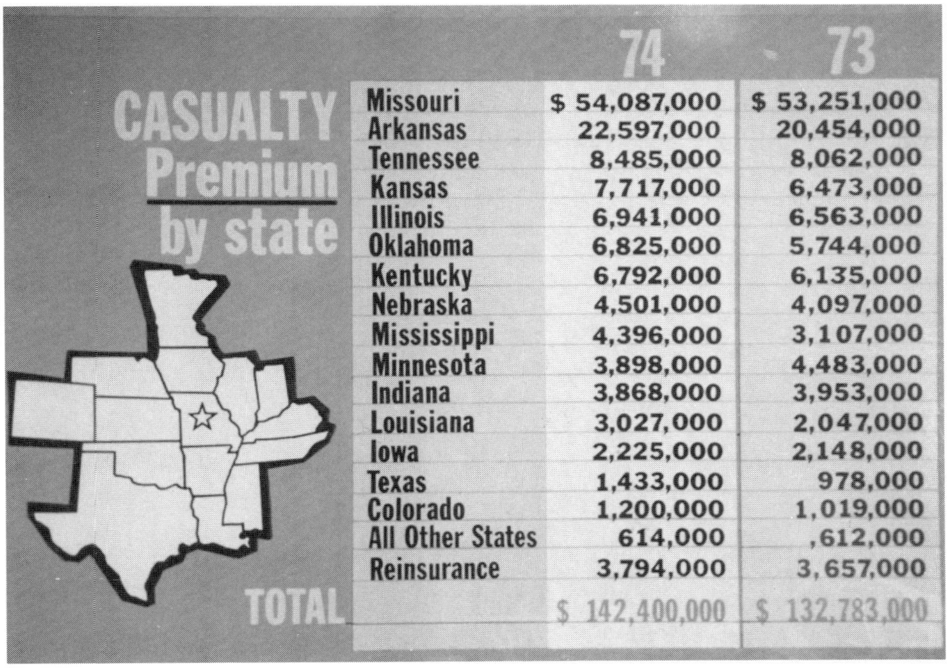

Slides such as this reported results to those attending MFA Mutual's annual meetings the first Wednesday of each April.

these changes with state insurance regulators. The actuarial staff could accurately project the impact of approved rate increases on company revenues. The improved financial reporting to the board and to company officers overseen by Paul Keithley and George Kent included monthly state-by-state underwriting results, begun in the early 1960s; and state-level consolidated reports for all MFA insurance companies, begun in the mid-1970s. Appearing in the 1970s were monthly marketing reports by Bill Conboy, claims reports by Arthur Lang, communications reports (including advertising and public relations information) by Jean Madden, and rates and filings reports by Jim Offutt.

Arguably President Sappington's most important change was the setting of profit as the central goal of company operations. In an undated overview of MFA Mutual and Countryside Casualty Company, probably written late in 1963 or early 1964, J. M. Silvey saw virtue in those companies' overall underwriting losses: "Policy holders have received their insurance for $2,538,890 less than cost. The surplus of the company has been built up from investment income." A. D. did not think of below-cost insurance as an advantage to policyholders, because it threatened the viability of the firm. As he said in 1970:

Why is profit one of our essential objectives? Not only is the rating assigned to our company [by Alfred M. Best Company] based largely upon the ratio of our surplus to written premium, but also the proper ratio of surplus to written premium is necessary for the financial stability and soundness of our companies.

By 1965, A. D. had established the goal of making a profit — that is, of adding to policyholder surplus not only from investment income, but also by holding losses and expenses to a level below the premium income. Speaking to employees on May 7, A. D. announced: "Our primary goal this year is to at least break even on our insurance operations." Beyond 1965, the company would realize an underwriting profit. "I know we can demonstrate to the entire casualty insurance industry that underwriting losses are NOT a necessary condition of being in the insurance business." He repeated the message in a letter "To all MFA Insurance Agents" dated July 9, 1965: "it is absolutely necessary that losses and expenses incurred do not exceed earned premium. Without question, our one most important job is to make an underwriting profit. . . ."

Table 5.1 MFA Mutual, Key Indicators of Growth,1964-1980

	1964	1965	1966
Earned Premium	$36,128,372	$41,791,688	$46,983,912
Cost of Losses & Adjustment	27,308,980	29,142,972	32,468,092
Underwriting Expenses	11,105,556	12,143,351	12,360,738
Net Underwriting Results	(2,313,717)	109,388	1,258,415
Total Investment Gain	2,788,635	1,867,047	1,898,434
Net Addition to Surplus	470,177	1,775,008	3,342,146
Year-end Surplus	10,747,941	12,249,949	15,592,096
	1967	**1968**	**1969**
Earned Premium	$48,234,233	$53,475,729	$58,771,867
Cost of Losses & Adjustment	33,036,077	40,352,359	44,304,878
Underwriting Expenses	13,269,960	14,967,445	15,709,477
Net Underwriting Results	796,021	(2,678,128)	(1,985,115)
Total Investment Gain	2,074,653	3,418,606	2,667,433
Net Addition to Surplus	2,522,761	3,700,807	1,282,343
Year-end Surplus	18,114,857	21,815,664	23,098,007
	1970	**1971**	**1972**
Earned Premium	$65,654,111	$80,506,145	$96,180,070
Cost of Losses & Adjustment	44,642,919	52,596,683	61,099,183
Underwriting Expenses	18,881,536	24,671,624	27,638,519
Net Underwriting Results	1,091,055	2,185,168	5,664,223
Total Investment Gain	3,005,646	3,191,244	5,417,202
Net Addition to Surplus	4,745,483	5,048,452	10,589,397
Year-end Surplus	27,843,490	32,891,942	43,481,337
	1973	**1974**	**1975**
Earned Premium	$110,803,763	$121,154,244	$131,898,286
Cost of Losses & Adjustment	79,037,680	94,401,586	106,072,393

One goal of this chapter is to see how successful the companies were in reaching their leader's major objective. What follows is an overview of the annual financial results, primarily of MFA Mutual, still the dominant member of the MFA Insurance family of companies, from 1964 through 1980. While Table 5.1 summarizes key data, the following paragraphs point out interesting and significant features of the statistics.

Board Chairman Fred V. Heinkel's straightforward explanation of insurance company finance is a good guide to the meaning in the statistics. As he told the April 1976 Annual Meeting:

. . . from the premium which we receive must be deducted the cost of claims or losses, as this is the reason people buy insurance. In addition, we must pay the expenses of salaries, commission, advertising, etc. Then there must be additions to reserves to keep the company strong. If there is anything left of the premium we have an underwriting profit, and to this we add the earnings from investments.

Underwriting Expenses	33,438,274	38,583,957	36,722,637
Net Underwriting Results	(3,939,343)	(13,241,266)	(11,553,281)
Total Investment Gain	5,535,310	4,169,662	6,062,732
Net Addition to Surplus	223,096	(14,521,685)	3,628,324
Year-end Surplus	43,704,433	29,182,748	32,811,072

	1976	**1977**	**1978**
Earned Premium	$136,274,031	$146,460,386	$162,910,241
Cost of Losses & Adjustment	90,343,418	90,471,123	107,820,936
Underwriting Expenses	36,785,515	41,308,910	44,955,570
Net Underwriting Results	5,680,922	9,980,564	7,975,438
Total Investment Gain	7,878,034	7,742,798	9,588,872
Net Addition to Surplus	24,438,122	19,468,177	21,389,543
Year-end Surplus	57,249,194	76,717,371	98,106,914

	1979	**1980**
Earned Premium	$179,742,259	$194,845,582
Cost of Losses & Adjustment	125,216,663	146,163,302
Underwriting Expenses	47,867,079	51,946,389
Net Underwriting Results	4,622,690	(6,217,665)
Total Investment Gain	12,174,534	19,778,076
Net Addition to Surplus	26,721,933	29,591,597
Year-end Surplus	124,828,847	154,420,444

An overview of the company's financial performance from 1964 to 1980 reveals three periods of contrasting experience. The decade from 1964 to 1973 was one of gradual, steady growth as measured by premium dollars earned and growth of policyholder surplus. But while the company made additions to surplus in each of these years, in 1974 — which Sappington termed "the worst year in our history" — surplus declined by one-third of the 1973 year-end total. Although surplus grew in 1973 and 1975, the company experienced large underwriting losses in those years. In the five years which followed these loss years, 1976-1980, the company's performance showed unprecedented, even spectacular, growth. Never before was MFA Mutual as strong financially as when the 1980s opened.

What of A. D.'s goal of making an underwriting profit each year in the casualty insurance business? In 11 of the 17 years under review, MFA Mutual did achieve an underwriting profit, ranging from $109,000 in 1965 (the first profitable year since 1960), to $9.9 million in 1977, the best year to 1980 from an underwriting standpoint. And 1978 was not far behind this achievement. In six of the 17 years the company suffered losses on its insurance operations, including staggering losses of $13.2 million in 1974 and $11.5 million in 1975. The impact of these years lingered into the good ones which followed. The cumulative three-year underwriting loss for 1973-1975 was $32,361,000. Even after hefty underwriting gains in 1976, 1977, and 1978, the six-year cumulative loss at the end of 1978 remained $4.3 million.

In 1971, A. D. Sappington, Judd Wyatt, Fred Heinkel, Arthur Lang, and R. J. Rosier celebrated 25-years of service, all having been a part of the company since 1946.

The company's poor years reflected the experience of the entire casualty industry. When it departed from industry-wide figures, MFA Mutual performed better than the average of all firms. The company, for example, pulled out of the trough of 1974 more rapidly than the industry. In the first quarter of 1976, while the company had an underwriting gain, the industry suffered a $1.06 billion loss. Still, to return to the question, MFA Mutual found that making an underwriting gain was a difficult challenge, whether the C.E.O. was A. D. Sappington or J. M. Silvey. For the life of both casualty companies, MFA Mutual and Countryside Casualty Company, as of December 31, 1976, the underwriting loss was $17.8 million. While Countryside had made over $2.2 million since its inception in 1957, MFA Mutual had lost over $20 million on its insurance operations since 1946. In 1980, Jim McTurnan made a ten-year review of MFA Mutual's underwriting experience. As of September 30 of that year, "the underwriting result was approximately break even" for the decade. Such figures spurred A. D. to greater effort rather than causing discouragement. Standing in the rubble of 1974, he found even that year filled with good signs: MFA Mutual's growth rate exceeded that of the industry, and it had been a good year for the sale of life and health insurance.

President Sappington's search for silver linings was not public relations; it was genuine, and characteristic of the man.

Many achievements distinguish these years. The total admitted assets of MFA Mutual grew impressively, passing $100 million in 1972, $200 million in 1977, and $300 million in 1980. The increase of assets by $42 million in 1979 surpassed the company's total assets of $39.8 million in 1963, J. M. Silvey's last year. In each of the years 1972 and 1976-1980, assets grew by more than $20 million. The amount added to surplus in 1977 — almost $19.5 million — was nearly double the total surplus of $10.7 million at the end of 1964, A. D.'s first year as president. The $29.5 million added to surplus in 1980 was nearly three times the total surplus in 1964. Two statistics demonstrate the impressive growth of surplus in the late 1970s. The net addition to surplus in 1976-1979 was $92,017,775. That amount was 74% of the total surplus in 1979. Compared to its pre-1964 experience, the MFA Mutual Insurance Company was so large by the late 1970s that the insignificant amount of dividends paid to some policyholders in some states, and the still sizable payments to MFA, were hardly noticed.

Senior Vice President Howard Lang speaks to employees in 1972.

Several milestones may stand for many others achieved between 1964 to 1980. In 1968, earned premium surpassed $50 million, and surplus exceeded $20 million for the first time. By 1973, earned premium exceeded $100 million. In 1972, the first annual addition to surplus in excess of $10 million occurred. In 1976, surplus passed the $50 million mark, three years later it shot past $100 million, and in 1980 it exceeded $150 million. Late in 1974, President Sappington reported that the companies had "over one million policies in force of all kinds." In 1968, the MFA Insurance Companies ranked as the 65th largest insurance group in the nation, and MFA Mutual was the 20th largest mutual company — a remarkable achievement over 22 years' time.

Within the industry the most widely accepted and respected measure of financial soundness is the rating of companies by the Alfred M. Best Company. As one might expect in a period that witnessed wide swings from profit to loss and back again, MFA Mutual's ratings did not remain constant. Early in 1967, A. D. Sappington met with officers of A. M. Best, Inc. in New York: "they commented on the splendid progress and sound financial condition of the company," and renewed its "A" rating. But by mid-1970, Best Vice President Robert J. Schraeder warned that the "A" rating was "in a very weak position" — though sales were soaring and the company would add almost $5 million to surplus by December 31. "For the second straight year [1968-1969] underwriting proved unrewarding and in addition the company encountered [investment] portfolio depreciation." By late 1973, however, after three years of strong performance, the Best Company awarded MFA Mutual a policyholder rating of "A+" and a "5-A" financial rating, the highest marks available. But the following three years of poor performance, 1973-1975, eroded the Best evaluation to an "A" policyholder rating in mid-1975, and a "B+" by May, 1976. It returned to an "A" one year later, and to an "A+" by mid-1979.

The late 1960s and the 1970s were particularly challenging for business leadership, and the MFA Insurance Group was quite fortunate to have A. D. Sappington at the helm during these years. He was aware of the threats to company success posed by such unprecedented conditions as stagflation — which A. D. defined as an economy "in a period of recession while at the same time [in] a period of inflation" — and recurring energy crises. The runaway inflation of the 1970s significantly increased the cost of losses, as auto repair and home replacement expenses soared. In addition, lagging economic growth and the increased cost of credit and fuel slowed new car and home sales — all bad signs for the insurance industry.

After 25 years on the board of directors, L. O. Wallis, right, retired at the April 1971 annual meeting, receiving a citation of appreciation from President Sappington and Chairman Heinkel.

The tools available to any casualty insurance company to correct flagging performance are limited. A. D. did not invent them any more than J. M. Silvey had. They were time-honored, common-sense responses used by insurers nationwide. What is interesting and instructive to note is the certainty and vigor with which President Sappington directed his management team to act in 1964-1965, his initial years as company head, and in subsequent years of profit and loss. Inheriting a record of underwriting losses in 1964, A. D. implemented a comprehensive program to reverse that situation: justifiable rate increases, "better agents, a better quality of business, and all full-time agents." These and other steps produced an underwriting profit in 1965 and 1966, so that A. D. could call the latter "the best year in the history of the Company."

Sappington loved to address agents and employees. Here he addresses a 1972 meeting; throughout the 1950s he was the motivational speaker for many company meetings.

In 1968 and 1969, and even more in 1973 through 1975, A. D.'s response to serious losses was quick and sure, based on intimate knowledge of his own casualty companies and of the nature of the business. The most visible action taken was the reduction of the MFA Insurance sales territory after nearly a quarter-century of expansion — a subject detailed in chapter 6. That step should not overshadow other constructive decisions that strengthened the company's financial condition, in the interest of its policyholders.

Scattered examples will suggest the comprehensive scope of the Sappington team's strategy. In 1968, based on detailed knowledge of frequency and severity of losses, the underwriting department conducted a state-by-state, agent-by-agent review of policies to identify bad risks and apply more stringent underwriting standards. In February, 1969, the company's loss-reduction efforts included increasing rates for younger drivers, reducing excessive loss ratios in the states of Arkansas, Illinois, and Tennessee, and meeting with 211 agents "on whose business in 1968 losses were in excess of $4 Million." A few of those agents "resigned rather than cooperate in good risk selection," and A. D. knew that their departure strengthened the company. Countryside Casualty Company proved its worth in times of excessive losses; agents were urged to convert MFA Mutual policies on accident-prone drivers to policies in Countryside "to obtain a rate commensurate with the risk involved."

Not much could be done about catastrophic storm losses, a major contributor to the underwriting losses of 1973, when, by July, storms had cost MFA Mutual over $3 million, and of 1980, in which storm losses exceeded $8 million. The company did, however, substantially increase its reserves against losses. In 1974, for example, MFA Mutual increased its loss reserves by $11.5 million, "about equal to the amount of decrease in surplus." Reduction of underwriting expense was another logical response to poor financial results, and in 1975 that kind of reduction and another in the agent recruitment program saved about $3 million.

Director Everett Osborne studies figures at a board meeting. He served from 1964 to 1970.

Table 5.2 MFA Mutual's Board of Directors February, 1964-July, 1981

Member	Residence	Years of Service
Fred V. Heinkel, Chair	Columbia	Chair 1964- April 17, 1981 Member 1964-1981
Howard B. Lang, Jr. (succeeded A. D. Sappington)	Columbia	Member April 11, 1979 Chair April 17, 1981
A. D. Sappington	Columbia	1964-April 11, 1979
Arthur Neuenschwander	Deepwater	1964-September 29, 1964
Lawrence Kullmann (succeeded Neuenschwander)	Warrensburg	September 29, 1964-1981
L. O. Wallis	Springfield	1964-April 7, 1971
Edwin F. Sachs (succeeded Wallis)	Rolla	April 7, 1971-1981
Miller Hern	Rocheport	1964-1981
B. M. Seaman	New Boston	1964-1981
Sam Murrell	Lancaster	1964-1981
Everett Osborne (succeeded Silvey)	Nixa	Feb. 28, 1964-April 1, 1970
Joe A. Marshall (succeeded Osborne)	Marshall	April 1, 1970-Sept. 28, 1972
Fred Brehe (succeeded Marshall)	Marthasville	September 28, 1972-1981
R. J. Rosier	Columbia	Secretary of Board 1964-March 8, 1973 Member of Board 1964-1981
Paul Keithley		Secretary of Board March 8, 1973-Sept. 1, 1978
J. Donald Duello		Secretary of Board September 1, 1978-1981

The MFA Insurance Companies relied not only on President Sappington and his management staff for informed leadership, but also on Chairman Fred V. Heinkel and other directors. Mr. Heinkel served nearly the entire period under consideration as board chairman, and, when he yielded that position on April 17, 1981, he remained on the board. Also providing stability and continuity for the era from February, 1964 to July, 1981 were R. J. Rosier, Miller Hern, B. M. Seaman, and Sam Murrell. Lawrence Kullmann served almost as long. A. D. Sappington was a director as well as president. Board members reflected the insurance company's close ties with MFA. The 1969 group, for example, retained three of the four men who had led the farm co-op's founding of MFA Mutual in 1945 — Heinkel, Rosier, and Sappington. Also on the board then was L. O. Wallis, an MFA official from Springfield, and four farmers with close MFA affiliations: Hern, Murrell, Kullmann, and Seaman. And Everett Osborne was a retired farmer.

Directors during these years were busy people. In addition to regular and special board meetings and the company's annual meeting in April, they attended informational sessions for agents and employees. And they traveled: all members were present for the May, 1974 board meeting in Little Rock. In July of that year, the board held the first of what would in the future be frequent two-day meetings, spending part of one day touring the facilities of affiliated companies Mid-America Auto Parts and KMMO radio.

Director Lawrence Kullman of Warrensburg served from 1964 to 1981 on the MFA Mutual board.

At Agent Jim Edwards' open house in Kirksville, Missouri, Director B. M. Seamon, second from right, greets a visitor.

Retiring director Miller Hern receives a citation of appreciation from Chairman Lang at the 1981 annual meeting.

One undeniable trend between the mid-1960s and the early 1980s was the greatly increased volume of data and data analysis available to directors. For many years, all of the minutes, reports, and supporting documents fit into one large bound volume per year. By the early 1970s the documents took two volumes, and after the mid-1970s they required three. These men were asked to digest an impressive amount of information! A latter-day reader of this material is impressed not just by the amount of information directors absorbed, but also by their command of it. Paul Keithley's minutes, beginning in 1974 and 1975, reported better than earlier ones had the dialogue between company officers and board members. As directors asked questions, they clarified for all present the meaning of the pages of information. It can be said with certainty that MFA Mutual's directors were not a passive group, not a "rubber stamp" for management — out of their element once they left the farm. The directors knew the insurance business.

And in return for their efforts, what sort of compensation did they receive? Not stock or stock options, of course, for in a mutual insurance company there are none of these. And not large salaries. From an annual compensation of $540 in 1967, directors' salaries grew to $2,100 in 1978. In 1980, the board set a mandatory retirement age of 71 years, created the title "Director Emeritus," and established a retirement plan for directors.

The directors' support of management was especially important from 1979 to 1981, as the transition from MFA to Shelter Insurance occurred. These men whose roots were firmly planted in the farmer co-op defended the interests of the insurance company and its policyholders when the rift with MFA developed. The directors might have remained loyal to MFA, even though Mr. Heinkel no longer led the organization. But they did not, and some might say that it was the board's finest hour.

Missouri's Lt. Governor Roger Wilson, a state senator at the time of this photo, presents a resolution honoring A. D. Sappington following his death in 1979. Mrs. Helen Sappington holds the resolution while her daughter and grandson look on.

The year 1979 ought to have been among the best in the company's history, and in some ways it was. The financial results for 1978 and 1979 will confirm that. But 1979 was also filled with events which rocked MFA Mutual to its very foundations. On February 27, A. D. Sappington died of cancer. On August 6, Fred Heinkel failed to gain re-election as president of MFA, and his successor soon confronted MFA Mutual's leaders with a fundamental challenge to the control and future of the company.

A. D. Sappington's death ended one living connection between the two organizations, of course. There were many monuments to his contributions to MFA Insurance's success, among them his prominent role in the national insurance industry (see chapter 8), and the company's remarkable comeback from the losses of 1973-1975. Perhaps his most critical achievement was the company's very survival during the hostile environment of the 1970s, which included not only the economic woes already suggested, but also legal and political difficulties to be discussed later. The 1970s were hard times, but with solid support from employees and agents, A. D. led the company through them. "He has left his mark," Howard Lang affirmed at the 1979 annual meeting, "and we are better insurance people because of him." In January, 1974 director Sam Murrell wrote to Fred Heinkel:

We are approaching the 10th Anniversary of Bastille Day . . . February 20. This is the day of the advent of A. D. Sappington becoming President. . . . Much water has passed under the bridge since that time, all of which has been for the better.

Howard B. Lang, Jr. served as president from 1979 to 1981 and chairman of the board of directors from 1981 to 1984.

Following A. D.'s death, the company faced the question of succession. At its meeting of April 11, 1979, six weeks after A. D.'s passing, Chairman Heinkel informed the board "that the next order of business would be the election of a President." Both Howard Lang and Gustav Lehr received nominations. The ballot count revealed a tie vote, four to four, as A. D.'s death had reduced the board's normal complement of nine members to eight. Following a discussion about the options open to the board in this unprecedented situation, Heinkel made a motion that resolved the impasse. His formula implemented discussions that he and Lang had already held, and a plan that Lang had outlined in a letter to Heinkel dated that same day, April 11. The board unanimously endorsed the plan: Lang would serve as president "until the first Wednesday of April, 1981" (later changed to June 30), which was the end of A. D.'s unexpired board term. Lang would also occupy that director's position. Heinkel then nominated Gus Lehr as executive vice-president, unofficially designating him as Lang's successor. The board confirmed this line of succession a year later at president Lang's urging, when Lehr was elected "President Designate."

President Lang's leadership abilities would be tested during the next two years, when circumstances often called for as much attention to press releases and legal documents related to the MFA dispute as to the business of insurance. But those abilities were soon evident. One evidence of leadership was the decision to name Lehr the next chief executive. Lang believed that the company needed a planned transition the next time that top leadership changed. Given Silvey's forced resignation and Sappington's death, MFA Mutual had not enjoyed an anticipated transfer of power from one president to the next since 1949. Lang's administration would benefit from the talents of two senior vice presidents in a tier of administration just below the president. In an organizational structure published in June, 1979, Executive Vice President Lehr had oversight responsibilities for claims, personnel, training and other areas, while Vice President of Administration Jack L. Pettit oversaw actuarial, accounting and other departments. Vice Presidents

Following his retirement as secretary of the Missouri Farmers Association, R. J. Rosier remained on the board of the insurance companies.

Madden (communications), Nelson (law), Conboy (marketing), Duello (finance) and McTurnan (underwriting) had responsibility for their areas. Organizationally, the company was poised for the challenge that soon would appear.

The dispute with MFA was complex and prolonged. This account will strive to present a factual narrative free of the rancor and tensions that surfaced at the time. For most of the years since MFA and MFA Mutual parted in 1981, the two organizations have been friendly partners in Columbia's business community. The cordial personal relationships of people like Howard and Arthur Lang, Ray Young of MFA and MFA Oil, Bob Maupin of both MFA and the insurance company, and their families, have overcome the rift of 1979-1981.

Between 1964 and 1979, the close and beneficial relationship between the farm cooperative and the insurance company followed the precedents already established. MFA Mutual employees participated in MFA's retirement plan and found it quite satisfactory. Legal agreements, periodically renewed, stated the obligations owed and benefits received by each organization — monthly payments by MFA Mutual, for example, for the right to use MFA's registered trademark. In 1977, following the operating losses of the mid-1970s, MFA voluntarily agreed to reduce temporarily the insurance company's monthly payments from $15,000 to $7,500, an accommodation typical of the 33 years when both organizations were headed by Fred Heinkel and interlocking boards of directors.

Other examples of close ties abound. At the insurance company's annual policyholders' meetings the MFA board of directors solicited and voted the proxies of policyholders when electing directors and making other decisions. In 1969, MFA Mutual, MFA Oil, and MFA joined to purchase an airplane for business use. For years, MFA and MFA Mutual jointly sponsored a breakfast for the Missouri congressional delegation in Washington, D. C. To funnel contributions to charitable causes, MFA Mutual gave funds ($60,000 annually by the late 1970s) to the MFA Foundation, as did other MFA divisions.

Eric Thompson succeeded Fred Heinkel as president of MFA in 1979.

Fred Heinkel's leadership of MFA seemed as permanent as the organization itself until a 36-year-old challenger, Eric Thompson, easily defeated him at the August 6, 1979, annual convention. An Air Force veteran of Vietnam, an MFA employee since 1974, and its director of employee relations since 1977, Thompson immediately made it known that the status quo was not sacred. The day after his defeat, Heinkel called Howard Lang to ask if he could move his desk into the Home Office. He was being evicted by the new MFA administration, just as several of Heinkel's associates would soon lose their jobs. Lang sent several men and a truck downtown to move the belongings of MFA Mutual's board chairman to 1817 West Broadway, where Heinkel kept an office until 1983. A few days later Thompson called Lang, demanding a seat on MFA Mutual's board and $1 million annually for use of the MFA emblem and name. Thompson acted on an assumption held by the new MFA leaders throughout the dispute: that the insurance company's success "was the direct result of its MFA affiliation." At one point Eric Thompson asserted that, if MFA terminated the licensing agreement with MFA Mutual, "we would want our share of the surplus . . . a lot of their surplus was made from Missouri MFA business."

Thompson firmly maintained this position in spite of the fact that the insurance companies operated far beyond MFA's influence in a thirteen-state region, and that farmers in all states represented less than 9% of MFA Mutual's and Countryside Casualty's auto policies. And Thompson's remark ignored the fact that legally, a mutual insurance company's surplus belongs to policyholders.

In an article in the September, 1979 SHIELD, President Lang stated that

Alfred Hoffman, left, in this early '50s photo with E. H. Van Ness, argued the 1980 case for MFA in the dispute over the insurance company's separation from its parent organization. Van Ness was described in this photo as a new type of claims adjuster, one with experience in automobile repairs rather than legal matters.

Heinkel's defeat "will have no effect on the management or directorship" of the companies. Thanks to the requirement imposed by the Iowa insurance department in 1960, though Lang did not mention that incident in his article, "there is no requirement that board members be associated with the Missouri Farmers Association." Clearly, however, MFA Mutual's management and directors were concerned about the future, in light of the changes at MFA. The best evidence of that is the review of the relationship between the two organizations that President Lang conducted at the August 17 board meeting. Gathered in executive session with officers absent, the board took a decisive step. Anticipating next April's annual meeting, when three members of the nine-man board would be elected, the directors agreed to solicit proxies from policyholders "on behalf of the current management of the company," not the board of MFA as had been the practice since 1945. The five officers named on proxy forms that policyholders received with their policy renewal notices over the following months were Howard Lang, Gus Lehr, Will L. Nelson, James McTurnan, and J. Donald Duello.

MFA Mutual officials did not inform Eric Thompson or his staff of the changed proxy solicitation. When MFA officials discovered the change after the first of the year, their charges of secrecy and deception — leveled often from March, 1980 onward — suggested their bitterness at being out-maneuvered by the legal talent at MFA Mutual. Officers Lang, Lehr, Pettit, and Nelson were among the lawyers who understood the use of the proxy tool as a defense against an outside threat to the company's independence. That, indeed, was the issue for Howard Lang, who spoke publicly for MFA Mutual in the months to come. As he said at the crucial board meeting on March 28: in the best interests of its policyholders, who in number and geographical distribution extended far beyond MFA, "the MFA Mutual Insurance Company must continue to operate as a separate and distinct corporate entity." Or as he stated the case fifteen years later: by 1979, "the insurance company was the tail that wagged the MFA dog." Originally the child of the farmer organization, it now was financially stronger than MFA and had to protect the freedom to set its own course.

MFA's position in the dispute, as stated by President Thompson, General Counsel Alfred J. Hoffman, and others, was equally clear. There was the note of betrayal: even the three MFA Mutual board members who also sat on the MFA board — Brehe, Sachs, and Kullman — had not shared their knowledge of the new proxy policy. But the main refrain was this: if the proxies were not returned to the MFA board, the insurance company's management would have "complete control" of the company. Who, then, would guarantee "the accountability" of those permitted to use the MFA emblem and good name? As Thompson said: the insurance company "should not use our name and shield without any control by our company" through representation on their board. As the disagreement developed, the use of MFA's name and emblem moved to the center of discussion, especially after it became clear that neither side would compromise on the proxies. Finally, Eric Thompson had another reason to oppose vigorously MFA Mutual's independence in the post-Heinkel era. If MFA Mutual could break away, so could MFA Oil, MFA Milling Company, and the other affiliates, "and this could have devastating consequences on MFA."

The actions taken at three board of directors meetings in March, 1980 were of critical importance in the unfolding controversy. On March 18, the MFA board met, and Al Hoffman revealed to its members that several conversations and meetings had not persuaded MFA Mutual officials to yield on the proxy issue. Therefore, he had nominated all members of the MFA board for election to the three vacancies on MFA Mutual's board at the April 2 annual meeting. Hoffman had also drafted a Supplemental Agreement to the current MFA-MFA Mutual contract. By approving it, the insurance company would agree to solicit proxies only in the name of the MFA board, and in return would receive an assurance that MFA would not interfere in the conduct of the insurance company's business. Although directors Sachs and Kullmann defended MFA Mutual at this meeting, the MFA board voted 19-4 to support their management's aggressive efforts to regain proxy control.

Prior to the next MFA board meeting, the farm co-op applied pressure on the insurance company. From whatever source, agents received unsigned letters questioning the wisdom of their leaders' actions. A petition bearing the signatures of 24 Higginsville-area MFA leaders demanded that MFA Mutual "return proxy

B. M. Seamon, A. D. Sappington, and Ed Sachs with Chairman Heinkel following their reelection to the board.

Advertising spokesman Joe Slattery, left, and President Sappington introduce the expression "Shield of Shelter" in this film introducing the 1972 advertising program. The years of equity in the words helped with the introduction of the new company name in 1980.

control" to MFA's board. Prior to the annual meeting, directors of MFA Mutual received letters from the MFA Executive Committee, stating that their "integrity" depended upon an acceptance of the Supplemental Agreement. The minutes of the board meeting on March 27 reveal two interesting points. One is that, privately, Eric Thompson already knew that the insurance company had won the proxy fight. The second was Alfred Hoffman's casual suggestion of the grounds for the compromise that would, six months later, help to produce a mutually agreeable separation of the organizations. If the two parted, Hoffman said, MFA Mutual could either pay for the true value of MFA's name and continue to use it, or "we could require them to change their name and emblem, and give them two years or so to get their changes made."

On the following day, March 28, one of the more important board meetings in MFA Mutual's history occurred. After President Lang reviewed developments and members discussed the proposed Supplemental Agreement, a recess was called to allow Thompson, Hoffman, and Glen Myers to arrive at the meeting. Each addressed the MFA Mutual board and officers, reiterating earlier arguments. Before the guests left, Lang made MFA Mutual's position entirely clear: the board would consider the Supplemental Agreement; it would work to have current directors reelected on April 2; the insurance company must retain its independence. As the meeting resumed, both Lang and Gus Lehr, who had consulted with the insurance regulators in five states including Missouri, stated the probability that the arrangement proposed by MFA would be rejected by these bodies. Lang then moved rejection of the Agreement, and the board unanimously passed his motion. Thus the outcome of the company's annual meeting on April 2 was determined. Although attorney Hoffman for MFA formally protested the new proxy arrangement, the proxy-holders cast those ballots for the reelection of Heinkel, Sachs, and Seaman. Control of MFA Mutual remained firmly in the hands of its board and management.

Both downtown and on West Broadway, the response to these events pointed toward an eventual solution of the dispute. At MFA, the predictable was joined by the unexpected. Predictably, Thompson canceled $4 million in casualty policies with MFA Mutual and vowed to redouble efforts to regain the proxies or deny MFA Mutual the use of the MFA name and emblem. The surprise occurred at the April 8 MFA board meeting. A majority approved a motion directing MFA officers and employees "to cease all activities which relate to removing MFA Insurance Company's right to use the MFA emblem" and to canceling the remaining insurance policies with MFA Life, until August 20. By that date, Thompson would have faced reelection in the annual MFA convention — a contested election, which he won. Though he fumed, President Thompson's hands were temporarily tied.

MFA Mutual's leadership took steps shortly after the April 2 annual meeting to remove the company's continued use of the MFA logo from contention. On the advice of the St. Louis law firm Arnold and Porter that, should MFA terminate the licensing agreement "our continued use of the 'shield' was questionable," the board authorized management to create a new emblem. As work on this shield proceeded, President Lang as early as April 30, 1980 also asked his colleagues to think about company names: possibly a title for the MFA Insurance Companies as a group. Suggestions included The Shield Group, The Shelter Group, The Shield of Shelter Group. Lang also raised the possibility of "a change even in" the name MFA Mutual Insurance Company. During the spring and summer staff developed a new company shield, a task the necessity of which no one doubted, as Eric Thompson renewed pledges to "pursue the proxy issue" to a solution satisfactory to MFA. By late July a new shield was ready, and at its September 12 meeting the board approved it. The

The term "Shield of Shelter" made its appearance in 1972, as shown in this Kansas life contest luncheon. State Sales Manager Bob Sloan addresses the group. Also at the head table are Director of Sales John Lenox and agents Clara and Van Ryan.

Howard Lang and his secretary, Frances McDonnell, served their careers together, having worked together before either joined the companies, and retiring together in 1981.

company planned agent meetings for fall to introduce the blue and red logo bearing the words "Shield of Shelter," a phrase used in MFA Insurance advertisements since 1972. The meetings in Missouri, where the MFA name and logo carried the greatest emotional attachment, would be conducted by company officers.

Within a month of the adoption of the emblem, a resolution of the dispute with MFA required a change in the company's name as well. In spite of heated rhetoric, contacts between officers of MFA and MFA Mutual had continued — by phone, at social functions, and in conferences. On September 25, 1980 Will L. Nelson and Terry Cox for the insurance company met with Cullen Cline, representing Eric Thompson. Memos and letters followed early in October, and a settlement of all disagreements emerged. Its broad outlines were simple: the insurance companies bearing the MFA name would find new names by December 31, 1981, and MFA would help to publicize that change. The newly-designated insurance company would have the opportunity to bid on MFA's policy needs, and MFA would not go into the insurance business for five years. The licensing agreements between the two companies would end on December 31, 1980.

An interesting sidelight to these events involved Robert W. Maupin, assistant general counsel for MFA. This future Shelter Insurance president, Howard Lang told the board at its October 3, 1980 meeting, had joined MFA Mutual as vice president of public affairs, the position that Gus Lehr had vacated. By October, 1980, the three chief executive officers-to-be of what would become Shelter Insurance were on staff. Lehr, Pettit, and Maupin would lead the company during the remainder of its first fifty years.

But in October, the name "Shelter" had not yet been chosen. The company decided it could settle on a good name without the need of an outside consultant. The selection process invited a broad spectrum of people to make suggestions: policyholders, agents, employees, and the company's advertising agency, D'Arcy McManus & Masius. A screening committee categorized and evaluated the suggestions, and the most suitable ones were presented to the board in early November, 1980. In this serious process there was room for humor. A Columbia newspaper reported that one Elton Fay had suggested to Jean Madden that the company adopt his mother's name: "Emma Fay." That was not a possibility, but on November 7, Lang presented these choices to the board: Shield, Shield American, Shield of Shelter, and Family Shield. Several votes produced a winner: Shield. But in November and December it developed that a Georgia insurance company whose name included the word "shield" had refused to sell the rights to that name to the company. Therefore, on December 19, 1980, President Lang proposed and the board approved the name Shelter Mutual Insurance Company. Beside the recognition value that "Shelter" had through the company's advertising, it announced the company's reason for being: protection from risk. The name was a natural.

"Changing names is difficult," Gus Lehr affirmed in his remarks to the Annual Meeting in April, 1981. "Enormously difficult, but we are well on the way toward completion." The changeover — of agents' signs, of stationery, of policy forms of all sorts, of the company's registration with thirteen state insurance departments, of a thousand other details — was led by an inter-departmental committee chaired by Don Goodwin, vice president of Information Services. Goodwin's preparation for the task included a visit with officers of American Family Insurance Company in Madison, Wisconsin, a company which had changed its name in 1962. The transition also deeply involved Jean Madden and his staff of public relations and advertising specialists in Communications. As Madden reported in April, 1981:

We are into transitional advertising; we have plans made to send all kinds of new materials to the agents, signs will be going up; but we need an event at each agent's office on July 1 to mark the occasion, and we are working on that.

A special policyholders' meeting held on April 17 officially adopted the new name, but July 1, 1981, was the important date. For although the company had until December 31 to complete the change, it was accomplished by mid-year. Known ever since as Shelter Day I, it was at 12:01 a.m. Central Time on that date that the MFA Mutual Insurance Company became the Shelter Mutual Insurance Company. And it was at that time that Howard Lang, who had performed so magnificently during two and one-quarter difficult but also exciting years, gave up the active management of the company to Gustav J. Lehr. An old and tested company had acquired a new name, and entered a new era.

Howard Lang and Will L. Nelson spend flying time between meetings in 1964 to stay current with daily office matters. The team of officers visited each state for a series of meetings, a tradition that continues today as an annual event.

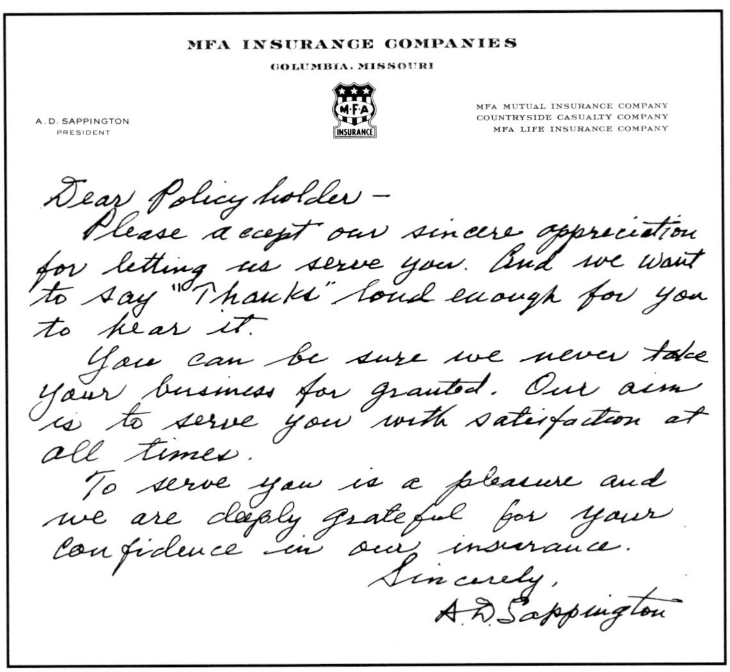

MFA INSURANCE COMPANIES
COLUMBIA, MISSOURI

A. D. SAPPINGTON
PRESIDENT

MFA MUTUAL INSURANCE COMPANY
COUNTRYSIDE CASUALTY COMPANY
MFA LIFE INSURANCE COMPANY

Dear Policyholder —
Please accept our sincere appreciation for letting us serve you. And we want to say "Thanks" loud enough for you to hear it.
You can be sure we never take your business for granted. Our aim is to serve you with satisfaction at all times.
To serve you is a pleasure and we are deeply grateful for your confidence in our insurance.
Sincerely,
A. D. Sappington

This note to policyholders from A. D. Sappington arrived with premium notices, and prompted numerous responses from appreciative insureds who wanted to thank him for taking time to write a personal note.

President Sappington presents Missouri football coach Al Onofrio with a bumper sticker created to show support for the coach and team. Virginia Etheridge wrote the copy, Bill Hume did the artwork.

chapter 6

Our Progress 1964-1981

Many of the topics discussed in chapters 6, 7 and 8 will seem familiar, for they represent recurrent themes in the company's history. These developments cast light on the internal growth of the MFA Insurance Companies and on the economic environment within which they operated in the 1960s and 1970s.

During his first decade as president, A. D. Sappington continued to promote the geographical expansion that he and Jack Silvey had begun in the 1950s. The ultimate goal was ambitious. A map displayed at the 1965 annual meeting revealed conscious decisions about 49 of the 50 states. MFA Mutual in 1965 operated in 11 states, had gained permission to operate in 11 more, had applications to operate pending in 14 other states and the District of Columbia, and expected to apply to ten additional states, including Hawaii. Company leaders had decided not to apply to three states that "have compulsory insurance laws which result in excessive losses." The only state not placed in any of these categories was Alaska. By the end of 1971, MFA Mutual had been admitted to 38 states and Washington, D.C. In four — New Hampshire, Massachusetts, New York, and New Jersey — admission was for reinsurance purposes only. If the company's plans had been realized, its operations would have reached from Maine and Florida to Hawaii, and stretched across seven time zones.

The two other insurance companies, Countryside Casualty Company and MFA Life, also expanded their actual and potential operating territories, though not as extensively as MFA Mutual. By December, 1971, for example, Countryside had gained admission to 16 states, and the Life Company to 15. As the company promoted "full circle sales," enabling its exclusive agents to market a full line of products, it was necessary for MFA Mutual's subsidiaries to enter other states, and that included the finance company, MFA Security Service Company. In 1966, a number of Kentucky agents urged A. D. to make available to them the auto financing that Security Service Company provided. "Just recently I lost another good T-1 to another auto insurer because of their finance plan," John Browning of Lebanon wrote. "We need Security Service in Kentucky," urged Richard Massamore of Dawson Springs. "We are missing the very best low-risk automobile business because 'they must insure where they finance.'" A. D. promised that in good time, Security Service would enter Kentucky.

In 1960 and 1961, MFA Mutual had begun operations in six states, a period of rapid expansion which was followed by nearly a decade of consolidation within the 11-state sales territory. It was in 1970 and 1971 that the company expanded into what is still the largest territory it ever served, 15 states. In 1970, agents in Mississippi, Colorado, and Texas began doing business, and those in Louisiana followed in 1971. Although it had ambitious expansion plans, the company was

President Sappington cuts the ribbon to the new Iowa State Office in Des Moines in the summer of 1975.

cautious and selective in its choice of new markets. Plans to begin operations in Alabama in 1971 were canceled when Governor George C. Wallace, in a speech to the legislature, asserted that he would not allow insurance rates to increase in his state.

Geographical expansion had its advantages and, perhaps less obvious, its disadvantages. New states took time to become profitable — some, a long time. Iowa and Indiana, for example, added in 1960 and 1961, lagged behind the other states entered in those years in terms of premium dollars and profitability. A 1967 overview of the Indiana operation reported that the investment made earlier in the state was now paying off. Ten years later Fred Heinkel observed "that it appears to be a little hard to get started in the state of Colorado." A. D. agreed, and mentioned one cause: with all our agents concentrated in Denver, "we need more . . . in the rural areas."

This old house gave way as Arkansas State Office in 1965 for a new office, the design of which was to become a model for other state offices. A ground breaking celebration was held at the site, just behind the old house, on November 16, 1964, with agent Ken Casey and his wife, Faye, turning the first dirt. The office staff gathers around the cake on the porch of the house.

Expansion was expensive, taxing the company's resources, especially when poor financial years replaced good ones. Late in 1974, Bill Conboy of Marketing noted a major expense that he would soon succeed in reducing: the 481 agents who were on the salaried agents program, many in new states. Expansion also meant a growing network of state offices and other locations maintained for marketing and claims personnel. In 1969, for example, the company operated 12 state offices (including two in Missouri, in the east and west regions), and 18 marketing offices. Salaries and benefits for these employees, plus rents and taxes paid on property, were funded throughout the operating territory by profits earned in those states that were profitable — most conspicuously Missouri.

In July, 1975, in testimony prepared for a committee of the House of Representatives in Washington, President Sappington described his company: "About 40% of our business is in Missouri, and the remainder is in the other 14 states in which we actively do business." Within six weeks, in this third of three years of serious losses for the company, A. D. initiated a major retrenchment program that would change his description of the sales territory. On August 26, A. D. created an Ad Hoc Committee of eight top administrators, including himself as an ex-officio member. Senior Vice President Howard Lang was the actual chairman.

Sappington and Heinkel presided at the dedication of a new state office in Little Rock, Arkansas on May 24, 1974.

The committee's mission was to deal with a mounting crisis: "a deterioration for all companies since December 31, 1974," serious underwriting losses since 1973 and a reduction in surplus in 1974, and a downgrading of MFA Mutual's A. M. Best rating. The Ad Hoc Committee's analysis of operations was comprehensive, as were its recommendations, made through the autumn and into 1976. The committee proposed several alternatives from which A. D. could chose, the most drastic of which would have pulled the companies out of six states: Minnesota, Indiana, Mississippi, Louisiana, Texas, and Colorado.

A lesser action — the one actually implemented — was the withdrawal from Minnesota and Texas. In addition, in some other states where MFA Insurance continued to operate, the companies withdrew from selected districts where relatively few agents had established a persistent pattern of losses. Districts in Arkansas and Mississippi are examples.

The explanation of the cessation of operations in Minnesota illustrates the thinking of Ad Hoc Committee members about several states: "terrific losses" which included high administrative costs, an unfriendly regulatory climate which included a 1972 no-fault insurance law mandating a 30% reduction of rates, and the state's remote location from the company's center of operations.

Finally, in 1977 and 1978, the company withdrew from 17 states and the District of Columbia, in which it had never actively pursued business. So ended an era of expansion that had begun in the early 1950s. The growth of MFA/Shelter Insurance in the future — and it would be impressive — would take place within the thirteen-state territory that has been stable since 1975.

Felix Hendrickson spent a long career in sales management, retiring as Arkansas state sales manager in 1986. He began his career as a Home Office underwriter in 1953.

This modern building accommodated the growing Arkansas operation, but has since been replaced by an even larger office, built specifically for the companies.

This early 1970s centerpiece for the fall life contest was typical of the creations by Scottie Garrett to cheer on the Missouri Tigers.

What was the response to and the result of the 1975 contraction? Of course, there was disruption and frustration as agents were terminated and policies canceled or not renewed. Some, like agent Arnold Wright of Benton, Arkansas, found strength in this experience and resolved to make the company a stronger presence in their state. "I have heard all I want to hear about MFA . . . staying in Arkansas," he wrote to A. D. "It is, so let's get on with the business of selling insurance." Arkansas insurance regulators ordered an inquiry into the company's recent rate hike, one reason for which was the allegation that MFA Mutual officers had known of the partial pullout from their state before they filed for the increase. The company rejected the charge as "wholly without foundation," and Howard Lang testified most of the day at a hearing held on October 14, 1975. The decision: MFA Mutual "had not acted in bad faith." The withdrawal from Minnesota and Texas went smoothly; the impact on agents, employees, and policyholders was minimal; and the results for the companies beneficial in the long run. MFA Mutual offered severance pay and jobs elsewhere in the company to employees, and allowed policies to run to expiration.

Table 6.1 suggests some results of expansion beyond Missouri. The data on earned premium which it reports shows the growth of sales across the sales territory for selected years. Missouri and Arkansas, Shelter's first two states, accumulated a majority of the mutual company's earned premium, but it was a declining proportion of the whole. In 1965, 76% of total earned premium came from those states, but in 1980, only 60%.

The window signs of the Bill Bell agency in Sapulpa, Oklahoma also promotes the financing available through agents and MFA Security Service.

Table 6.1 Earned Premium by States, Selected Years (thousands of dollars)

States (dates signify start of operations)	1966	1970	1974	1979
Missouri (1946)	$28,308	$35,138	$50,478	$78,930
Arkansas (1950)	6,776	10,456	19,416	30,153
Kansas (1950)	2,040	2,764	6,259	11,362
Nebraska (1954)	963	1,943	3,912	4,854
Illinois (1956)	2,649	3,666	6,050	7,336
Iowa (1960)	671	829	1,938	2,339
Kentucky (1960)	1,085	1,661	5,302	7,860
Tennessee (1960)	2,231	3,833	6,653	10,059
Minnesota (1961)	557	1,186	3,662	——
Oklahoma (1961)	1,426	2,210	5,519	10,272
Indiana (1961)	617	1,266	3,347	3,888
Mississippi (1970)	——	57	3,465	3,463
Colorado (1970)	——	50	1,030	2,514
Texas (1970)	——	135	1,247	——
Louisiana (1971)	——	——	2,283	6,702

Sources: **1966:** **"Report of Examination of the MFA Mutual Insurance Company as of December 31, 1969"**
1970: **Minutes, March 4, 1971**
1974: **Minutes, March 25, 1975**
1979: **Minutes, March 28, 1980**

As it had before 1964, MFA Mutual continued to organize subsidiary companies during the Sappington years. MFA Insurance's organizational charts suggested the best way to think about these companies. At the top were the three insurance companies, without which there would have been no need for the remaining companies. MFA Mutual in the center owned the two stock insurance companies, Countryside Casualty (1957) and MFA Life (1958). Two of the non-insurance subsidiaries pre-dated 1964: KMMO radio (1951) and MFA Security Service Company (1956). In the period under review, four more subsidiaries came into being, plus KMFL-FM, a companion station to KMMO in Marshall. In 1965, MFA Mutual organized Daniel Boone Underwriters, Inc., an insurance brokerage through which agents could obtain for clients policies that were unavailable directly from MFA companies. In 1971 came Mid-America Auto Parts, Inc., a salvage company whose function was "to dispose of automobiles and damaged parts from automobiles on which we take title in settlement of claims." In 1973, the company created May Fair Advertising, Inc., which received a commission for placing some company advertisements. Finally, in 1978 came MFA Service Company, formed to make installment loans in Nebraska.

Mid-America Auto Parts provided the companies a market for salvage vehicles acquired through claims, and was a state-of-the art salvage yard. Another benefit was the use of automotive repair experts to repair minor damage and to aid in the instruction of claims adjusters through practical, hands-on use of repair equipment.

KMMO manager Harold Douglas, center, and station engineer Bill Williams receive a certificate of appreciation from Al Kreek of the Social Security Administration in February 1970. The station had broadcast Social Security programs as a public service.

The purpose of all subsidiaries was straightforward. First, to reduce the costs of doing business by eliminating middlemen and gauging the costs of items such as bumpers and broadcasting time. And second, to strengthen the position of agents, who were made more versatile by these companies. Since the role of the non-insurance subsidiaries was secondary and supportive, most remained small — and vulnerable in times of financial stress. One suggestion of the Ad Hoc Committee in 1975 was that the company "abolish" Daniel Boone Underwriters and consider selling KMMO and Mid-America Auto Parts.

The growth of the two insurance subsidiaries deserves emphasis. As measured by the total premium of the three insurance companies, Countryside Casualty Company and MFA Life Insurance grew impressively relative to MFA Mutual. In 1963, the latter took in 89.6% of the three insurers' total premium; in 1980, that figure stood at 74.5%. Additional data will highlight Countryside Casualty's experience after 1964. In the 14 years from that year to 1978, the company's total assets grew from \$4.3 million to \$35.9 million. Its net operating gain of \$115,000 in

1964 grew by a factor of 18 by 1978, and Countryside's total surplus grew by 1,000% during the 14-year period. Total surplus in 1978 was nearly $13 million.

Although "MFA Insurance" during the 1960s and 1970s meant casualty coverage to most people, the life and health policies provided by the MFA Life Insurance Company grew in relative importance. In 1978, President Sappington wrote to a fellow insurance executive: "there is no type of insurance as sure of making a profit after it gets off the ground as a company which engages in life insurance." When the Life Company passed the "one billion of insurance in force" milestone in 1975, another insurance man noted that "few companies have ever reached the billion dollar mark in such a short time." By 1979, President Lang could call the Life Company "a real factor in the industry." The life and health policy count in 1973 of 144,500 grew to 179,000 by 1978. The value of policies written in 1973 was over $219 million, while insurance in force was nearly $768.5 million. Five years later the corresponding figures were $410.5 million and $1.407 billion. The woes that the casualty industry experienced in the 1970s — including the increasing cost of losses attributed to inflation and storms — could not adversely affect life insurance operations, though rising medical costs certainly affected health insurance. When the casualty business slowed, the MFA group made special efforts to market life insurance. As the 1970s matured, the 1958 decision to create a life insurance company seemed wise, indeed.

During the years 1964-1981, MFA Mutual, with its subsidiaries, remained a multiple-line company, enabling its agents to serve nearly any insurance need. As of 1969, to illustrate the point, the company was licensed to write these lines of business in Missouri: Accident and Sickness; Automobile Full Coverage; Boiler, Steam; Burglary and Theft; Credit; Employers Liability; Fidelity; Fire and Allied: Liability (B.I.), Liability (P.D.) and Collision other than Automobile; Livestock Full Coverage; Machinery; Marine; Mortgage Guarantee Insurance; Plate Glass; Rain; Surety; and Workmen's Compensation Insurance.

The companies innovated new coverages and phased out others as policyholder needs changed, as the economy fluctuated, as the industry created new products, and as legislation changed. For example, in 1965, the federal government created Medicare. The following year the company responded by discontinuing hospitalization insurance for Medicare-eligible policyholders, and created in MFA Life a Medicare Supplemental policy — an adjustment made by the industry as a whole. In 1966 also, as an internal administrative adjustment, MFA Life took over all health insurance policies from MFA Mutual.

To meet changing recreational practices in wintry areas, MFA Mutual offered a snowmobile policy in Minnesota beginning in 1969. In 1973, the company pursued commercial business more aggressively, developing a multi-peril policy for employers

President Sappington signed the pact in 1968 which made MFA Mutual the tenth assuming company of the Mutual Reinsurance Bureau, a pact that remains in effect today. Signing for MRB was Walter Schiltz, manager. Looking on are Don Tripp, MRB secretary, and Paul Keithley, MFA Mutual secretary-treasurer.

and retailers. As relatively fewer Americans owned single-family dwellings and more rented, the company developed improved apartment policies. The cut-backs in 1975 were in lines of coverage as well as in geography. MFA Mutual stopped writing mobile homeowners and boatowners insurance in the "high loss states" of Tennessee, Mississippi, and Louisiana that year, and Workmen's Compensation in Illinois in 1976. The following year, the company withdrew from Workmen's Comp in all states but Missouri and Arkansas.

A couple of examples of new policies and policy features illustrate the underwriting and marketing departments' innovations of these years. New homeowners policies in 1979 insured the replacement cost of homes. Older policies that allowed insureds to cover only partial replacement frustrated policyholders whose actual losses were not met by their policies, and failed to provide the company with a premium equal to the risk involved. By 1979 also, auto and homeowners' renewal notices gave policyholders' the option, without contacting their agents, of increasing their coverage. Called the roll-up, this feature was voluntarily selected by more than 80% of policyholders. In addition, Bill Toler and his staff worked hard to offer attractive policy features to those seeking life insurance. These included annuities marketed as early as 1969, savings plans with tax advantages that involved no insurance features at all. The Golden Emblem life policy marketed in the late 1960s combined ten years of term insurance with whole life coverage paid up at age 65, and added double accidental death and dismemberment benefits that tripled payments if death occurred on a bus, train, or other common carrier.

Soon after the Arkansas office was completed in 1965, work began on this office in Springfield, Illinois.

When MFA Mutual began in 1946, it was an auto insurer. Other lines of coverage grew in importance over the years as a proportion of the companies' total business. Still, auto insurance remained the single most important type of business MFA Insurance wrote into the 1980s. In 1977, the premium income collected for auto policies was 71.7% of all premium income for MFA Mutual and Countryside Casualty Company. Figures from other years, including those which report all casualty and property policies in force, underline the central importance of auto insurance to the companies.

This 1966 view shows construction of the top two floors on the north side of the office, four years after the lower level had been completed.

During J. M. Silvey's administration, the Home Office building grew to include roughly the front half of the present two-story plus basement structure, plus the underground floor of the back half, added in 1962. By the fall of 1965, A. D. Sappington began a construction project which would complete the Home Office to the dimensions it retains in 1996. Employing the architectural firm Childs and Smith of Chicago and the J. E. Hathman Construction Company of Columbia, the company added a 45,000 square-foot addition in two floors over the 1962 underground section. The top floor provided space for the future, as it was not finished and used immediately. By the time this project was ready for occupancy in 1967, changes in physical plant also had occurred behind the Home Office. Early in 1966, the company erected a new warehouse and drive-in claims facility north of the existing Annex building. In the Annex, an improved space for physical damage training was created. Work on these two buildings in 1974 expanded the warehouse and added two classrooms/meeting rooms to the Annex, which was evolving into the company's training facility.

In the late 1970s, the company made important functional improvements to the Home Office facility. Early in 1976, for example, a new security system employed television cameras to scan building entrances and hallways. For the first time plastic cards replaced metal keys for those with building access. In 1977, as part of the development of MFA Gardens (see chapter 8), the company sunk a deep well in the northwestern portion of its property. True to its growing reputation as a company that valued efficiency and the latest technology, MFA Mutual used the well water to service the gardens and lawn, to flow through the beautiful fountain on Broadway, and to operate the building's cooling system. Also in 1977, an engineering consultant investigated the possibility of using the heat generated by the main frame computers to heat and cool the building. Changes in the Home Office work space, implemented from late 1977 to early 1979, improved the working environment for employees. Carpet replaced tile on the floors, and office modules with movable walls replaced "a pasture of desks," in the words of the interior

Many current Home Office employees would not recognize this work area of the brand new headquarters building. The area is divided with office modules and permanent walls, there is new lighting, and the floor is carpeted.

designer who planned the project. The changes, everyone agreed, improved office morale and productivity.

The same innovative spirit that created building improvements pushed MFA Mutual to the forefront of applied computer technology. A. D. Sappington's leadership included an enthusiastic willingness to invest in the latest office equipment, even in years when profit was difficult to achieve. To this day that same commitment motivates the company's leadership. Between 1967 and 1980, MFA Mutual changed its central computer system on four occasions. In 1967, it purchased from IBM a Model 360 Series 30 and a Model 360 Series 50 at a total cost of $850,000. Four years later it purchased a Model 360 Series 65 to replace the Series 50. The new computer delivered four times the power of the old machine, at a purchase price of $1.75 million. In 1973, following a visit to IBM's headquarters by A. D. and Don Goodwin, the company ordered two Model 370 Series 158 computers for a combined cost of nearly $5 million. And in 1980, Goodwin recommended and the board approved purchase of the new IBM 3033N for $2.8 million. In addition to realizing income on the sale of replaced computers when new ones were acquired, management proved that the purchase, rather than lease, of hardware saved the company hundreds of thousands of dollars over the life of each computer.

What did the latest in computer technology enable the company to do? A few examples suggest an answer. In 1976, A. D. reported that MFA Insurance was "one of the few companies to get statistics from our computer twice a year," making possible a more frequent review and adjustment of rates than would otherwise be possible. When GTE installed a new phone system in 1977 it was tied into the

Sappington had always been dedicated to providing the best tools with which to work. The computer room as it appeared late in his administration is indicative of the company's continuing interest in the latest technology.

The roster of the Springfield, Missouri branch claims office in November, 1968, reads like a claims hall of fame list: in the front row, left to right are Al Herbert, George Lionberger, Ken Slankard, Howard Winget, Charles Riley, Jerry Cantrell, and Norman "Bud" Kruse; in the middle row are Mack McClanahan, Jim Hyde, Fred West, Warren Medley, Bob Barnett, and Jim Groves; in the back row are Bhurle Sossamon, Gale Huffmaster, Roger Hutchins Sr., Wade Shelton, John Kollmeyer, Bob Leonard, and Darrell Ledbetter.

company's computers, making agent and policyholder telephone services more efficient. Two years later the firm's computers were tied to state motor vehicle departments, greatly increasing the speed of access to motor vehicle reports by underwriters.

The Word Processing Center, started in 1969, as it appeared in 1972.

Another major contributor to office technology was the Word Processing Center introduced in 1969. "It is much more than the old familiar 'typing pool,' A. D. told employees. It was "the newest and most modern system of dictating, preparation of communication material, and the actual typing, gathering, and mailing of all types of communications." In performing these functions, Jack Pettit affirmed after the Center had operated for some months, "our company was further advanced than any other company in the country." Indeed, MFA Mutual was the first U. S. insurance company, and only the second business firm in the nation, to have a Word Processing Center.

A quick look at the Claims Department, headed by Vice President Arthur Lang, shows that innovation at MFA Mutual happened independently of expensive technology. Throughout the sales territory, drive-in claims facilities appeared. In 1974, Claims experimented with its FACS Program: Fast Action Claims Service. Its goal, achieved by October and then applied company-wide, was to settle small claims by branch office personnel, often over the phone. This allowed claims adjusters to concentrate on the larger cases. Claims also had too many occasions to use its catastrophe teams of adjusters, as the weather periodically caused widespread destruction. In June and July, 1979, teams assisted policyholders after separate storms hit towns in Oklahoma, Arkansas, and Kansas. In 1980, catastrophe units traveled to 17 storm sites to handle 10,386 claims. The expenses of the teams themselves that year amounted to $278,965.

Phil Dysart became director of training upon the retirement of Henry Kilburn in 1975 after 27 years of service.

The Claims Department made heavy use of the training staff and its courses, which became a more central part of MFA Mutual's operations under President Sappington. By 1966, two years after A. D. took over the company's leadership, Training Director Henry Kilburn had the assistance of five supervisors, including Warren Connor and Kilburn's successor upon his retirement in August, 1975, Phil Dysart. Company training prepared both agents and employees to do their jobs better. The menu of courses and seminars offered was bewildering in its variety. In

The aftermath of the Topeka tornado of 1966 illustrates why such catastrophes are so costly to insurers.

Physical Damage Supervisor Hank Schmidt shows the equipment and supplies the 1976 catastrophe teams carried to the scene of a major storm.

Since the mid-1960s the companies have used corporate aircraft to conduct business throughout its operating area. Shown in flight are the company's King Air and Queen Air during the peak of the corporate aircraft program. This means of travel remains an important part of the company today, with one owned King Air and other planes leased as needed.

1965 they totaled 2,000 hours of instruction involving more than 1000 students in 45 classes. A group of Missouri vocational training teachers went to school at the Mid-America Auto Parts facility in July, 1978. The session on auto body repair gave the teachers "an insurance point of view of handling physical damage auto claims so they might . . . teach this to students who are learning body work." An anecdote suggests the payoffs of a sound training program. A young claims specialist in Lincoln was able, with one phone call, to educate the crew at a body shop and save the company money. In MFA Mutual's physical damage training she had learned about a repair kit for rubber bumpers that the shop knew nothing about.

The Communications Department under Jean Madden's leadership had responsibility for advertising, public relations, publications, art, the two radio stations in Marshall, and May Fair Advertising Agency. In the late 1970s, the

An early claims office was in Joplin, Missouri, longtime branch manager Paul Trousdale, checks the sign in front of the new office in 1969. The office housed the claims branch and two agents.

department's personnel was a mix of veterans like Bill Hume (art) and Judd Wyatt (public relations), and younger talent like Gene Baumann, director of Publications, Bruce Meentemeyer, associate editor of SHIELD, and Jan Ferlisi, editor of CONTACT. The company's advertising budget was a good index of developments within and outside of the company. MFA Mutual joined MFA as sponsors of the radio broadcasts of University of Missouri football and basketball. In the 1970s, before LIFE magazine disappeared from American newsstands, full-page ads appeared in it and in LOOK. Those advertisements and the commercials that appeared much more frequently on radio and television carried a new slogan beginning in 1972: "The Shield of Shelter."

The company's advertising dollar was divided in several ways. To take 1972 as an example, MFA Mutual spent $2,060,000 on advertising and agents spent an additional $580,000 on their own. Of the company's expenditure, $1,230,000

Marilyn Maye, popular Kansas City vocalist and RCA recording artist, sang MFA Mutual radio jingles throughout the 1960s.

facing page: One way to promote the finance operation of MFA Security Service was sponsorship of this little league team, the Orioles, here getting instructions from its coach, longtime sports information director for the Missouri Tigers, Bill Callahan.

BIG 8

Jean Madden, vice president for Communications, visits with production staff from the D'Arcy advertising agency during the filming of 1974 television commercials.

supported the agents cooperative advertising program, while $830,000 went for production costs and corporate television time. Always eager to persuade more agents to join the company in cooperative advertising, Madden reported a successful month in June, 1979: 543 agents helped pay for commercials on 248 radio stations, for example, and 545 agents advertised their services in 485 different newspapers. The figure for newspaper advertising was the highest ever. As underwriting losses mounted in 1973, 1974, and 1975, reduction in advertising expense was inevitable. Spending, which had been 2.75% of earned premium in the first half of 1974, dwindled to approximately 1% by 1976. Nevertheless, ever-increasing premium income insured a large advertising budget. Jean Madden's first year with the company, 1971, was the first in which advertising spending topped $1 million; it well exceeded $1.5 million, in fact. From 1972 to 1974, expenditures were over $2 million annually, and although they dropped below that figure in 1975 and 1976, from 1977 to 1980 the company spent over $2 million a year on direct advertising of its name and products.

As in an earlier period, though with a decreasing emphasis on films for public viewing, MFA Mutual promoted safety among the general public. As well, its efforts continued to win recognition. In June, 1969, President Sappington proudly informed the board of directors:

Due to the good work done by Judd Wyatt and other company personnel, the MFA Mutual Insurance Companies won for the sixth year the Alfred P. Sloan Award for safety. . . . this was a high honor since the competition was nation- wide . . . this was the first time any company had won this award for the sixth year.

Together with its earlier National Safety Council Public Interest Awards and honors for specific films — such as the Industrial Oscar given "Fair Game" in 1964 — MFA Mutual was, indeed, recognized for its unique industry-wide contributions.

This Kansas City office served the claims branch and three agents in 1959.

chapter 7

Our People 1964-1981

An insurance company does not sell an impersonal product, such as automobiles or cans of soup, to unknown consumers. Companies like those in the Shelter Insurance Group market a quite personal service — protection from peril — to known policyholders and their particular property. The relationship established between the company and the insured, through agents especially, is something akin to that between lawyers and their clients, or teachers and their students. To an important degree, that same bond applies to the insurance company's relationship with its employees and agents. Particularly in a medium-sized company like MFA/Shelter Mutual, people know each other. They associate outside of work time as well as within it. They are not merely personnel files and Social Security or agent numbers.

Table 7.1 Employee Numbers

	Total	Home Office	Elsewhere in Missouri	Outside Missouri
12-1-'65	1025	655 (63.9%)	181 (17.7%)	189 (18.4%)
12-31-'73	1783	1013 (56.8%)	259 (14.5%)	511 (28.7%)
12-31-'80	1651	867 (52.5%)	302 (18.3%)	482 (29.2%)

Source: minutes of MFA Mutual board of directors meeting meetings and accompanying personnel reports.

The number of MFA Mutual employees correlates well with the company's financial experience: long-term growth over the whole period, with a peak in the number of employees coinciding with the onset of the difficult mid-1970s, a reduction in the workforce, then a gradual increase again. Some of the employees represented in Table 7.1 worked for other companies in the group besides MFA Mutual. At the end of 1975, for example, MFA Life employed 95 and Security Service Company 62. At that time, fully 1,514 of 1,708 employees worked for MFA Mutual, which meant that they also did the work of Countryside Casualty Company. Most of the company's employees were full-time; 1,461 of 1,574 at the end of 1976, for example. The workforce shrinkage of 1975 and 1976 came through attrition, and, like reductions in the advertising budget and other expenses, was necessary in light of huge underwriting losses. Personnel Director Bill Redmon reported in mid-1975 that expected savings in salaries and benefits for the year attributed to personnel reductions would exceed $1.3 million. Two years later, as losses had turned resoundingly into profits, Howard Lang concluded: "we may have reached the time where it is necessary to increase the number of personnel." While numbers of employees fluctuated, two other statistics changed in linear fashion. As

left: Clowns have become a staple item for the spring fountain turn-ons. This one is the late Bertha Dowding, secretary in general services.

Nellie Colson, who simply ignored comments about a woman being a claims adjuster, at work in an eastern Kansas body shop in 1973.

the proportion of the total workforce located in the Home Office fell steadily, the proportion working beyond Missouri increased. By this and other measurements, MFA Mutual became less a Missouri company, and increasingly one that was truly regional in presence and importance.

Most new employees went through a series of established steps to gain a job with the company. But the company was small enough, and its president interested enough in dealing personally with employees, that the hiring process could be very personal. In the summer of 1964, Ray Jones applied for a job. President Sappington responded with a letter and a job application:

. . . which you should complete and return to me. Then, if you will . . . tell me what day you can come to Columbia, I will see you at that time and discuss your associating with our companies.

A. D. also took time to deal with employee grievances. In 1976, a group of from 60 to 70 women in the Underwriting Department sent him a petition requesting a system of merit pay increases, promotions from within employee ranks, and other changes. The policies resulting from his meetings with the group included a Home Office merit-pay plan whose total dollar amount exceeded $210,000 annually.

Another result of A. D.'s response to these women's concerns was the promotion to supervisor of another female worker. In the 1960s and 1970s, MFA Mutual gave other women increased opportunities for professional growth. In the mid-1960s, artist Jeanne Stultz and writer Phyllis Mussman served on the staff which produced CONTACT, then a bi-monthly magazine. Donna Gallo, Commercial Auto underwriter, used her expertise in the article "Truck Rating Primer" in a 1968 issue of ACTION! June LaRock and Marie Gardner, secretaries in Home Office Claims, also handled small auto claims. In 1967 they attended a special auto claims training course in Pennsylvania.

In 1974 and 1975, the Claims Department's FACS Program created a number of openings for women as small claims specialists. A company study showed that in October, 1970, MFA Mutual employed no female field claims adjusters or claims specialists. In October, 1975, 13 field adjusters (3% of the total) and 79 claims specialists (17%) were women. Early in 1981, a Columbia newspaper featured senior MFA adjuster Lucille Schwartz, who had been doing her job for 15 years. Boonville native Marilyn Robb, in 1979, moved from the Home Office Marketing Department to the position of DSM in Kansas District 9.

During these years racial minorities also found employment opportunities with MFA Mutual. Affirmative action records compiled in the 1970s and early 1980s provide snapshot views. On September 15, 1980, for example, the company employed 47 African-Americans and eight other racial minorities, which amounted to 3.23% of total company employees. In the Home Office, minorities constituted

The Home Office has been described as a mini-city with its own post office, travel agency, food service, infirmary, and bank in the form of the credit union, with president Linnie Kalaf in 1974. Kalaf celebrated 30 years of service in 1995.

Mail clerks sort the morning's mail in this 1978 photo.

One of the early husband-wife teams, Dale and Mabel Magness of Batesville, Arkansas. While Dale finished up his time for railroad retirement, Mabel took care of the agency.

3.67% of all employees, and 2.79% of all field employees. In Underwriting, two African-Americans were underwriters, one a senior underwriter, and one, hired in 1966, was a regional manager. Minority group claims adjusters and underwriters worked in field offices in Arkansas Kansas, Louisiana, Missouri, and Tennessee.

Table 7.2 Total Employee Salaries and Benefits Paid by MFA Mutual, Selected Years

	Salary Expense	Retirement Fund	Other Benefits	Profit Sharing
1964	$3,625,819			
1967	5,443,338			
1970	8,685,652			
1973	12,487,845	$292,182	$749,264	$105,208
1976	16,278,109	593,583	583,772	1,307,761
1979	21,530,553	782,404	1,068,981	484,085
1980	24,883,018	1,427,936	1,054,419	

Source: Annual Reports of Underwriting Expense

Company fringe benefits had begun with the retirement plan of 1951. Over the years they had not only grown in number, but also moved from the "fringe" to the center of importance. Table 7.2 summarizes information about the salaries and benefits expenses of MFA Mutual. One way to see these data is as a contribution to local economies, especially in the Columbia area, where a majority of company employees lived. By the 1960s and 1970s, MFA Mutual's employee benefits package was large and diverse. Until September, 1980 it included participation in the MFA's retirement plan, when — "in view of the change in the relationship between MFA and MFA Mutual" — the company formed its own plan. Amended several times over the years in the employees' favor, the plan became noncontributory early in 1980, with all payments into the plan made by the employer. When the insurance company separated from MFA, it formed group plans to continue other benefits shared with the farm co-op and its subsidiaries: life, health, long-term disability, and accidental death insurance. Employees had enjoyed these and other benefits for years — in 1964-1965, to cite another, the company had adopted a sick leave plan for salaried employees. Other programs joined this package of insurance protection. In 1973, MFA Mutual established a COLA (Cost of Living Adjustment) program, just in time for the most severe inflation since the 1940s. Also in 1973, the company inaugurated a Profit Sharing and Thrift Plan, offered to employees on a voluntary basis. Participating employees contributed a percentage of their annual salaries and the company a proportion of profits, when there were profits. As of 1976, the company had contributed only in 1973, but the positive financial results of the late

1970s translated into substantial growth in the plan's balance. By August 31, 1979, the Profit-Sharing Plan enjoyed total assets of $7.7 million, employees having contributed nearly $2 million and the company $4.4 million. The investment income for the life of the plan was $1.17 million. The credit union likewise continued to grow. Chartered by Missouri in 1958, but grown into a multi-state membership operating under multiple state regulations, the re-named MFA Insurance Federal Credit Union received a federal charter in 1979.

Management remained sensitive to the need for improvements in the benefits package. In the 1970s a Fringe Benefits Committee considered modifications in various plans, such as increasing hospital room allowances in the health plan, and adding dental care. Committees also considered adopting flextime in the Home Office and an employee physical fitness program. More social than strenuous, probably, were the annual company bowling tournaments, held in the 1960s in Columbia. In 1965, 61 teams from seven states, representing both agents and employees, participated.

The Shelter Insurance Federal Credit Union operations are guided by a board made up of members, with officers elected at each year's annual meeting. These 1993 officers are, left to right, Gerald Brooks, treasurer, Dennis Rooney, vice chair, Maggie Wood, chair, and Gene Baumann, secretary.

Table 7.3 Total Number of Agents, Selected Years

1964 . . . 1668	1973 . . . 1525
1967 . . . 1088	1976 . . . 1056
1970 . . . 1284	1979 . . . 1185

Source: 1964-1973 figures from tables attached to Minutes, March 22, 1974; 1976 and 1979 figures from table attached to Minutes, March 20, 1981.

Table 7.4 Numbers of Agents by States, Selected Years

Gary and Joyce Hanlon, Greenfield, Indiana, accept the 1970 Agent of the Year Award from President Sappington in Boston.

	On March 30, 1972 *	On March 31, 1975 **	On December 31 1980 ***
AR	157	161	155
CO	23	29	40
IL	106	97	75
IN	104	70	52
IA	45	40	42
KS	100	110	87
KY	79	79	99
LA	44	51	50
MN	58	56	—-
MS	36	65	41
E. MO	176	167	163
W. MO	218	202	196
NE	80	80	50
OK	80	98	93
TN	85	90	75
TX	30	29	—-
Total	1421	1424	1218
MO % of total	27.2	25.9	29.5
MO & AR of total	38.8	37.2	42.2

Sources: * Bill Conboy, "Marketing Observations," part of his Report to the Board, April 30, 1972
**** Conboy's Report, with Minutes, April 25, 1975**
***** Conboy's Report, with Minutes, March 20, 1981**

Tables 7.3 and 7.4 contain information about the number of agents affiliated with MFA Insurance during the years from 1964 to 1980. The statistics are related to several parts of the discussion which follows. Also of interest are the kinds of people represented by the numbers — who, exactly, "agents" were. There are several criteria. For one, MFA agents were exclusively MFA Mutual agents; the company had decided that during Jack Silvey's time. But as many as half of his agents had been part-time, and the proportion of part-timers had been even greater during the company's earliest years. One of A. D. Sappington's major decisions was that the company would recruit only full-time agents, and that is the second distinction. One cause of declining agent numbers was the departure of these agents whose commitment to their business was less than total, and who as a result often had high loss ratios.

But as circumstances change, so does policy. In March, 1977 Bill Conboy of Marketing announced that "we had started the practice of hiring part-time agents." They, he pointed out, "would be less costly than our financed agents program." And that comment leads to a third distinction among MFA Mutual agents. Most agents were commission agents, totally independent business people. However, some were salaried agents, financed by the company for a limited period as they established their agencies, often in new sales territories. At the start of 1975 the company had 440 agents on salary, and Conboy launched a program to reduce their numbers as a part of the company's efforts to cut expenses. By June, 1977, only 118 of them remained, and the goal was to phase out the program completely in 1978. In 1980, however, a new, carefully-controlled salaried agents program began. By the end of the year, 41 agents were on the plan.

Director of Sales John Lenox, agent Don Silkey, and State Sales Manager Bob Sloan at Silkey's agency in Topeka in 1971.

President Sappington visits McCook, Nebraska agent Lyle Blauvelt, holding his son Jay, and Chamber of Commerce member Ken Foster at Blauvelt's 1971 open house.

MFA LIFE INSURANCE COMPANY
SALUTES
TOP AGENTS
GEORGE & DON PEARSON

Harold and Ella Riekhof accept their Hall of Fame Plaque from President Sappington at the 1968 Conference in Miami Beach.

Total agent numbers fell in two waves: one from 1964-1969, when many part-time agents left the business, and the second following the underwriting losses in 1973-1974. But if the quantity of agents slipped, the quality of business improved — which was the whole point. As A. D. commented in mid-1968:

. . . at the time he became president, the company had 1,830 agents, but that this number had been reduced to 1,071 who now write considerably more volume of better quality than the larger number of agents.

The work of the Ad Hoc Committee in 1975 and 1976 included an agent-by-agent review of the entire agency force. In meetings that sometimes ran all day and continued over a period of months, members of the Ad Hoc Committee considered each agency as a micro-insurance company, analyzing the profitability of each as the A. M. Best Company evaluated MFA Mutual. For those agents showing losses, the Committee prepared a program of remedial action: requiring some to re-rate drivers to accurately reflect the risks; canceling other policies; perhaps restricting an agent's authority to approve repairs on damaged cars or homes. The agency reviews turned many into profitable businesses. Twenty years later, Howard Lang remained convinced that the Ad Hoc Committee's stringent review did more than anything else to save the company during its deepest crisis.

left: George and Don Pearson were honored for their results in the 1964 life contest.The pair earned the 1961 Agent-of-the-Year Award at the New Orleans President's Conference.

Table 7.5 Total Commission and Bonus Paid to MFA Insurance Agents, Selected Years

	Agents' Commission and Salary	Agents' Bonus	Total
1964	$3,810,155	$393,541	$4,203,696
1967	5,152,747	705,452	5,858,199
1970	7,478,254	868,616	8,346,870
1973	13,246,072	1,996,993	15,243,065
1976	13,605,783	1,804,594	15,410,377
1979	17,895,133	3,433,068	21,328,201

*** Salary first mentioned in 1971 statement. Source: Annual reports of underwriting expense.**

Table 7.6 Average Agent Income

1963 . . $2424	1972 . . .11,090
1964 . . . 3093	1973 . . .12,475
1965 . . . 4424	974 . . . 13,791
1966 . . . 5472	975 . . . 14,934
1967 . . . 6587	1976 . . .15,792
1968 . . . 7722	977 . . . 19,152
1969 . . . 8312	1978 . . .20,601
1970 . . . 8258	1979 . . .21,959
1971 . . . 10,505	1980 . . .21,951

Sources: 1963-1973 data from table attached to Minutes, March 22, 1974; 1974-76 data from table attached to Minutes, March 21, 1977;1977-1980 data from table attached to Minutes, March 20, 1981.

facing page: The Ad Hoc Committee of 1975-1976 did not invent agency review, which had its start in 1962, then was enlarged in 1965. Here, in 1968, John Ader, seated, is manager of the program, with Dave Ruse, center, and Leo Struglia as part of his staff.

For many MFA Mutual agents, professional success grew from a mixture of factors, one of which was good management from sales management. Jack Maxwell, shown with wife Helen at a life contest victory luncheon, received recognition.

Tables 7.5 and 7.6 reveal information about agents' commission and bonus income, and average annual income. Recall that the average agent income went both to full- and part-time agents, and involved salaried as well as commissioned agents. The agent contract, which changed over time, determined the rate of commission. In 1969, the commission on new policies was 20%, with a 7% renewal commission. In 1966, a revised Agents' Incentive Bonus Plan tied the bonus both to total premium and an agent's loss ratio over three years. Loss ratios of 40.0 and under earned the maximum bonus rate of 5%; those over 60.0 no bonus at all. For 1978, MFA Mutual paid a record bonus, and Bill Conboy attributed the large increase over previous years "to the agent's desire to only write quality business and keep his loss ratio at an acceptable level."

As in earlier years, of course, sales contests for agents and sales incentive plans for district and state sales managers helped to motivate those who marketed the companies' life, health, and casualty policies. In 1970, there was a life contest, an auto finance contest, a health contest, and a property contest — each with a list of prizes to be won. But the greatest single reward for outstanding sales achievement was the Conference of Champions and, beginning in 1976 for life sales, the Millionaire Trip. Tables 7.7 and 7.8 summarize essential information about these highlights of each year in the life of the companies. Enjoying luxurious accommodations in exotic and exciting surroundings, the companies' best agents, DSMs and state sales managers, plus Home Office managers, came together for an

The fall life insurance contest of the 1960s carried football themes, with victory luncheons and college football games part of the reward for the winners. Harold and Ella Riekhof sign in for this 1962 luncheon. Among the winners were Dean Rauer and Don Glasford.

Gerald and Genny Brandorff, Kearny, Nebraska, with their 1974 Agent-of-the-Year plaque.

Top MFA Life agent in Arkansas, Ben Whitaker, Rogers, sold $110,302 during the 1961 fall contest. Ellen Whitaker receives a mum from Mary Ann Miller of the Arkansas state claims office at the victory luncheon.

Agent Carl Durtschi, Dixon, turned the agency over to his son, George, following retirement.

experience equaled in few professions. And among the events repeated each year, perhaps the most warmly recalled by those who heard them were A. D.'s words uttered after a delicious dinner: "Well, here I am again . . . passin' out awards."

Table 7.7 Conference of Champions, 1964-1980

	Location	Number of of Agents Attending	% of Agents Attending	Agent of the Year
1964	Quebec	66	——	Troy Hightower, AR
1965	Nassau	70	4.2	Jim Sawyer, AR
1966	San Francisco	101	7.3	Same
1967	Estes Park	89	7.5	Same
1968	Miami	94	8.6	Richard Harp, AR
1969	Galveston	126	12.1	Bob Riley, MO
1970	Boston	133	12.9	Gary Hanlon, IN
1971	Honolulu	248	19.3	Jim Greene, AR
1972	Las Vegas	267	19.5	Bill Bell, OK
1973	Acapulco	176	11.9	Harrell Brawner, AR
1974	Spain	267	17.5	Gerald Brandorff, NE
1975	Freeport	235	15.3	Dave Bunn, LA
1976	Los Angeles	94	7.8	Vernon Golden, AR
1977	Maui, Hawaii	176	16.7	David Jeffs, OK
1978	Rio de Janerio	204	19.1	Joe Neil, AR
1979	Montreux , Switzerland	300	26.3	Curtis Watts, MS
1980	San Diego	165	13.9	Frank Riekhof, MO

Table 7.8 Millionaire Trip, 1976-1980

	Location	Sappington Award/Chairman's Award
1976	Marco Island	
1977	Bermuda	
1978	Aruba	
1979	St. Maarten	Bill Bell, OK
1980	Paradise Island	Frank Riekhof, MO

Management learned that Conference site selection did affect agent motivation and attendance. Early in 1970, A. D. asked agents how many would commit to qualify for a Conference held in Hawaii, and over 400 responded positively. March, 1970 was the biggest in sales volume in company history, and the Hawaii trip was the reason. In 1974, Gene Baumann assembled a film with scenes from Conferences since 1965, to show to agents as an additional motivator. The company's poor financial performance in the mid-1970s had an affect on agents' trips. The 1976 Conference of Champions remained in the continental United States and the standards for qualifying increased, both successful efforts to reduce the cost of the experience. It is perhaps no coincidence that the first Millionaire Trip happened that same year, at the end of several bad years for earnings on casualty insurance sales, but good years for life sales and profits. As an illustration of how the agents who attended the Conference of Champions excel, consider these facts about the

Richard Harp, who won the 1968 Agent-of-the-Year Award in Miami Beach, has attended more Conference of Champions trips than anyone. He qualified but chose to not attend the first trip to St. Louis in 1960. He hasn't missed since.

Howard and Mary Kay Lang greet the 1979 Millionaires at the hotel on St. Maarten Island.

Bob Riley, 1969 Agent-of-the-Year, has continued as a perennial leader. Here Mark Zimmer presents Riley a citation for authoring an article for INSURANCE SALES MAGAZINE.

129 who attended the Galveston event in 1969. Although they represented only 12% of the total agency force, these agents in the qualifying year 1968 wrote 24% of total casualty business as measured by premium, 25% of the new casualty business, 38% of the new life insurance and 32% of the new health insurance business. Their loss ratio over a three-year period was 52.83, compared to a company-wide figure of 60.67. At the 1965 Conference, a special group of these outstanding agents was inducted into the Hall of Fame, seven who had earned trips to all six conferences held so far. They were Bob Brown, Mexico; George and Don Pearson, Columbia; Harold Riekhof, Higginsville; Ralph Ross, Chillicothe; and Don Shuey, Unionville — all in Missouri — and Ben Whitaker, Rogers, Arkansas. In spite of the considerable expense of sponsoring the Conference and Millionaire trips, MFA/Shelter Mutual considers them not only as rewards for past achievement, but also an investment in the future.

A company newsletter and magazine continued to provide effective communication with agents and employees. From 1964 through 1967 the company's magazine for agents, a glossy, well-illustrated piece appearing in seven to nine issues annually, was CONTACT. Containing occasional articles by President Sappington, issues included a regular column by Gene Baumann: "The North-East Corner." From 1964-1967, "published for MFA Insurance Employees," was the newsletter "Close Contact." In January, 1968, amidst the disruptive debates and events that still form the general image of the sixties, appeared the first issue of

ACTION!, the re-named agents' magazine. Beset on all sides by burning cities as well as heated criticism in legislative halls and the media, the insurance industry faced unprecedented challenges. "These are times for action," A. D. asserted in an editorial. Insurance people needed to put their case forward and defend their independence and social contribution. "The new name ACTION! . . . is most appropriate for the work which lies before us."

After a decade of ACTION!, in January, 1978, THE SHIELD magazine made its appearance — "for MFA Insurance Agents and Employees." A. D.'s editorial explaining the changes in format and title emphasized the same source that his successors identified in 1980 when changing the company name: "The Shield of Shelter" advertising slogan. That phrase provided "a solid and significant corporate identification," and an appropriate publication title. An interdepartmental Publications Committee, under the chairmanship of Ray Jones from Marketing, initiated and oversaw the changes in the magazine, from greater use of color photography to a wider range of articles.

It is a hard task to adequately convey a sense of the bonds with agents that A. D. Sappington developed during the 33 years that he helped lead the company. But a few of the letters that passed between them suggest the dimensions of that relationship. Most of the letters used here were written in 1978, at a time when the illness that would soon take his life already caused him to miss work. Some agents wrote to express their satisfaction with their jobs. "I never thought a man could fall in love with a job and a company but I have," wrote Jerry Lannan from Indiana. "Thanks for helping change my life for the better." When veteran agents retired, A. D. contacted them personally. In 1977, he thanked Harold Remley, Sr. for 26 years of service to MFA Mutual, and in 1972 a similar note went to Maggie Elliston of Montrose, Missouri, who had represented the company for 25 years. She responded: " . . . you have all seemed so personal and interested in all my interests." Agent Roger Arnold of Colorado brought a problem to A. D. in 1978: the Home Office did not inform the agent until after the policyholder learned of an application rejected or an existing policy canceled. A. D. promised to take the matter up with underwriting. When several Kansas agents pointed out that MFA homeowners' policies were not price competitive in their state, Sappington agreed and outlined a solution. When Jim Sawyer wrote from Arkansas with a suggestion that the rate of commissions on Countryside policies be increased, A. D. said no, that was not possible now. But he added: "I want you to write me anything about our company, its management or operations because you always write in a constructive manner." That was this

Agent Bill Bell presents a gift from the agents attending the 1977 Millionaire Trip in Bermuda to A. D. and Helen Sappington.

The late 1970s Law Department: seated, Will L. Nelson, vice president and general counsel, standing left to right are Doris Bartolacci, Terry Cox, Shirley Johnson, and John Clark.

"agent-oriented President's" attitude toward most of the thousands of agent letters that came to him.

From 1964-1981 the company's officers met regularly with and reported to the board of directors. They shaped policies to respond to the financial crisis of 1973-1975 and to the changed relationship with MFA in 1979-81. Chapter 3 discussed key members of this group to February, 1964. This discussion will catch up with those careers, and examine more closely a group of managers who emerged to prominence after 1964. Taken together, the veterans and the younger group spanned the entire history of the company. A. D. Sappington, one of the former, who became president in 1964, had been a founding father in 1945. Gus Lehr, who became president in 1981, remains chairman of the board in 1996. It was A. D. and Howard Lang in particular who spotted the talent of these younger executives and served as their mentors in the 1960s and 1970s.

A look at those who attended meetings of the board in 1964 and 1981, most having attained the position of vice president, will distinguish one group from the

Administrative Vice President Jack Pettit gives employees the okay sign at a 1972 meeting.

other. In the mid-1960s, the key executives of MFA Mutual and its subsidiary companies were President Sappington; Senior Vice President Howard B. Lang, Jr.; Vice President and General Counsel Will L. Nelson; Secretary-Treasurer Paul Keithley; Vice President of Marketing Bill Conboy; Vice President of Underwriting James L. McTurnan; and Vice President of Claims Arthur Lang. All had been born prior to 1920, and all had begun their careers with the companies by 1954. With the exception of Keithley, who retired in 1978, and Sappington, who died in 1979, all experienced the break with MFA, with which several had old ties. When Shelter Mutual was born on July 1, 1981, Howard Lang retired as president and chief executive officer, while he remained board chair until 1984. Joining him in retirement were his brother Arthur and Will Nelson, as well as Judd Wyatt of advertising and Bill Redmon of personnel. Jim McTurnan became vice president of Claims on July 1, 1981. He and Bill Conboy continued their careers into the 1980s.

Agent Bill Moutell, Murphreysboro, Illinois welcomes open house guests Charles Allen, left, Underwriting, and Delbert Galloway, Claims, to his 1972 event.

A few of the newer officers who attended board meetings in 1981 had not even been with the company in 1964, though most took their first jobs with MFA Mutual between 1949 and 1959. Most of this group was born between 1927 and 1934, and a good share occupied vice presidencies in 1981 that had not existed in 1964 — a sign of the growing complexity of the company itself and that of American (and global) business. Listed in the order in which they became vice presidents, this group included Gustav J. Lehr (1966), Jack L. Pettit (1966), Donald Goodwin (1970), Jean Madden (1971), James A. Offutt (1972), J. Donald Duello (1978), Robert W. Maupin (1980), and Charles J. Dysart (1981).

Future chapters will have much to say about the presidencies of Lehr, Pettit, and Maupin. As already noted, during Howard Lang's presidency from 1979 to 1981, Lehr as executive vice president and Pettit as administrative vice president served as super vice presidents, having oversight of multiple departments and functions. Gus Lehr has described himself as "Mr. Outside" and Jack Pettit as "Mr. Inside," as he for years dealt with the company's legislative interests and other matters pertaining to "public affairs," while Pettit specialized in the internal administration of the company. Thus Lehr took the lead in representing MFA Mutual in the 1979 investigation of its arson program (chapter 8), while one of Pettit's special projects was the Word Processing Center. As a new historical era began on Shelter Day I, Gus Lehr became president and CEO, while Jack Pettit replaced Lehr as executive vice president.

Bill Conboy served as vice president of marketing for 18 years, from 1964 to 1982, when he became vice president for industry affairs. Conboy retired in 1984, with combined service for Missouri Farmers Association and the insurance companies of more than 40 years.

Two of these officers came to MFA Mutual from careers begun elsewhere. Bob Maupin, a native of Carrollton, graduated from the University of Missouri (B.A., 1954), and that institution's School of Law (1959). Coming to the insurance company as it severed its ties with MFA, he symbolized its historic roots in the farm organization. Maupin spent the years 1959-1980 with MFA, leaving his positions as

The annual bowling tourney attracted agent-sponsored teams from throughout the operating territory as well as home office league teams.

Defending champs who managed a runner-up spot in the 1970 MFA Mutual agents and employees bowling tournament, the Weldon Jones team from Columbia received their trophies from President Sappington.

associate general counsel and secretary/treasurer of the cooperative in September, 1980. From November of that year to July, 1981, he held Lehr's old post of vice president, Public Affairs, an appropriate role for a man who had represented MFA in Jefferson City during the years that Lehr represented MFA Mutual before state government. The two had been effective partners as lobbyists. On July 1, 1981, Maupin became vice president and general counsel.

Jean Madden came to the insurance company in 1971 following several careers at the University of Missouri, as the first vice president of Communications. Under his direction were all forms of internal and external communication, including public relations. Madden found his job to be especially interesting in 1979-1981 as the name and emblem changes occurred.

This new officer was accustomed to a whirl of activity. A track star and honor student at MU, where he took a B.S. in Education in 1950 and an M.A. in 1951, Madden had coached high school football, served in the military during the Korean conflict, taught freshman English classes, and been a television sports director before settling into the development and alumni relations office at his alma mater.

At Bill Bell's 1978 Kiefer, Oklahoma open house, Dale Ball, Tulsa claims manager, left, and Bob Reid, auto underwriter.

Charles Dysart had already enjoyed a long career with MFA Mutual when he became vice president of Underwriting. Hired full-time in 1957, this Columbia native had established a broad experience in underwriting and other departments. Named a senior vice president in 1994, Dysart retired early in 1995 after 39 years with the company.

Don Goodwin, vice president of Information Services, Jim Offutt, vice president of Actuarial, and Don Duello, vice president of Finance, oversaw areas of increasing importance to the company. Although Duello took over many of Paul Keithley's duties, the titles these men acquired originated in the 1970s. And although their areas of expertise were not exactly new, computer technology, actuarial prediction, and financial planning became more central than ever before to the company's success. All of them graduated from the University of Missouri; all held jobs briefly with companies outside the insurance industry before arriving at MFA Mutual; and all were specialists in areas that creatively support the company's main task of selling and servicing insurance policies.

Chapter 11 will include a further analysis of persons who served in Shelter Mutual's key management posts. Many of their names have not yet appeared in this history. But most had begun their careers with the company well before 1981, as three brief examples will illustrate. John Lenox, Ray Jones, and Terry Cox started with MFA Insurance between 1961 and 1965. Members of what might be called a third generation of company executives, all were vice presidents by 1986, and they continue in key leadership positions as the first 50 years of MFA/Shelter come to an end.

Leaders of the insurance industry trade organizations, both from MFA Mutual. Howard Lang, left, was president of the National Association of Mutual Insurance Companies, while A. D. Sappington was chairman of the board of governors for the National Association of Independent Insurers. Their terms overlapped by one month in 1971.

he became executive vice president, Gus Lehr reflected on an "extremely active [role] in industry matters over the years." He had served on the trade associations' legislative and solvency committees, for example, and soon would become a member of the NAII board of governors. Beyond the 1970s, the group now called the Professional Insurance Communicators of America gave its Sheila V. Meredith Award for "outstanding contributions" to two veterans of Shelter Insurance's publications staff: Gene Baumann in 1986 and Bruce Meentemeyer in 1993. What does this catalog of honors and elected positions amount to? An unerring sign that their peers in the national industry placed trust in and valued the leadership of MFA Insurance talent.

Their national prominence gave key MFA Mutual leaders opportunity to speak on insurance-related public issues, in an era of renewed governmental activism and media criticism of insurance practices. Sappington, Lehr, and Lang in particular

Agent Paul Brumaghim, Danville, Illinois and actor Fess Parker, TV's Daniel Boone, join in the 1970 Cancer Crusade. Parker was national chairman, Brumaghim district chairman.

With the help of its own expert auto body shop people in 1979, the companies built and donated this special vehicle to the Rusk Rehabilitation Center in Columbia. The car chassis is designed to assist victims of accidents to relearn how to enter and exit vehicles with their disabilities.

Vice President Hubert Humphrey addressed the 1966 MFA Convention. Here he and his wife, Muriel, left, visit with Fred and Dorothy Heinkel at the picnic served by insurance company employees.

articulated clearly the public service role of the private but intelligently-regulated insurance industry, and publicized their view of the role of business in the political process. They did this even during an uncomfortable "media event" which A. D. did not live to see — the Missouri Insurance Department's Market Conduct Survey of the company's regional fire program in 1979.

Arson as a means of defrauding insurance companies must be as old as insurance. Well before the 1979 events, MFA Mutual employed a former Missouri State Highway Patrolman, Harry Hansen, to investigate suspicious fire claims. Hansen was so good at his work that he trained police and fire department arson investigators and those employed by other insurance companies. In the mid-1970s, the arson problem grew more serious. Art Lang, in May, 1977, distributed to the board an article entitled "Arson Problem Out of Control." MFA Mutual developed a program to get tough on arson fraud. In cases over a certain amount of loss, a special team investigated the fire, and in a number of cases found evidence of arson. The team's claims adjusters employed special methods of questioning claimants and gathering and analyzing evidence. The fire program had two goals, explained Bob Crouch, its director. "One is to take the profit out of a fire." The second was to develop a reputation for exposing arson fraud, to deter those bent on such a scheme from insuring with the company.

While MFA Mutual developed its program, Missouri voters in 1976 sent Joseph Teasdale to the governorship. Teasdale was an energetic young Kansas City attorney who campaigned successfully as a consumer advocate. His initial target was

The company's strong stance against arson was both economical and to support the firefighters who risk their lives to protect property.

A 1977 meeting of the Fire and Allied Lines Claims Committee to decide on payments on large losses in major fire claims. From left to right are Jim McDonnell, Bob Crouch, and Joe Duncan.

privately-owned utilities such as Union Electric of St. Louis, but later in his single-term administration Teasdale set his sights on another regulated industry, insurance. In 1978, with his active backing, the General Assembly passed the Unfair Insurance Practices Act. It replaced an older statute's vague language with clear directives about how and within what time frame companies must respond to the loss claims of their policyholders. The stage was set for a confrontation between a governor with a cause to defend and a re-election campaign to wage in 1980, and an insurance company facing a growing arson problem and employing some hard-nosed methods to solve it. And ready for a story were the St. Louis media.

Several cases in which MFA Mutual refused to pay the full amount the policy called for because of the suspicion of arson were in the St. Louis area. Steve Trenkmann, whom Gus Lehr recalls as a "fair but aggressive reporter" for KMOX-TV, began a series of reports on policyholder complaints on the 6:00 News. That was in May, and by June the television news investigation, bolstered by POST-DISPATCH articles, had spread negative publicity across Missouri, though its

This Bill Hume editorial cartoon from a 1980 Shield magazine expressed a viewpoint on the arson problem.

strongest concentration was in metropolitan St. Louis. The publicity prompted President Lang to appoint a management committee "to review the handling of major fire losses," and caused the Missouri Division of Insurance to begin its own investigation. That inquiry of thirty-eight complaint reports and 122 randomly-selected fire claim files from three MFA Mutual claims offices for the period January 1, 1977 to August 31, 1979 proceeded through the summer into the fall.

Events climaxed in November, 1979 upon completion of the Market Conduct Survey. On Monday, November 5 the Division of Insurance gave a draft copy of its report to company officials, and by Wednesday morning Gus Lehr and Jack Pettit had carefully analyzed its charges. The report, citing violations of law, presented a list of required changes in the company's fire investigation procedures. Lehr and Pettit also found inaccuracies and unnecessarily inflammatory language, especially the charge that the company displayed "corporate paranoia regarding arson." That phrase did not survive the initial draft, and the final version contained other changes as well. A copy of the survey was illegally leaked to the POST-DISPATCH on Tuesday the 6th, so that it carried a story on the state's charges against MFA Mutual even before company representatives could confer with state officials.

On Wednesday, November 7, Pettit and Lehr met in Jefferson City with Richard J. Fredrick, director of insurance, in a day-long conference in which the parties discussed in detail the language of the report, its substantive content, and the company's response. The critical event was Governor Teasdale's public intervention into these proceedings. During the lunch break on Wednesday, Teasdale summoned a surprised Fredrick to a "hastily-called news conference" at which KMOX-TV cameras were set up, to denounce MFA Insurance's violations. "I find the conclusions of this report very distressing," Teasdale said of what was only an initial draft. "I'm not going to tolerate insurance companies using arson as an excuse to delay or deny legitimate insurance claims." Showing restraint, Gus Lehr told reporters he was "disappointed" that the state's chief executive would make public comment on an administrative matter which his director of insurance was handling through established procedures.

The results of the incident are quickly told. For its part, MFA Mutual — while not conceding that it had done anything wrong — changed its arson investigation program. Wishing to comply fully with the report, the company changed all eleven procedures criticized by the Division of Insurance, and paid a $10,000 penalty to the state. By December, the company had abolished its regional fire program in response both to the state's investigation and the recommendation of the study committee appointed by President Lang. Second, the adverse publicity did hurt business in the short run. The company's quick alteration of arson investigation methods aimed to ease the anxieties of Missouri policyholders and agents, as did a series of agent

President Jimmy Carter, waving, enters the Hearnes Center in Columbia to address the 1978 MFA Convention.

meetings in November and December. Third, as the special arson investigators blended in with other claims adjusters following the end of the fire program, they brought their expertise with them. In spite of the negative publicity, Arthur Lang concluded, "the program was not all bad. . . . We gained much valuable experience."

Finally, the mundane subject of MFA Mutual's fire claims program casts light on an important matter: the nature of our political system and the proper role of business firms in it. In the incident's wake, Governor Teasdale blasted what he described as the political machine put together by the state's insurance companies. "It's a highly organized, well-financed program complete with public relations firms and lobbyists." According to the Teasdale administration's scenario, the national insurance industry saw Missouri as a battleground in their resistance to state regulation, and was creating a $2 million "war chest" to fight the stronger regulation that the governor would propose to the General-Assembly in 1980. In addition, a Teasdale aide charged, companies were mobilizing their agents to lobby the legislature, under threat of losing their contracts if they did not cooperate.

Gus Lehr, MFA's seasoned lobbyist, called these charges "preposterous." He argued, first, that insurance firms were mounting no special legislative efforts for the 1980 session. A trade association pamphlet of ten pages, defending the principle of open competition in insurance pricing, was "hardly . . . a massive undertaking," Lehr said. All the wild charges of agent coercion and huge expenditures by the industry were simply wrong. Yes, his company occasionally did ask agents to contact their legislators on pending bills — if they agreed with the company's position. Yes,

President Sappington visits with North Carolina Senator Sam Ervin, later of Watergate fame, at the 1971 NAII Annual Meeting.

MFA Mutual did spend policyholders' money to fund its political efforts. The governor spent taxpayer money to denounce insurance companies and advocate measures like prior state approval of policy rates. The documentary record, indeed, shows that MFA Mutual's political expenditures were small. In 1979, with MFA, the company formed a PAC — a political action committee — and authorized an expenditure of no more than $5,000 per year to support or oppose candidates and proposals. When the break with MFA occurred in 1980, MFA Mutual formed its own PAC with similar purposes and of like size. Gus Lehr's fundamental point was this: if the company could not do these things, if the industry could not do them, "democracy is on the decline."

Do business firms have a right to try to influence legislation and election outcomes? Of course they do, since legislation proposed by elected officials vitally affects the conduct of a business. Is lobbying a dirty word, or a legitimate exercise of political rights? Although any use of power may become corrupt, the second choice is true. Is corporate lobbying as much a part of the democratic process as the lone citizen casting a ballot? Yes, again. These were the views of MFA Mutual's fifth president Gustav Lehr, who spent a good share of his first twenty-two years with the company as its chief lobbyist in Jefferson City. Lehr quoted the remark of the late senator from Oklahoma, Robert Kerr, to a group of insurance executives: "Whether or not you want your business in politics, politics is in your business, and if you want to survive you had better learn how to lobby." Lehr did not shy away from the word "lobbyist." By supplying busy, non-specialist legislators with information and points of view, "lobbyists perform a vital public service," he asserted in 1972. Lehr was proud of his role, fascinated with the legislative process, and an effective, highly-respected lobbyist. Preceded by A. D. Sappington, who was MFA Mutual's first legislative representative in the 1940s and 1950s, and succeeded by Robert Maupin in 1980, Lehr began practicing his lobbying skills in 1960. As vice president of public affairs from 1966 to 1979, he continued to represent the company at the state capital and to keep track of legislation in the other states in which it operated. Specific examples of issues and legislative proposals will explain further why MFA Mutual was rather deeply involved, through the roles of Gus Lehr and A. D. Sappington especially, in politics. An issue that persisted through the 1960s and 1970s was no-fault insurance. And national no-fault bills in Congress raised a larger issue: federal intrusion into what had been a state responsibility. Lehr and Sappington had much to say about both issues, since they perceived them as a threat to the welfare of the insurance industry. In 1967, for example, Lehr and Jack Pettit attended a meeting of insurance executives whose goal was to make policy recommendations to NAII's board of governors.

One of these was "that the NAII staff should continue to aggressively and

This 1974 editorial cartoon by Bill Hume depicts President Sappington in his role as industry spokesman and his appearance before the Judiciary Committee of the U.S. Senate in opposition to a federal no-fault program.

realistically support state regulation" over federal. In July, 1974 Sappington testified before a House Committee in Washington on no-fault, and in June, 1977 Lehr made a similar statement before a U.S. Senate Committee. A. D. made it clear that he had not come to praise one of the two bills before the House over the other. Both were bad, because they "constitute an intrusion by the federal government into the regulation of the automobile insurance business." With the opening wedge of no-fault, Sappington feared, other laws would follow, creating uniform federal policy provisions, pricing schemes, and costly administration. Lehr made the same point, but added others. One was that the states were useful laboratories which ought to continue to experiment with the no-fault principle or reject it. Turn to federal legislation, and a deadening uniformity would fall across the industry.

Missouri's U.S. Senator Stuart Symington gets the insurance industry perspective from Fred Heinkel, Harold Douglas and A. D. Sappington. Symington was in Columbia to address the 1968 Missouri Farmers Association annual convention. Company leaders maintained a close relationship with state and national legislators, and influenced the passage of many laws which have stood the test of time. That tradition has continued to the present, with strong lobbying support through industry trade organizations and direct to office holders.

It was no-fault, plus compulsory insurance, prior approval rating laws, and other ideas current during the 1960s and 1970s, that made an active political role necessary for MFA Mutual and the casualty industry as a whole. They help to explain Mr. Lehr's years in Jefferson City and the company's PAC. They reveal why MFA Mutual officials joined with those from MFA to host an annual country ham breakfast for the Missouri congressional delegation in Washington. These legislative issues motivated the occasional letters Lehr sent to agents, in other states as well as Missouri, asking them to contact their representatives in state government on key bills. And they made sensible Gus Lehr's regular legislative reports to the board.

One final issue requires discussion: the decade-long contest with the Internal Revenue Service over the taxable status of agents. In March, 1982, President Gus Lehr testified before a House subcommittee in Washington in support of a bill which would clearly define what were known as independent contractors. From its beginning in 1946, MFA Mutual had considered its agents to be independent contractors — people in business for themselves, who maintained their own offices, set their hours, hired their staff, and paid their own taxes, while agreeing to sell exclusively MFA insurance policies. Until November, 1972 the IRS, in numerous audits of the company's tax returns, agreed with this understanding. But at that time the federal tax agency changed its interpretation. It now argued that agents were employees, not independent businesses affiliated with the company. Lehr appeared before the subcommittee of the Committee on Ways and Means on behalf of NAII, for many other insurance companies were affected by the ruling. And so were other industries, from real estate firms to home sales companies like Avon, all of which used independent contractors.

President Lehr spoke to members of the House Ways and Means Committee because the issue was taxes. Independent contractors paid their own taxes and provided for their own retirement. Employees did not; their employers paid Social

Security taxes and unemployment insurance taxes, withheld a portion of salaries for income taxes, and paid into company retirement plans. The IRS assessed MFA Mutual $19,148,563 for unpaid back taxes on employee-agents for the years 1968 through 1974. An additional assessment for 1975 and 1976, while not formally levied, would have added $8,900,000 to the bill. The change in IRS policy created a fundamental threat to the MFA Insurance Companies. Facing a tax bill of at least $20 million, while attempting to build onto a $57 million policyholder surplus, "we were," Lehr admitted, "apprehensive about our ability to continue as a viable organization." In addition, the MFA pension plan was jeopardized. The IRS ruled that the company had discriminated against agents by not including them in the plan, and removed its tax-deferred status. The plan received a tax bill of over $1 million, and many within MFA as well as MFA Mutual had visions of a bleak retirement.

Campaign Chairman John Lenox paints the final tally on the 1978 United Way Goal sign.

In his March, 1982 testimony, Lehr reviewed his company's experience with the Internal Revenue Service to illustrate to members of the House the imperative need for a resolution of the matter. Firmly opposing the tax agency's interpretations, MFA Mutual employed the law firm of Arnold and Porter, Washington, D.C., to represent it. Administrative appeals to the IRS failed to reverse its policy. The company then brought a suit to Tax Court, but without satisfactory result. The entire matter had become very costly, including the expense of obtaining verification from past and present agents across thirteen states that they had, indeed, paid their taxes for the years in question (information that the Internal Revenue Service had, of course, but would not release). As of 1982, the only resolution achieved was a temporary one. A section of the 1978 Revenue Act had established a moratorium under which the IRS was prohibited from pursuing companies like MFA Mutual for payment of taxes allegedly owed, while the Congress considered legislation clearly defining "independent contractor." But as Lehr's visit to Capitol Hill in 1982 suggests, the threat of a destructive and unjust tax bill still hung over the company as the era here under consideration closed.

MFA Mutual's public roles extended far beyond the defense of its business interests through political action. The final subject of this chapter might be called community service. In an article published in RESPONSE, a magazine of the Clearinghouse On Corporate Social Responsibility, President Sappington and Chairman Heinkel had this to say:

Like all responsible insurance companies, MFA participates in many philanthropic activities and encourages its employees to participate in many others. We believe in paying our dues to the community and to society at large.

They cited several examples of the community activities that they had in mind.

The kickoff for the 1976-1977 United Way campaign was held at the Shelter flag pole.

In 1972, Gus Lehr received a special citation from President Richard Nixon for his years of service as appeals agent for the Boone County draft board.

The company itself and individual employees were committed to United Way campaigns throughout the operating territory. Each fall in Columbia, the United Way's "thermometer" measuring the building of contributions toward the goal sat on MFA Mutual's front lawn. John Lenox led the Columbia campaign in 1979. Two years earlier, employees contributed $32,827 to the drive, a per capita gift of $36.80. As for other fund-raising campaigns, Heinkel and Sappington mentioned "extensive company and employee participation in" those of the Easter Seal, Multiple Sclerosis, and Muscular Dystrophy organizations, as well as activities of the Girl and Boy Scouts and the Jaycees. Sponsoring Red Cross blood drives at the Home Office and supporting CARE's efforts to feed the hungry overseas became annual activities. Funding the yellow-ribbon campaign in 1979-1980 in remembrance of the American hostages in Iran was a unique cause.

MFA Mutual received frequent appeals for funds from many sources, far and near. There were two attempts during the 1960s to regularize the company's giving. In 1966, the board authorized the president to use his discretion on gifts up to $500, and by the following year the insurance company was contributing funds to the MFA Foundation which, among other worthy purposes, underwrote college scholarships for rural youth. In 1967, the company added $50,000 to its regular $10,000 annual contribution to the Foundation's endowment. In 1980, as the separation with MFA occurred, the insurance companies received a share of the funds of the MFA Foundation and established their own charitable trust. But the board continued to respond to specific appeals for monies, and initiated other gifts. In 1977, for example, the company gave real estate to the Urban League of Little Rock, and in 1976 it donated one of its replaced computers to the Quincy public schools.

Through its cash donations, MFA Mutual supported a myriad of causes. Gifts helped to build the Oklahoma Highway Patrol building in McAlester; to establish the new Rock Bridge State Park south of Columbia; to purchase a new fire truck for Galt; to support the Missouri Association for Retarded Children; to purchase television sets for the new Veterans Hospital in Columbia; to expand the state cancer research facility there; to construct a building for the American Royal horse show in Kansas City; and to support the Hubert H. Humphrey Institute of Public Affairs.

The most distinctive and lasting community project that MFA Mutual accomplished during this era was the beautification of its Home Office property. In the minds of visiting agents and employees, the many tourists who flow through Columbia, and most Mid-Missourians, the most distinctive feature of Shelter Insurance is the fountain on Broadway and Shelter Gardens on the northwest portion of the grounds. Both were projects of special importance to A. D.

Judd Wyatt, director of advertising, received the Presidential Award of the National Association of Mutual Insurance Companies, the group's highest service award. He received similar accolades from the other trade association with which he worked closely, the NAII.

During his lobbying days for the farmer's association, Bob Maupin was well-known for his bow ties. He and Gus Lehr worked as a team to influence legislation that would be favorable to farmers and the insurance business.

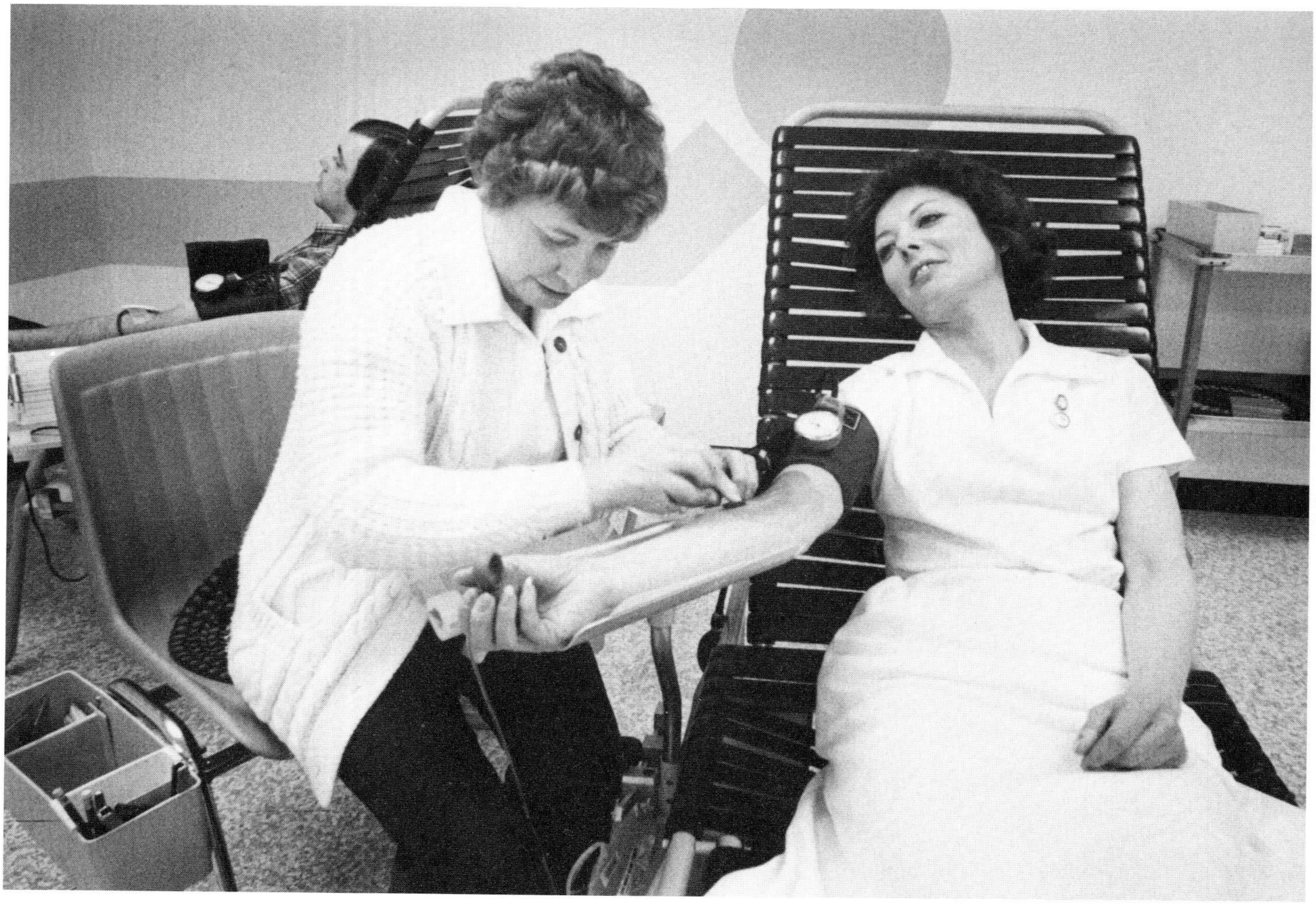

Companies nurse Shirley Stockton set a good example by joining a Home Office blood drive in 1980.

The lighted fountain is a popular gathering place for the community.

As often as not, the first day of spring and the fountain turn-on is held in less than spring-like weather.

Sappington, and they brought an instant identification to the company when it dedicated them in 1966 and 1975, respectively.

A. D. proposed and obtained board approval for the fountain in May, and oversaw its dedication on September 16, 1966. Scottie Garrett, superintendent of Buildings and Grounds, was in charge of the project. During its first weekend of operation the splashing waters of the colorful lighted fountain attracted viewers in more than 4,000 cars. For Columbians, especially Home Office employees, the fountain has been the focus of two annual events: the welcoming of spring as the fountain is turned on in March, and the start of the holiday season as a large Christmas tree is lighted in December. No matter that celebrants often enjoy a warm evening for the winter rites and wet snow for the rites of spring. Hundreds of people turn out to enjoy bands, choral groups, and a Santa, as well as what the fountain holds.

Even before the company created the MFA Garden, an editorial writer used the grounds surrounding the Home Office building as a model for Columbians. Noting that the city's "commercial and public areas generally leave much to be desired" in

This 1978 Christmas tree continued a tradition that has become a Columbia tradition. To celebrate the tree's lighting in the fountain to welcome the holiday season, huge crowds gather for music and a visit from Santa Claus. Here Jan Lucchesi and Teresa Howard from Communications help Santa.

The addition of the gardens in 1975 accelerated the popularity of the Home Office grounds as a place for the public to visit, the fountain in the front, the gardens in the northwest corner.

Board Chairman Fred Heinkel breaks ground with a team of mules and a plow for the gardens and replica of the Newcomer School on March 10, 1974, the 60th anniversary of the Missouri Farmers Association.

Virgil Bachtel, left, grandson of the farmer who called the first meeting in 1914 which led to the founding of MFA, visits with Gene Baumann, chairman of the Garden Committee in July 1975. Bachtel attended the original Newcomer School, and lauded the accuracy of the reproduction for this replica.

the way of beauty, the writer pointed out that the MFA Insurance property "show[s] what can be done with regular attention." With Gene Baumann as chair, members from both MFA Mutual and MFA, and guests A. D. and Fred Heinkel, the MFA Gardens Committee first met in April, 1972. From the start it was established that MFA Insurance would pay for the project; that the organization of the first MFA Farm Club in the Newcomer School near Brunswick would be memorialized by a replica of that building; and that trees and flowers native to Missouri would beautify the area in a series of gardens. On March 10, 1974, ground was broken in ceremonies for both the school and garden, and while the MFA convention met in early August, 1975, the whole project was dedicated. Beginning in 1976, Jean

The flag at Newcomer School flies at half-mast on August 4, 1976 in memory of U.S. Representative Jerry Litton, who was killed the night before in a plane crash, along with his wife and two children. Litton had just won the Democratic nomination for the U.S. Senate from Missouri and was en route to a victory celebration in Kansas City.

Al Price, president of Boone County National Bank, rings a school bell the bank gave to MFA to commemorate the ground breaking and anniversary.

This 1976 concert in the gardens used the school house as a backdrop. Present day concerts, held each Sunday in June and July, use the gazebo as a stage, and the lawn for seating of thousands.

The gardens are a year-round attraction, making them truly four-season gardens.

Early in the life of the Shelter Gardens the trees and shrubs allow long distance views, shortly after dedication in 1975.

Madden scheduled a summer concert series in the garden, and these bring-your-own-lawnchair affairs have attracted thousands of people each season since. The garden received landscaping awards for Scottie Garrett's expert work and hosted numerous weddings and other events, including the picnic lunch on Shelter Day 1.

On that day, as Gus Lehr became president and Howard Lang left that office but remained chairman of the board, a monument to their friend and mentor stood nearby. The entrance to the garden and the fence along its eastern border were erected with memorial funds contributed after A. D. Sappington's death. The strength that he had built into the companies would be a valued resource as MFA became Shelter in mid-summer, 1981.

Sixth graders from Columbia's Russell Boulevard School role-play pioneer education in the one-room Newcomer School in Shelter Gardens in the spring of 1977.

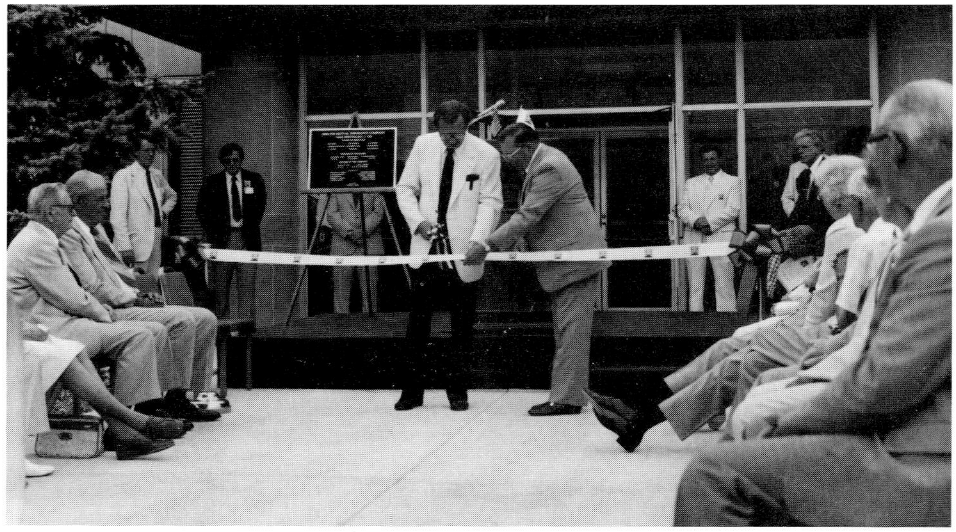

Shelter Day I — President Gus Lehr and Chairman Howard Lang cut the ribbon to a new era, officially dedicating the new name, Shelter Insurance.

Part Three

A MATURE AND CONFIDENT COMPANY: SHELTER INSURANCE 1981-1995

chapter 9

Overview 1981-1995

Board Chairman Gus Lehr, who was asked in 1995 if the Shelter Insurance Companies had become so financially strong and diversified that their very existence would never again be threatened as in fact they had been in 1974-1975, answered with a smile. The smile surely expressed satisfaction with the impressive strength and stability of the enterprise he had led for so long. The smile may have betrayed a temptation to answer yes. But the answer was "no." No casualty and property insurer, given inevitable disasters like Hurricane Andrew in 1992 and the Southern California earthquake of 1994, can ever allow past success to breed complacency. Then there is the normal swing from good times to bad and back again inherent in the insurance business. As President Bob Maupin noted in 1994: "The property and casualty industry is starting into another downturn in the insurance cycle. These cycles are not new, but occur in almost a predictable pattern."

Shelter's history since 1981 illustrates that the reappearance of underwriting losses, and even a decline in accumulated surplus, make a bit foolish an interviewer's mention of invulnerability. On the other hand, Shelter Mutual and its subsidiary companies rebounded impressively from several years of poor results in the first half of the 1980s, and again in 1990. In the last phase of its development, Shelter has matured into a company of imposing strength, one whose presence is felt far beyond its thirteen-state operating area.

The companies obtained new names on July 1, 1981, an event celebrated each year on Shelter Day. Jim McTurnan struck an appropriate note in his invocation: "Midst the blossoms of the garden and the sparkle of the fountain, a new name is born. . . . New child, born of MFA and christened Shelter, grow strong and reach for the stars." Those to whom officials spoke that day included Home Office workers, plus employees assembled at branch offices who listened by amplified telephone. The picnic lunch served in Shelter Gardens featured a huge birthday cake; employees elsewhere shared their own cakes. Agents, too, marked this special day with office open houses, as their new Shelter Insurance signs replaced those advertising MFA Insurance. In Shelter Gardens employees watched the burial of a time capsule containing contemporary company literature. "Won't they be surprised in 25 years how cheap our insurance was," remarked President Lehr on his first day in office.

Shelter officials prepared for the name change with great care, and found that all constituencies accepted "Shelter" with an ease that was very satisfying. "What's in a name?" A company's identity with present and future customers, an identity which means recognition and familiarity, but also trust — the earning of respect over time. A name change may jeopardize such treasure, and some in the company

Don Goodwin, long time head of information services and senior vice president at his retirement in 1992, chaired the committee that executed the name change from MFA Mutual to Shelter Mutual in 1980-1981.

Ed Berg and Zen Thomas unveiled the new Shelter sign as part of the Shelter Day I ceremony marking the name change.

This 1980 newspaper ad explained the change in logos, but at the time the company name remained MFA until 1981 when the Shelter name was adopted.

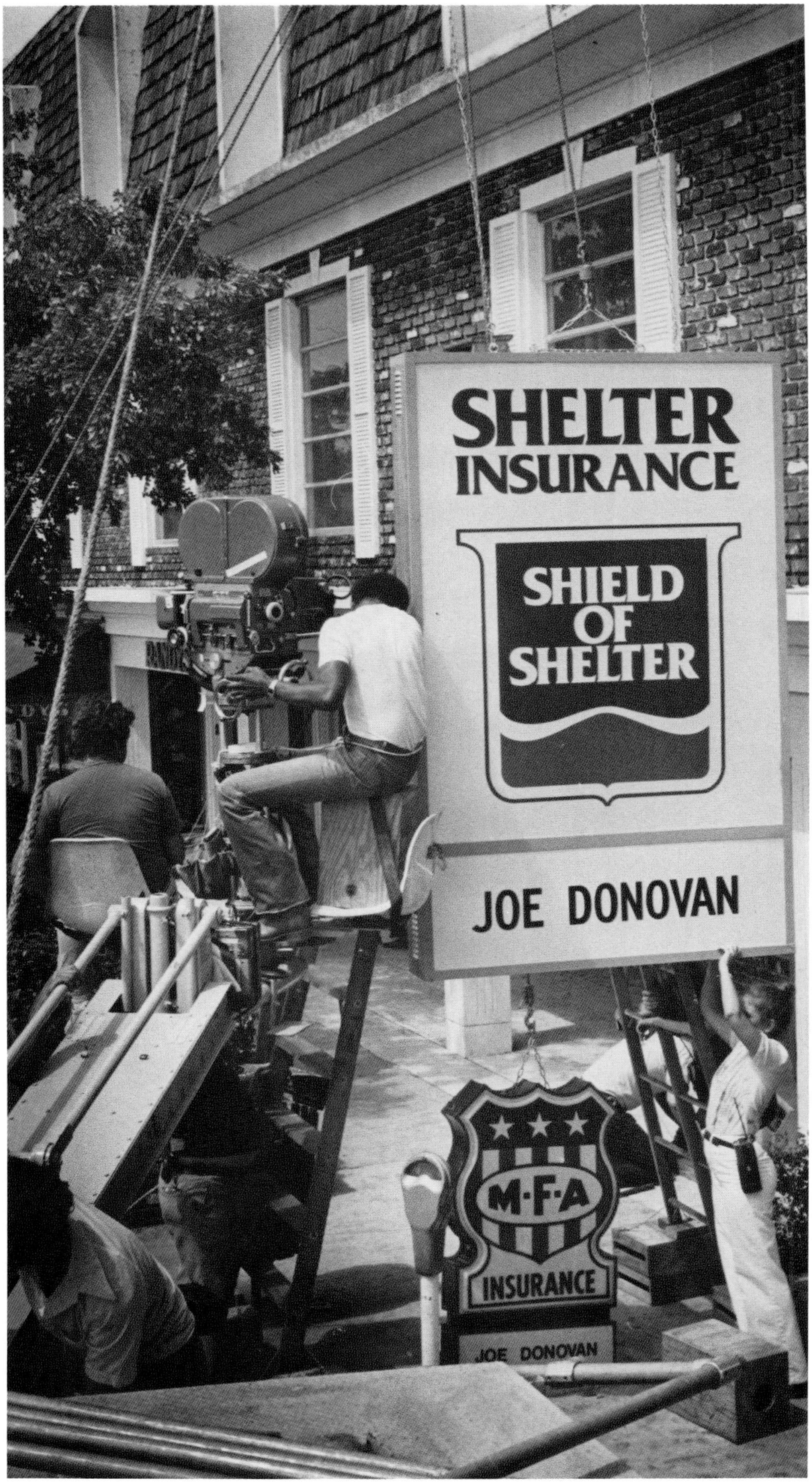

One of the most important, and most effective TV commercials ever produced for the companies was this sign-changer spot, in which the spokesman describes the change in name for the companies.

A major aspect of the name change was in agent signs, a sample held here by Jean Madden and Gary Mayfield.

wondered how many policyholders would go elsewhere for insurance. In fact, hardly any of them did. The name-change was costly and time-consuming: Don Goodwin reported "1,200 forms to be changed . . . 40,000 forms to be filed with the Insurance Department." But after it was over Bill Conboy recalled the "positive approach agents took toward the name change," and that was true of employees and policyholders too.

Changed on July 1, 1981 were the names of the three companies called MFA, plus Countryside Casualty Company. It became Shelter General Insurance Company and continued to write higher-risk auto policies. The parent company changed its name to Shelter Mutual Insurance Company, while the third insurer, MFA Life, became Shelter Life. The finance company, MFA Security Service Company, did business from that day on as Shelter Financial Services. What sounded a bit strange and unnatural then now has the endorsement of 15 years' usage.

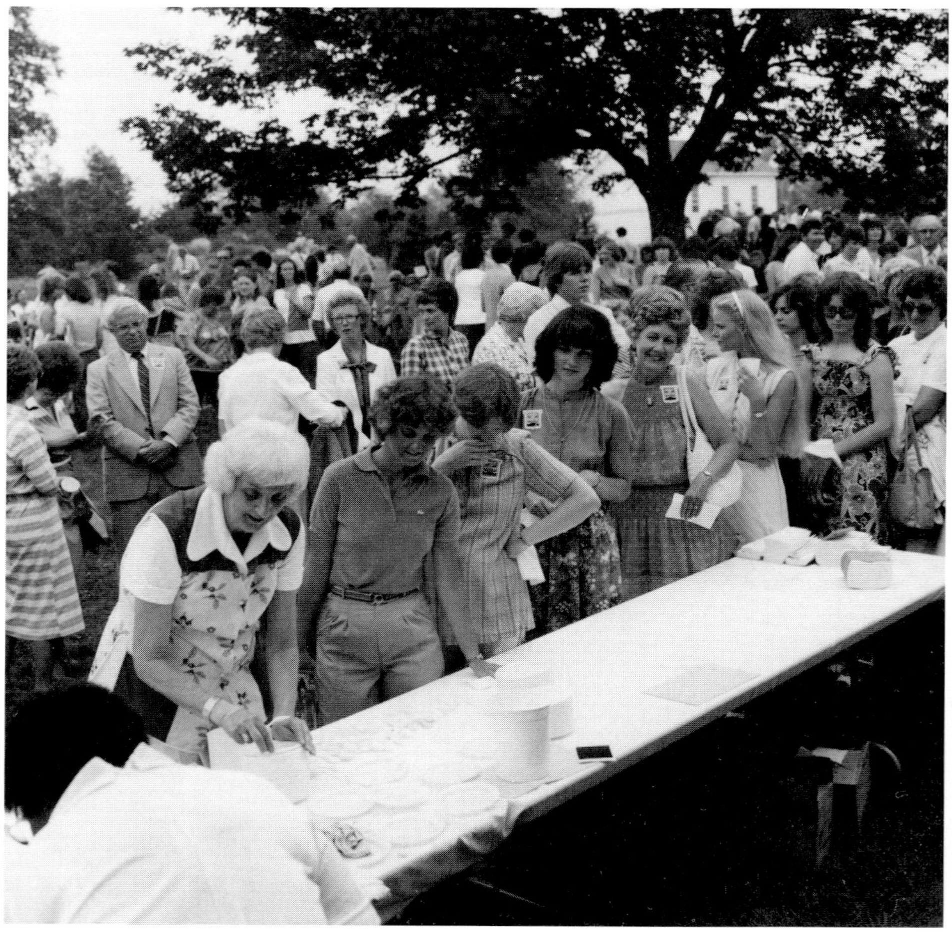

The change was cause for celebration in the gardens, a tradition that continues.

Table 9.1 Shelter Mutual, Key Indicators of Growth, 1981-1994

	1981	1982	1983
Earned Premium	$207,699,404	$225,916,643	$261,803,885
Cost of Losses & Adjustment	148,289,407	186,852,379	222,156,812
Underwriting Expenses	60,731,396	69,117,165	79,730,980
Net Underwriting Results	(2,560,004)	(32,157,763)	(41,226,820)
Total Investment Gain	22,889,787	21,265,104	18,637,387
Net Addition to Surplus	6,139,515	1,197,584	(13,852,177)
Year-end Surplus	160,559,959	161,757,551	147,905,377

	1984	1985	1986
Earned Premium	$286,109,944	$277,366,716	$281,313,917
Cost of Losses & Adjustment	249,191,806	195,402,523	187,963,428
Underwriting Expenses	79,822,763	77,089,501	82,850,496
Net Underwriting Results	(45,276,772)	542,707	7,209,927
Total Investment Gain	22,521,968	24,008,706	28,824,338
Net Addition to Surplus	(17,963,304)	58,233,204	42,391,128
Year-end Surplus	129,942,072	188,175,275	230,566,406

	1987	1988	1989
Earned Premium	$279,653,148	$310,507,323	$327,217,654
Cost of Losses & Adjustment	182,051,190	215,731,115	249,914,361
Underwriting Expenses	91,670,998	94,293,312	97,188,396
Net Underwriting Results	18,733,367	(4,953,692)	(24,075,230)
Total Investment Gain	32,159,634	35,582,257	37,584,242
Net Addition to Surplus	21,347,100	31,348,791	35,553,702
Year-end Surplus	251,913,512	283,262,303	318,816,002

	1990	1991	1992
Earned Premium	$354,976,228	$387,453,042	415,218,088
Cost of Losses & Adjustment	294,913,229	295,124,134	297,443,106
Underwriting Expenses	106,023,112	113,467,985	127,276,720
Net Underwriting Results	(50,835,062)	(26,611,353)	(18,155,278)
Total Investment Gain	41,115,162	54,219,473	41,378,771
Net Addition to Surplus	(13,058,340)	41,165,851	26,372,087
Year-end Surplus	305,757,662	346,923,513	372,045,600

	1993	1994
Earned Premium	$445,913,429	$485,227,092
Cost of Losses & Adjustment	312,527,410	346,557,800
Underwriting Expenses	138,563,268	161,801,072
Net Underwriting Results	(15,099,802)	(34,933,531)
Total Investment Gain	40,907,210	86,037,349
Net Addition to Surplus	58,014,258	24,905,087
Year-end Surplus	430,059,859	454,782,150

What was the financial experience of these firms in 1981 and after? What appears below are responses to that question for Shelter Mutual, the original and still the largest, most important of the Shelter insurance companies. Chapter 10 will offer a briefer discussion of the other Shelter insurers.

Shelter Mutual's earned premium, $207 million in 1981, doubled by 1992 and grew by another $70 million in the next two years. In 1994, it had nearly reached the half-billion dollar mark. In 1983, earned premium surpassed $100 million in Missouri alone, and three years later it exceeded $50 million in Arkansas. By 1994, earned premium in Missouri was $165 million and almost $94 million in Arkansas. Accumulated policyholder surplus, too, pushed toward the half-billion dollar milestone at the end of 1994. Twice — in 1985 and 1993 — Shelter Mutual added over $58 million to surplus. Under Gus Lehr's leadership, and with the knowledgeable advice of Don Duello, the investment committee of the board of directors kept a careful watch on invested funds. The payoff was the generous returns of the late 1980s and early 1990s. The company earned a spectacular $86 million on investments in 1994, over $30 million more than it had ever earned in a single year. That increase in returns was greater than the entire investment gain for any single year between 1981 and 1986.

John Lenox, executive vice president, board member since 1989.

Bob Maupin, president and chief operating officer from 1988 to 1993, when he also became chief executive officer. He has been a board member since 1982.

Jim Offutt, executive vice president, board member since 1984.

Gus Lehr, first president under new name, Shelter, serving from 1981 to 1984, when he became chairman of the board; a board member since 1982.

In 1981, President Lehr pointed out to directors and officers that the Shelter companies had over one-half billion dollars in assets. "We are a very large company," he reflected, "and have great responsibilities as such." By 1987, the assets of Shelter Mutual alone exceeded one-half billion dollars. And in 1990, consolidated assets (all companies) stood at $1.12 billion.

The data in Table 9.1, as well as consolidated statements which provide the long view, show problems as well as strength. The 40-year combined results of the two property and casualty companies, for example, showed a $130 million underwriting loss. And that dilemma — how to make money on the writing of insurance, as opposed to other sources of income — plagued top company leaders Lehr, Jack Pettit, and Bob Maupin just as it had Jack Silvey and A. D. Sappington. In 11 of the 14 years under review, Shelter Mutual lost money on its insurance operations. In the worst years, the underwriting losses ran $45 to $50 million. In 1983, 1984, and 1990, surplus declined significantly. Unusual storm losses were the major cause of the early 1980s failure to earn a profit. But management developed an active intervention program to correct aspects of operations which were not "acts of God." "This is a cyclical business," President Lehr recalled in 1984; "1974, '75 and '76 were equally distressing for Shelter."

The record shows overall growth in spite of poor financial results for particular years. The basic soundness of the companies and management's ability to take corrective actions to meet adverse circumstances persuaded the A. M. Best

Company to award the Shelter Insurance Companies either A or A+ Superior ratings during this era. As Shelter Mutual struggled to reverse underwriting losses in 1984 and 1985, Best gave it an A rating. For that company leadership was grateful, given "the significant loss in surplus in 1984." Two years later the mutual company retained its A rating, while both Shelter General and Shelter Life retained the A+ marks that the Best Company assigned them throughout the 1980s. In 1987, Shelter Mutual regained its top rating. As President Bob Maupin told the companies' Annual Meeting in 1990, the A+ truly had meaning: " . . . of 1,800 property and casualty companies and 1,400 life and health companies rated, only 14% are A+ Superior."

Dr. Sid Leeper, vice president, board member since 1986.

Ray Jones, executive vice president, secretary, board member since 1992.

The top three company leaders whose strategies dealt with unsatisfactory financial results, and who basked in the glow of superior industry ratings, were Gustav J. Lehr, Jack L. Pettit, and Robert W. Maupin. While Pettit enjoyed retirement in 1995, the other two-thirds of this management team continued to lead the companies as Shelter Mutual turned 50. They were a team, with Gus Lehr as its captain. Ray Jones has described Pettit and Lehr as "bookends" to A. D. Sappington. During A. D.'s long administration, they were indispensable aides, performing a variety of tasks rather than settling into lengthy tenure in a particular department. Like Sappington, both were lawyers. Maupin, after joining MFA Insurance in 1980, followed in A. D.'s and Lehr's footsteps as chief lobbyist. Lehr promoted Pettit to the president's office when he vacated it in 1984. And he "vigorously" pursued Maupin's talents for the insurance companies when the split with MFA occurred. Good friends and knowledgeable colleagues, the three men have provided Shelter with a remarkable unity and continuity of leadership since 1981.

The most efficient way to summarize their careers since 1981 is in the following chart:

Gustav J. Lehr:
President and CEO, July, 1981 to April, 1984;
Board Chair and CEO, April, 1984 to December 31, 1992 (Howard Lang continued as Chairman of the Board until April, 1984);
Continued as Chairman of the Board of Directors to the present.
Beginning in April, 1984 Lehr, Pettit, and Maupin constituted three-fifths of the Board's key Executive and Compensation Committee.

Jack L. Pettit:
Executive Vice President, succeeding Lehr, July, 1981 to April, 1984;
President and COO, April, 1984 to June, 1987;
President (no longer COO) until September, 1988;
Became a director in December, 1982, chosen Vice Chair of Board, January, 1989, and left Board in September, 1994;
Named President Emeritus, February, 1994.
Pettit was the primary leader of the important Management Advisory Committee beginning in 1983; Lehr especially, and then Maupin, also played key roles in this group's efforts, described below.

Robert W. Maupin:
Executive Vice President, following in the footsteps of Lehr and Pettit, April, 1986 to July, 1987;
President Designate and COO, July, 1987 to October, 1988;
President and COO, October, 1988 to January, 1993;
President and CEO since January 1, 1993.
Became a director in April, 1982.

It is difficult in every case clearly to distinguish what initiatives belong to one member of this team. Gus Lehr's guiding hand has been a continuing presence in the company's development during the entire decade and one-half following 1981. Pettit's active role diminished in that time, and Maupin's increased, as one replaced the other as companies president.

Both J. M. Silvey and A. D. Sappington had to formulate plans of action to counter serious underwriting losses and erosion of policyholder surplus. So, too, did the Lehr team. In all three instances, the responses to financial distress were similar: increase rates within the limits imposed by state regulation and marketplace competition; reduce underwriting expenses, or the costs of doing business; and underwrite the company's business more carefully. The solutions to the crisis in 1983 and 1984 were no mystery. "Mr. Pettit explained that he and Mr. Lehr know how to fix the problem," one set of board minutes recorded. "It is the responsibility of management to see that the proper improvements are made." Agents, as well as management, felt the pressure to improve business. As front-line underwriters and sales personnel, they were partly responsible for accepting only quality business. As he met with agents in 1983 and 1984, Gus Lehr praised their part in Shelter's recovery efforts. "The agents' attitudes remain very good," he reported in October, 1984. "The agents are very supportive of the actions of management."

One source of the poor financial returns in 1982, 1983, and 1984 was extraordinary storm losses. The year 1984 recorded the greatest storm-related losses ever in the property and casualty insurance industry. Shelter Mutual experienced catastrophe claims of $17.4 million in 1982, $12.6 million in 1983, and a colossal $28.7 million in 1984. But when the weather temporarily improved in the first half of 1983 "while underwriting losses continue to be recorded," it was clear that there were other problems. While Lehr initiated steps to counter poor results in 1982, formation of the Management Advisory Committee in 1983 launched the company's major assault on underwriting losses and decline of surplus. Chaired by Executive Vice President Jack Pettit, its members were Don Goodwin, Ray Jones, Charles Dysart, Mark Zimmer, Bob Maupin, John Lenox, and Don Duello. One of the MAC's initial steps was to gather the state sales managers in Columbia and ask them to review their state's operations. Later the committee devised a "business improvement program" unique to each state's situation, while the company sought to increase rates and to reduce expenses. In 1985, for example, the advertising budget was cut by $1 million and travel to industry meetings ceased for the first six months.

But these early steps did not reverse the losses. As Gus Lehr, now board chairman, informed agents in mid-1984: "Financial results for the first six months of this year are terrible." Shelter Mutual's surplus had plunged by $24 million since the year-end 1983 total, and by $58 million in two years. "Management feels that [the] current financial situation has changed from serious to grave," President Pettit told the board. The "serious actions [that] must be taken" included not permitting agents with high loss ratios to write new policies "until they improve the quality of their current book of business." With the MAC's help, the Marketing Department created a specific business improvement plan for each agent, sales district, and state with the largest loss problems. The recovery efforts included cancellation of policies, a freeze on hiring, and the termination of some agents' contracts. In the spring of 1985 the company placed 77 agents on probation, restricting their freedom to write policies. Echoing A. D. Sappington in 1964 and 1965, Jack Pettit asserted late in 1984: " . . . profit is now our number one objective. We have the skill to produce profit." As Table 9.1 reveals, the Management Advisory Committee's business improvement program turned losses into a profit in 1985. The MAC continued to monitor loss problems in particular states into the late 1980s, when Bob Maupin reported on its activities. In 1990, when storm losses and the inability to increase prices again produced problems, the Committee met regularly to review operations state-by-state and impose remedies. When Jack Pettit's retirement approached in 1988, Gus Lehr gave his leadership of the Management Advisory Committee due credit:

Jack Pettit, succeeded Lehr as president, serving from 1984 to 1988, and on the board from 1982 to 1994.

Mr. Lehr stated that Mr. Pettit has been the individual most responsible for the recent turn-around in our companies' financial position. . . . we were indeed fortunate to have had a man of Mr. Pettit's talent, knowledge, and skillful leadership guiding our companies through the turbulent times in recent years.

When introducing Pettit to a crowd, Lehr often called his colleague the best insurance executive in America.

If leadership means responding positively to current circumstances, it also means planning for the future. The Lehr team — Lehr and Bob Maupin in particular — were quite conscious of their responsibility to prepare the Shelter Insurance Companies for the 1990s and the early 21st century. From the start of his term as president and CEO, Lehr brought a previously unknown concern for planning to Shelter. It stressed annual and long-term goals and monitoring progress toward them. In 1985, officers held regular discussions "about the manner [in] which we want to grow in the future." Beginning in 1982, a regular feature of board of directors' meetings were the planning and research board reports of Vince Bartle and Gary Ford.

These reports compared actual company performance to the current year's goals, and spending compared to budgeted expenses. Company goals for 1983 included a 10% growth in written property and casualty premium over 1982, a 15% increase in life insurance premium, and 1425 agents, 300 of them in the salaried agent program.

Both Presidents Silvey and Sappington, in addition to Fred Heinkel, had spoken of sales and other goals. But under Lehr, goal-setting became a process rather than a slogan. Naturally the company fell short of goals some years and exceeded them in others. If planning worked, it was not batting averages for prediction that counted. The point was to gain a better control of the companies' future in order to avoid the need to grapple with crises of profit and loss. As part of the corporate planning process, Shelter produced a statement of "Continuing Corporate Values." This companies' mission statement listed these important long-range commitments:

1. "Make 'personal service' and personal pride a reality at Shelter Insurance."

2. "Continue to provide excellent service and protection to our growing number of customers."

3. "Help each agent to improve his/her economic position through commissions earned on increased sales and bonus earned on a profitable agency."

4. "Afford greater opportunities to employees for the good jobs that come with profitable growth and pay fair wages and salaries."

5. "Exercise responsible care and control over expenses so as to be a cost effective provider of insurance service and protection."

President Bob Maupin has continued the practice of annual financial goal-setting and of maintaining the prominence of corporate values like those stated above.

With all the Shelter companies in splendid financial condition, Bob Maupin's job required less attention to current operations, allowing him greater freedom to plan for the company's long-range future. Two matters will serve as examples. Through its own Shelter Reinsurance Company, participation in reinsurance pools has made Shelter Mutual a company with global interests that extend far beyond the 13-state operating region. Hurricane Andrew, both when it hit south Florida and when it devastated Louisiana in 1993, caused the largest single loss in Shelter's history. Exposed to the storm's wrath through its own policyholder losses in Louisiana, Shelter faced losses in Florida through reinsurance agreements. Disasters in Europe and Asia can affect the company's financial condition. But where there is risk, so is there opportunity for profit and growth, and in recent years the Shelter companies have realized those benefits. Though he resides in mid-Missouri and deals with agents, employees, and policyholders in the mid-continental United

States, Maupin's vision of leadership must be worldwide.

He also must seek the most efficient and effective ways to handle the many transactions — new policy applications, premium payments, claims, and so on — that fill each business day and involve thousands of field representatives, Home Office personnel, and customers. In 1995, Shelter began the change to two new data processing systems that will improve the ways employees and agents work. President Maupin, his officers, and the board of directors know that the long-term cost efficiencies achieved by these systems will make for a stronger company, better able to compete in the next century. As the company's first half-century ended, Bob Maupin defined his job as positioning Shelter for continued success in the 21st century.

A third example of leadership exercised since 1981 — in this case some new directions set by Gus Lehr — involved changes in the board of directors and the

Board member Ken Mihill, Chesterfield, 1984 to the present.

Roscoe Creed, Advertising, left, and Warren Conner, Training, work with Shirley Ruppel and an unidentified staff member on a slide show to be used to train agents in the early 1960s.

assignments and compensation of company officers. First, this account must identify board members from 1981-1995.

Deaths, retirements, and replacements transformed the boards of directors of Shelter Mutual and its affiliated companies between March, 1982 and July, 1984. What had been a farmer-MFA member board became one of college-trained businessmen, including selected company officers who now performed double duty

Board member Marshall Chatfield, Kansas City, 1994 to the present.

Bill Bates, Columbia, board member from 1985 to 1992.

B. M. Seamon, LaPlata, board member from 1947 to 1989, at which time he became an advisory director.

Board member Art Oliver, Columbia, 1987 to the present.

Table 9.2 Shelter Mutual's Board of Directors, July, 1981-1995

Member	Residence	Years of Service
Howard B. Lang, Jr. Chairman	Columbia	1981-April 4, 1984
Gustav J. Lehr Chair April 4, 1984--1995	Columbia	Member March 22, 1982-1995 (succeeded Brehe)
Fred Brehe	Marthasville	1981-March 22, 1982
James A. Offutt	Columbia	April 4, 1984-1995 (succeeded Lang)
Edwin F. Sachs	Rolla	1981-April 2, 1986
Sidlee W. Leeper	Columbia	April 2, 1986-1995 (succeeded Sachs)
Bernice M. Seaman	LaPlata	1981-April 5, 1989, at which time he became Vice Chair Emeritus and Advisory Director
John W. Lenox	Columbia	April 5, 1989-1995 (succeeded Seaman)
Lawrence Kullmann	Warrensburg	1981-July 1, 1984
Kenneth W. Mihill	Chesterfield	August 9, 1984-1995 (succeeded Kullmann)
Miller Hern	Rocheport	1981-April 7, 1982
James L. McTurnan	Columbia	April 7, 1982-April 3, 1985 (succeeded Hern)
William H. Bates	Columbia	April 3, 1985-April 27, 1992 (succeeded McTurnan)
Raymond E. Jones	Columbia Member	April 27, 1992-1995 (succeeded Bates) Secretary 1986-1995 (succeeded Duello)
R. J. Rosier	Columbia	1981-December 22, 1982
Jack L. Pettit	Columbia	December 22, 1982-February 7, 1994 (succeeded Rosier)
H. Marshall Chatfield	Kansas City	February 7, 1994-1995 (succeeded Pettit)
Sam Murrell	Lancaster	1981-April 7, 1982
Robert W. Maupin	Columbia	April 7, 1982-1995 (succeeded Murrell)
Fred V. Heinkel	Columbia	1981-April 6, 1983
James E. Godfrey	St. Louis	April 6, 1983-November 15, 1986 (succeeded Heinkel)
David A. Oliver	Columbia	March 2, 1987-1995 (succeeded Godfrey)
J. Donald Duello		Secretary of Board, 1978-1986

as directors. The board which celebrated the rebirth of Shelter Insurance on July 1, 1981 consisted of Chairman Howard Lang; Fred V. Heinkel and R. J. Rosier, MFA executives and founders of MFA Mutual; and six farmers or retired farmers who had long relationships with the Missouri Farmers Association. All had given lengthy and dedicated service to the insurance company. In February, 1982, Fred Brehe died, and in April Miller Hern and Sam Murrell retired from the board. R. J, Rosier left the board in December, 1982 and died in early 1983. In April, 1983, Fred Heinkel left the board which he had chaired for 35 years. And in July, 1984, Lawrence Kullmann retired. In 28 months these six vacated the nine-man board, and Howard Lang joined them in April, 1984. In 1986, Edwin Sachs died, and in April, 1989 Bernice Seaman, a director since 1947, gave up his active role for honorary ones, which he still held to this writing. Thus, within eight years of Gus Lehr's assumption of company leadership, there was a complete turnover of board membership.

Ed Sachs, Rolla, served on the board from 1971 to 1986.

James E. Godfrey, St. Louis, board member from 1983 to 1986.

Charter Agent Otto Young poses proudly with his agency sign in Union, Missouri. The Young agency continues today under Otto's nephew, Harlan Young.

Lehr found new directors in the post-MFA era among those already a part of Shelter Insurance, primarily officers, and men outside the company who had ties to and knowledge of it. The outside board members included James E. Godfrey, a St. Louis attorney who served for three and one-half years before his death in an automobile accident in 1986. A member of the Missouri House of Representatives from 1960 to 1972 and speaker of the House starting in 1966, Godfrey went to Jefferson City about the time that Gus Lehr did, and the two became friends in the capitol's political setting. Godfrey's seat was filled by David A. Oliver, a Columbia attorney whose firm had done work for Shelter. William H. Bates, also from Columbia, was president of Boone County National Bank from 1976 to 1984, and then its board chairman. Kenneth W. Mihill was an executive with Shelter's advertising agency, D'Arcy MacManus, Inc., in St. Louis. Marshall Chatfield was

Ten years before his retirement, while Underwriting vice president, Jim McTurnan and his wife, Helen, presented the companies with this grandfather clock for Christmas 1972, in appreciation for 20 years McTurnan had served the companies at that time.

MFA President Eric Thompson had pledged that the farm co-op would not engage in the business of insurance; would not, that is, compete with Shelter for five years. In mid-May, 1982, Howard Lang reported "receiving some indications" that MFA "was giving serious consideration to the formation of an insurance company." By fall, MFA had filed papers with the Missouri secretary of state to form MFA Financial Services, a corporation "to engage in the business of a general insurance agency and insurance brokerage business." In addition to forming this agency, by the summer of 1983 MFA had endorsed the American Hardware Mutual Insurance Company to its members. In an advertisement directed at "MFA Customers," Thompson wrote: "You owe it to yourself to give American Hardware Mutual the opportunity to cut your auto insurance rates." Many MFA members, of course, retained Shelter as their automobile insurer.

Having "lost" what MFA had never owned in the 1980 agreement of separation — MFA/Shelter Insurance — Thompson looked for ways to regain property and casualty insurance business for his organization. It was probably early in 1981 that he asked J. M. and Jim Silvey, owners of a successful insurance company headquartered in Columbia, to help him organize a firm to compete with Shelter. The Silveys refused. Bill Conboy reported second-hand information indicating that, in 1983, Thompson had again approached the Silvey Company, and also Nationwide Insurance of Columbus, Ohio, about an agreement to market insurance. In the summer of 1983, Shelter's lawyers sought an injunction against Thompson and MFA, a court order which would force them to live up to their legal commitment "to refrain from carrying on, engaging in or being connected with any insurance business directly or indirectly for a period of five years" in states where Shelter did business. On March 27, 1984 the Circuit Court in Boone County, Missouri issued the injunction, and the incident was closed.

Lawrence Kullmann, Warrensburg, board member from 1964 to 1984.

For Shelter Day III, flagpoles carrying the flags of Shelter's operating states were dedicated.

chapter 10

Our Progress 1981-1995

As in past eras, those who wish to chart Shelter's growth from 1981 to 1995 must look at more than the mutual company's year-end financial data. Several measurements reflect expansion, including the development of key subsidiary companies and the marketing of new coverages. Developments in several Home Office departments also help trace the evolution of an increasingly complex and technologically sophisticated company.

With the exception of Shelter Reinsurance Company, the Shelter group did not push into new geographical areas after 1981. Nor did the number of Shelter agents increase markedly. (See chapter 11) Instead, the growth of sales indicated in Tables 9.1 and 10.1 resulted from a more intensive cultivation of a sales territory that had been stable since 1975. A greater variety of attractive coverages marketed by an increasingly professional agency force, backed by effective company training, advertising, and other support, explain the growth of sales within a fixed geographical area.

Table 10.1 Earned Premium by States, Shelter Mutual (in thousands of dollars)

(states in order of date of admission)	1982	1986	1990	1994
Missouri (1946)	92,972	113,048	130,700	165,421
Arkansas (1950)	38,779	50,225	72,707	93,945
Kansas (1950)	13,857	18,108	17,843	24,898
Nebraska (1954)	5,279	7,117	9,180	13,168
Illinois (1956)	7,149	8,047	10,641	14,380
Iowa (1960)	2,885	2,709	3,476	6,150
Kentucky (1960)	11,833	15,396	21,517	27,266
Tennessee (1960)	11,364	16,132	22,743	27,310
Oklahoma (1961)	18,826	23,307	23,918	38,260
Indiana (1961)	4,315	5,981	9,475	14,149
Mississippi (1970)	3,816	4,814	7,554	13,204
Colorado (1970)	4,759	7,003	9,848	19,474
Louisiana (1971)	10,077	9,422	15,368	27,602

Source : Year end financial statements

Missouri and Arkansas, Shelter Mutual's first two states, continued to pull in over half of all earned premium after 1981. But as was true earlier, their combined proportion continued to decline. In 1982, those two states accounted for 58% of Shelter Mutual's earned premium, but in 1994 only 53%. The mutual company's most rapid growth came in southern states, with Kentucky, Tennessee, Oklahoma, and Louisiana showing particular strength. Theories about why sales and the size of

A Marketing Concepts Committee was developed to bring agents, sales management, and marketing staff together to discuss matters directed at improving the marketing of Shelter's multiple lines of products.

their agency force lagged in Iowa and Indiana, while both indicators surged in Oklahoma and Louisiana, vary among past or present company officials being interviewed. The explanations include competition from well-established casualty and property companies headquartered in Des Moines, and a particular way of doing business in small southern communities that Shelter's MFA background prepared it to understand. Whatever the reasons, Shelter's states did not grow in relation to the company's length of service in them.

Shelter's overall growth also resulted from the maturing of some older subsidiaries and the establishment of new ones. Table 10.2 names the companies in the Shelter family early in the period under consideration, and near its end.

Table 10.2 The Shelter Companies

1983	1993
The insurance companies:	**The insurance companies:**
Shelter Mutual	Shelter Mutual
Shelter General	Shelter General
Shelter Life	Shelter Life
	Shelter Reinsurance Company
The support companies:	**The support companies:**
Shelter Financial Services	Shelter Financial Services
Shelter Service Company	Daniel Boone Underwriters
KMMO, Inc.	Daniel Boone Agency, Inc.
Daniel Boone Underwriters Inc.	DBU, Inc.
Daniel Boone Agency, Inc.	May Fair Advertising, Inc.
DBU Inc.	Shelter Enterprises, Inc.
Mid-America Auto Parts	
May Fair Advertising Inc.	

The lists reveal several additions and deletions during the decade. Shelter Service Company (originally MFA Service Company), an automobile loan company operating in Nebraska, was liquidated in October, 1984. Unique state laws caused the proliferation of insurance brokerages named Daniel Boone. Daniel Boone Underwriters, chartered in Missouri, did business there and in ten other states. Shelter chartered Daniel Boone Agency, Inc. in Illinois, and DBU, Inc. in Mississippi. The board of directors sold radio station KMMO in Marshall on

November 30, 1984. The companies gradually phased out the auto parts facility located in Columbia during 1985 and 1986, officially closing Mid-America Auto Parts on December 31, 1986.

The Shelter group gained two new companies after 1981. The smaller of the two was Shelter Enterprises, Inc., formed in 1989 to manage assets formerly owned by Shelter Financial Services and to make new investments in such assets. Real estate owned in Columbia and the companies' airplanes are examples.

More important was the creation in 1986 of a property and casualty reinsurance company, Shelter Reinsurance. At its meeting of June 2, the board authorized creation of this company as a wholly-owned subsidiary of Shelter Mutual. Vice President for Finance Don Duello made clear the advantages of such a company. They included the promise of favorable returns on investment of the mutual company's funds in reinsurance contracts — a means of sharing the risk of the original insurer for a fee. In fact, the companies were already "assuming more reinsurance business," and Shelter Reinsurance was a way to specialize in it. By November, 1986 the new company was operating.

The increased exposure created by Shelter Reinsurance led to losses incurred far from home. In 1989, Hurricane Hugo caused a $7.3 million loss, and severe European storms in early 1990 also produced poor operating results. But from 1987 through 1994, the new company's assets grew from $42 million to over $100 million. In the latter year Shelter Reinsurance's earned premium was $39.7 million, and its Retained Earnings Balance (surplus) exceeded $8.6 million. The assets that Shelter Reinsurance had invested provided a good return for the companies.

The two most important subsidiaries were Shelter General and Shelter Life, which did what Shelter Mutual did: insure policyholders directly. While both companies grew impressively in size, they did not grow in relative terms. Shelter Mutual's share of the combined earned premium of all three insurers increased from 72.5% in 1982 to 79% in 1994. When applied to Shelter General and Shelter Life, the term "subsidiary" is misleading, for it denotes a subordinate role. In truth, each company could stand alone as a good-sized and financially-sound firm. Shelter General's assets grew by $50 million between year-end 1981 and 1994, more than doubling in that time and approaching $100 million in 1994. Its surplus was $81 million in 1993.

1982 Heinkel Award winners Sheila Holzworth and Dr. Horace Thomas visit with Scottie Garrett, the "father of the Shelter Gardens." In the dark dress is Ginger Downing, coach for Miss Holzworth, a blind athlete who, among other achievements, climbed Mt. Rainier, and raced on foot, bicycle, and skis. She was named Most Courageous Athlete in 1979. Dr. Thomas is a Columbia surgeon.

Without question, Shelter Life Insurance Company by itself would be an important regional company among life insurers. In 1994, its assets were well in excess of one-third billion dollars; its net premium income was almost $90 million; its benefits paid to policyholders nearly $79 million; and its total surplus over $60 million. Perhaps the best indicator of growth is life insurance in force, reported in Table 10.3.

Table 10.3 Shelter Life Insurance Company, Dollar Value of Life Insurance in Force, Selected Years (year-end figures; in thousands of dollars)

Year	Value	Year	Value
1983	$2,636	1991	4,933
1985	2,856	1993	5,813
1987	3,385	1994	6,308
1989	4,062		

Source: Various reports of the Marketing Department to the board of directors.

Toward the end of his term, President George Bush visited the Shelter Gardens for a face-to-face visit with families to discuss their needs.

Shelter officials carefully watched these mounting figures wishing, among other things, to identify the newly-insured whose policy pushed Shelter Life past another milestone. To celebrate $3 billion of insurance in force, officers of the company journeyed to Mountain Home, Arkansas on January 13, 1987 to recognize the policy sold to the Michael Shero family by agent Tim Martin.

Although the Life Company contributes greatly to the Shelter companies' financial profile today, its growth to importance was slow. One reason is that life insurance is a "harder sell" than property and casualty policies. State drivers' laws and mortgage-holder requirements require the latter, while no one insists that heads of families or other wage earners plan for their heirs' welfare. The life sales approach is different than that for casualty, but company training courses and life marketing incentives have helped bring Shelter Life Insurance to the prominence it has enjoyed in the 1980s and 1990s.

The insurance industry reflects a changing society. During the 1980s, Shelter offered, through the Life Company, a very good comprehensive health policy. But the company could not charge policyholders enough to make the

Chairman Lehr welcomes President Bush to the Gardens.

coverage profitable, given "the continuing and unrelenting increase in health-care costs," in Gus Lehr's words. So in 1991 Shelter stopped sales of its comprehensive health policy. Although an insurance company's data collection and analysis make most aspects of its world predictable, this is not always true. Through 1990, "Shelter had paid out a total of nearly $2 million . . . on AIDS-related claims" — for a disease unknown a decade earlier, still spreading, and still incurable. The changing American family posed perhaps the greatest challenge to insurers' ability to adapt. The aging of the huge baby-boom generation, the increasing importance of women in the workplace, the emergence of single-person and single-parent households in very large numbers, and the growing volume of retirees with generous disposable incomes — such demographic trends hold implications for Shelter that MFA Mutual's founders could not have imagined in 1946.

Arkansas Agent Pete DeWoody at the plaque dedicating a desert garden in Shelter Gardens to agents and employees who were called to active duty during the Desert Storm action in 1991. DeWoody was one of six who served.

Those who designed Shelter's coverages were demographic experts, and the statisticians' analyses revealed important facts. For example, the "loss behavior" of insureds age 48 and older differed from that of those below that age. As drivers of automobiles and owners of homes, older insureds simply had fewer claims. Therefore, Shelter Mutual offered them reduced rates at age 48 rather than 55, as most other companies did. An industry innovation in the late 1970s, universal life insurance policies became a mainstay of Shelter Life's sales by the mid-1980s. Compared to traditional life policies, universal life's levels of protection and premium payments are exceptionally flexible, and thus adaptable to the financial circumstances of many policyholders.

By the 1990s the series of concerts in the gardens drew crowds numbering in the thousands each Sunday in June and July.

From 1988-1990, the Home Office building underwent significant renovation. Projects included removal of asbestos and installation of several new systems: heating and air conditioning, lighting, and telephone. In 1990, Shelter added an Energy Center to the northwest corner of the building to hold the heating and cooling equipment.

Other construction projects continued in Columbia and across the operating territory. Shelter put millions of dollars into larger, more conveniently-located, and more efficient state office buildings and branch offices. Two of the new state office buildings were those in Colorado and Indiana. The erection of a new claims office in Columbia and the transformation of the Annex Building into a training facility was another project. The Training Center, completed in the summer of 1988, housed the Audio Visual Department, a training library, classrooms and offices. It is an educational facility which few companies of comparable size could match. In front of the Home Office there was another addition in 1983: flagpoles to hold the flags of each state where Shelter did business.

Shelter Insurance's part in a global economy in the late 20th century is evident in more than its reinsurance business. On May 19, 1995 the company signed a contract with IBM-HUON Solutions to replace its current information systems with new ones, "customized to fulfill our needs well into the next century," in the words of Ray Jones, executive vice president. During the 1980s and into the 1990s, Shelter regularly enhanced the capacity of its mainframe computer. During the 1980s also the companies began an important innovation which the commitments made in 1995 will complete: bringing its agents on-line, linking them electronically

The original building on the Home Office grounds, the Annex, is hidden beneath this modern training center, dedicated in 1988. The structural walls were used to anchor this new building. At the dedication open house, tours revealed to employees and the business community a state-of-the-art facility, from auto repair shops to a television studio, being explained by Media Services Manager Tom Apple to tour guide Mary Lou Mills and Columbia Chamber of Commerce members George and Nadine Trial and Shelter retiree Bill Conboy.

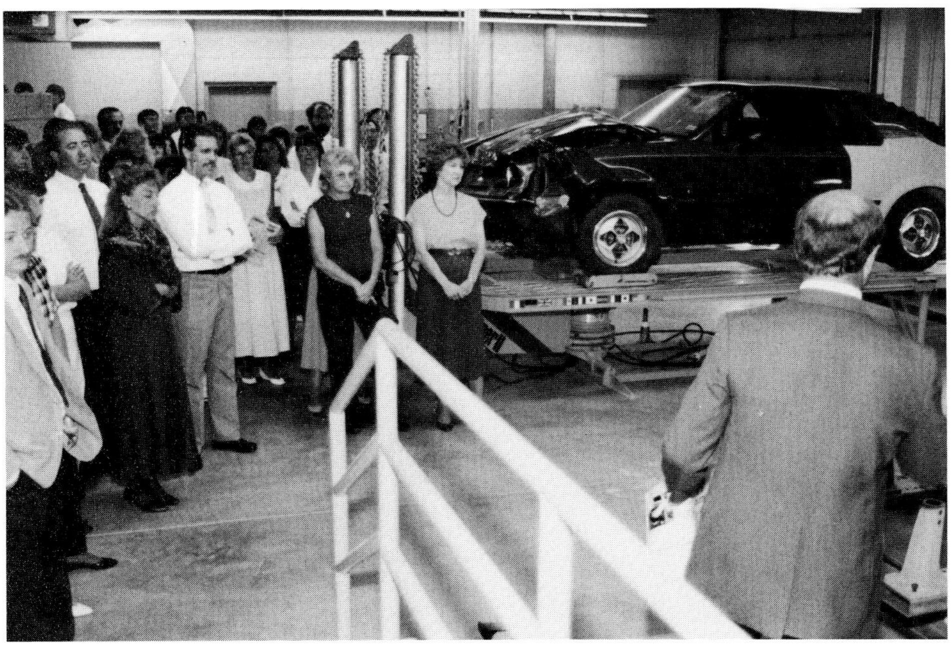

This group of information service employees joined with representatives of user departments to determine the needs of data processing and how a new system, from Australia's Huon Corporation, could meet those needs into the 21st century. Throughout 1995 this team worked toward implementation of a new client-based system of policyholder information.

to the Home Office data base. Projects begun in 1983, in fact, put all field claims offices and some agencies on-line. In February of that year the first branch claims office was connected to the Home Office, and in 1985 all claims offices were so linked. By 1988, claims representatives in the field could process claims in other lines as well as auto. Beginning in 1983, also, the company began installing computer terminals in selected agents' offices on a voluntary basis. Besides providing electronic mail, the system allowed agents to access policy files, obtain rate quotes, and enter policy changes and new business. Agents agreeing to test this project included Bill Bell, Dave Jeffs, Tommy Hight, and Gerald Brandorf. As of December, 1984, 19 agents were on-line.

But even with these and other improvements, the company's information systems left much outside the system. To gain the cost efficiencies necessary to compete in the next several decades, Shelter began two large and significant projects in 1995 with the signing of the HUON contract. In a presentation made at the fall, 1994 agent meetings, Ray Jones has described the new systems, which will become fully operational in 1997. One, the client-based Policy Administration System, will organize data in a different, more effective way than at present. Instead of arranging information by product line (auto and homeowners, for example), the system will file all data on a policyholder under that person's name, as well as information on other "clients" under their names — lawyers, body shops, and so on. The second system does what its title announces: The Agency Automation System. The company will provide the hardware and Shelter-specific software to all agents, linking them to the Home Office in what will truly be an interactive computer network connecting many points in 13 states.

In mid-1995, work on both systems went forward, with the placement of equipment and the training of agents in Tennessee being the first step in implementing the Agency Automation System. Two comments convey the great importance that Shelter's leadership placed on these changes. Ray Jones told agents in 1994:

. . . as we move from a paper environment to an electronic environment, we all must be willing to change the way we perform our day-to-day tasks. Our investment will pay huge dividends down the road, but only with the full participation and cooperation of all agents and employees.

And as President Bob Maupin addressed the Conference of Champions in Geneva in June, 1995:

We are putting all available resources into these two programs and they will remain the central focus of our activities for the next 18 months. . . . We are putting this company in a position to be able to compete in the industry for the long term.

Shelter, as Don Goodwin once affirmed, has "always . . . been in the forefront

For Shelter Day III, flagpoles carrying the flags of Shelter's operating states were dedicated. Members of the PACC raised the flag from their respective states; Dickie Cooper is shown ready to fly the Commonwealth of Kentucky flag.

Before color television, MFA Mutual commercials appeared in the form of still slides, then animation from the art table of Bill Hume.

. . . in using the computer." Shelter is the first U.S. insurance company to adopt the Australian-developed, European-applied HUON system.

"Technology," of course, means more than computers. In the 1980s, Shelter's Audio Visual Department gave valuable support to other departments, including Training. Tom Apple joined the companies in 1982 as AV's only staff person, and he moved his equipment from the lower level of the Home Office building to the refurbished Training Center in 1988. Apple and his staff have recorded training and marketing presentations, public service safety messages for use on television stations, and interviews with retired company officers and veteran agents, among many other applications. Early videos included these titles: "Employee Orientation," "New Homeowners Policy," and "Munich — Conference of Champions."

One of the changes initiated by President Lehr in 1981 was the consolidation of all Shelter's training programs in a new Corporate Training Department headed by Bob Decker. Offering industry courses such as those sponsored by the Life Underwriter Training Council, the training staff also offered company training in sales, claims, physical damage, and the human resources area — secretarial training and performance appraisal being examples of the latter. Sure signs of Shelter's commitment to training is the money spent on it and the numbers trained. In the years 1982 to 1988, the company averaged $1.28 million a year in support of employee and agent training. In 1988, a total of 1,726 people were trained, including 638 in agents' courses, 485 in claims courses, and 603 in other employee courses. In addition, 400 persons took industry courses through the Training Department in 1988. Shelter's training program was part of a vast educational enterprise, as American business annually spent close to $100 billion in employer-sponsored educational activities in the early 1990s.

Shelter's Communications Department, led by Vice President Jean Madden until February, 1992 and by Vice President Lanny Barton since then, continued to support the companies' insurance operations in numerous ways. Among them, advertising was the best known and most easily-identified by the public, and it did much to tie agents to the companies in a common effort. The central message of Shelter's advertising was "personal service" offered by agents, by claims representatives, by all personnel with whom policyholders came into contact. Proud

Actor Wally Dalton portrayed Shelter agent Joe Donovan through most of the 1970s.

Director Don Keeslar explains a shot during the filming of TV commercials in 1992. In the center is Bill Tyler, producer of the commercials, and at right is Communications Vice President Lanny Barton.

An affiliation with the National Association of Intercollegiate Athletics proved popular for agents who made local presentations of funds for student athlete travel to championship tournaments. Lanny Barton, left, and Bob Maupin were on hand for the national women's softball tourney, where Maupin threw out the first pitch. Among the participants at the Tennessee presentation were Julie Adkins, Toby Sircy, Vonnie Hall, Steve Hall, Mike Pate, Phil Sartin, Steve Saunders, Ginger Grona, Jack Grona, and Randy Swayze.

of his firm's commercials and advertising philosophy, Gus Lehr urged agents to increase their participation in the cooperative advertising program, in which they and the company shared costs.

Referring to the figures for 1986, Lehr noted that "Shelter's spending of 1.38 percent of earned premium on advertising ranks among the industry's highest." Madden's reports to the board detailed the advertising dollar expenditures, with special emphasis on co-op advertising, "where we spend 50-cent dollars." To take 1985 as an example, when the company spent $2.9 million on all advertising, or 1.08 percent of earned premium, the figures for the most important categories of cooperative advertising were these:

Television: 567 agents spent $511,000 on 101 stations; Radio: 559 agents spent $487,000 on 271 stations; Newspapers: 695 agents spent $809,000 on 572 papers;Billboards: 209 agents spent $234,000 for 193 billboards.

Shelter matched agents' spending in each medium. The company also carried on a separate corporate advertising campaign, and it underwrote the production of commercials.

The great number of departments which make up the Home Office prevent a discussion of more than a few. Chapter 11 will continue consideration of Shelter's people: employees, agents, and officers. The progress that the present chapter has addressed was borne upon their effort and intelligence.

Claims employee Molly LaBarge shows the 1980 Almanac on which she graces the cover. A tested advertising tool for more than 40 years, the Almanac continues to be a popular giveaway for agents.

Longtime sponsorship of the Missouri Show Me State Games has given the company exposure throughout the state. Agent offices are used to distribute entry forms for the games. Games director Gary Filbert addresses a rally at the Home Office for the final leg of the 1991 torch run.

As State Senator Roger Wilson listens behind him, Joe Duncan waves a Games program to the crowd as he prepares to send Paul LaRose toward the arena in the final leg of the torch run.

Missouri Governor John Ashcroft visits reporters at a late 1980s kickoff in Shelter Gardens, as Games mascot, Sport, arrives in background.

President Bob Maupin welcomes Missouri Governor Mel Carnahan to the Games kickoff in the Gardens in 1993.

Longtime voice of the Home Office, Bridget Sebastian operated the switchboard before her retirement, and was known for her recognition of callers by their voice.

chapter 11

Our People 1981-1995

Two features distinguish this chapter from earlier accounts of Shelter's people. It singles out some of the top agents who have led the company's sales efforts over the years. These few will represent the many more men and women who have reached a high level of achievement in the most challenging job associated with the Shelter Insurance Companies' operations: that of agent. The second feature is an attempt to profile the officers who constitute the third generation of Shelter leadership. Along with statistics, then, this discussion uses biography as a way to understand the companies' people during the last 15 years of Shelter's first half-century.

Table 11.1 Employee Numbers, Selected Years

	Total	Home Office	Outstate Missouri	Outside Missouri	Total Field
12-31-'82	1,689	940 (56%)	293 (17%)	456 (27%)	749 (44%)
12-31-'85	1,694	952 (56%)	271 (16%)	471 (28%)	742 (44%)
12-31-'88	1,636	950 (58%)	231 (14%)	455 (28%)	686 (42%)
1-29-'92	1,649	931 (56%)			696 (42%)
1-31-'94	1,609	916 (57%)			679 (42%)

Beginning in 1989 data no longer separated into outstate and outside of Missouri.

Total includes some temporary agency secretaries.

Source: Personnel Department/Human Resources Department Reports.

Table 11.1 conveys information about employee numbers. What is notable here and in the agency force statistics in Tables 11.3 and 11.4 is the stability which the company experienced in this era. In contrast to earlier periods of sharp growth and decline, Shelter's employees numbered 1,689 in December, 1982 compared with 1,595 in November, 1994. Its agency force stood at 1,228 in December, 1981 and 1,252 in late 1994. The overwhelming majority of employees were full-time workers who participated fully in the company's benefits package: 1,581 full-time to 108 part-time in December, 1982, for example, and 1,577 to 54 in December, 1990. And, as before, most employees worked for the two casualty companies: 1,522 of 1,785 at the end of 1983; 1,469 of 1,631 in 1990.

Under Ray Jones's leadership, in 1981 Shelter began a laborious process which involved employees from beginning to end: writing job descriptions of approximately 150 jobs performed within the companies and establishing procedures for evaluating employees' performance in those positions. A healthy, growing firm provides opportunities for reward and promotion, and Shelter's leadership wanted employee recognition to be as objective and merit-based as possible.

Some organizations see nepotism as an obstacle to objective performance appraisal. It has not been a problem at Shelter, in part because, as a mutual company, top personnel do not own the company. Shelter's 1995 employee roster reveals that the children and other relatives of company veterans have invested their careers in this insurance firm. Names like Kiethley, Lang, Lehr, Sappington, Aufranc, Offutt, Dysart, and Maupin are present at Shelter into the second generation.

Employee turnover rates are important to any company, and in 1992 Bob Reid of the Human Resources Department presented a revealing study to the board. Using data that reached back to 1965, Reid noted that the company experienced annual turnover rates of 20% to 30% in the 1960s and 1970s. In 1969, the worst year, 370 employees, or 31.8%, left their jobs. In 1982, Shelter experienced a less than double-digit turnover rate for the first time: 8.9%. Ten years later, to cap an amazing reversal, the rate was 5.2% Shelter's salary and benefits package was one explanation.

Another was the job-posting program. Personnel Director Vic Ohman, reporting on the first quarter, 1983, noted that of 33 job openings, 22, or 67%, "were filled by internal promotions." Job posting "continues to provide opportunities for employees who prepare for and seek promotions." Begun on a small scale in 1977, and expanded to include higher job grades in 1979 and 1981, the program eventually encompassed field as well as Home Office positions ranging from clerical to managerial. One reading of job-posting's results showed that for job grades four through six, from January 1, 1979 to January 31, 1985, the company filled 168 of 202 job openings through promotions. In 1982, Ohman evaluated the program in a non-quantitative way. It had achieved its goal: to increase opportunities available to employees. Job posting "has increased the morale and motivation of many employees. . . . It certainly has made promotions from within visible."

When applied to particular employee groups, job posting and hiring outcomes showed mixed results. In an age when women and minorities entered the mainstream labor force in unprecedented numbers and levels of job skill, what was Shelter's experience? Vic Ohman gave a partial answer in 1981. The job posting program "has been a very positive factor in providing upward mobility for women." But for two reasons it had less impact on expanding opportunities for minority persons, especially African-Americans. Job posting favored present employees over outside applicants, but Shelter lacked "a sufficient source of black employees in the lower [job] grades from which to draw." In addition, low employee turnover "limits our need to recruit new employees." Beginning in the 1970s, the personnel department had monitored minority hiring, and learned that during the 1980s between 3-4% of company employee were minorities, and less than 3% black. Home Office percentages were higher than those in the field. In the 1990s, the figures rose. A Minority Report dated September, 1991, revealed 71 minority persons working for Shelter, 51 in the Home Office and 20 in the field. The proportions were 4.29% of all employees, 5.43% in the Home Office, and 2.79% of the field staff. Shelter Insurance made active efforts to recruit minority employees, among them the summer intern program. In 1994, for example, seven minority students, five at the Home Office and two in St. Louis, learned about insurance and the companies' operations. Begun in 1988, the internship program had produced six full-time employees by 1993.

Board Chairman and CEO Gus Lehr made this evaluation of employee compensation in 1985:

It is my opinion that for most employees we do an excellent job. Until employees' earnings equal $45,000 per year, they are protected from inflation by our COLA program. In addition, we have a salary range for each position and specified time periods for salary review. . . . salary adjustments for most employees are regularly made.

Table 11.2 Employee Salaries and Benefits Paid by Shelter Mutual, Selected Years

	Salary Expense	Retirement Fund	Other Benefits	Profit Sharing
1981	$27,222,699	$2,701,132	$1,294,215	$ 499,817
1985	33,913,301	4,219,358	2,377,689	1,650,524
1989	40,384,844	232,208	3,303,283	2,735,850
1993	51,757,467	5,619,538	4,695,976	4,449,236
1994	53,792,872	17,577,953	4,594,230	3,816,587

Source: Year-end Financial Statements, Underwriting Expenses, Shelter Mutual

The information in Table 11.2 elaborates on Lehr's judgment. Readers of that chart should realize that to Shelter Mutual's contributions in the profit-sharing column were added monies from other Shelter companies in profitable years. More

Long careers run throughout the companies. Carl Kenney, who supervises night maintenance, raised and lowered the flag each day for many years. Carl and E. W. Buckner carried a large share of the responsibility for the clean, comfortable work areas of the office.

meaningful, perhaps, than gross company spending on salaries and benefits are the amounts spent by Shelter per employee. As of January 31, 1994, for 728 hourly employees, the average hourly rate of pay was $10.16; and the average annual cost to the companies of an hourly employee was $28,529. Both figures included COLA, while the annual total included a 35% benefit factor. For 881 salaried employees, the average monthly salary was $3,808, and the average annual cost to the company $61,690 (both figures included COLA; the annual amount included a benefit factor of 35%). Good jobs at good pay: they are concentrated in Columbia, of course, but also spread across 13 states for 1,600 workers in 1994.

The companies' benefits package included the following plans in December, 1992: retirement; savings and profit sharing; group accidental death and dismemberment insurance; group travel-accident insurance; group long-term disability insurance; group health and dental insurance; and group life insurance. Employees were able to fund their contributions to these plans on a pretax basis.

Other employee benefits included a tuition-reimbursement program; paid vacations and holidays; sick leave; maternity disability; paid time-off for jury duty; personal days; and the services of the Shelter Credit Union. An array of other programs served employees. In May, 1994 the company cafeteria added breakfast to its schedule, for example. Pam Bruenjes, R.N., of Health Services offered cholesterol and prostate screenings in the Home Office in April of that year. Indeed, wellness became a byword at Shelter during the 1980s and 1990s. Noontime seminars on preventive medicine; CPR classes; professionally-conducted stop-smoking programs financed by the company for field and Home Office employees; blood-sugar screenings and blood pressure checks; and free flu shots were among the health-related benefits available to personnel. Some employers still give turkeys to workers during the year-end holiday season; Shelter made available items in a gift catalog at company expense.

Since 1981, Shelter has paid greater attention to employee recognition. In 1982, a service award program began with a luncheon at the Home Office to honor those who achieved five-year milestones of full-time service with the company. A dinner in Columbia recognized field employees and agents with 20 or more years of service, in five-year increments. Special awards recognized unique achievement, such as the James L. McTurnan Award, first given in 1983 to the underwriter of the year, Jerry Livingston. Other departments, too, added recognition awards during the

Douglas "Scottie" Garrett, longtime manager of buildings, grounds, and food service, was the first winner of the Gustav J. Lehr Award. He received the award from President Jack Pettit, left, and Chairman Lehr, right.

President Sappington meets with agents in the spring of 1974.

1980s. Claims gave the Lang Award for Excellence in Claims, for example, to senior adjuster Virgil Karstens of Lincoln in 1984.

In the 1990s, awards were a major focus of Shelter Day ceremonies held in late June or early July. Perhaps the most prestigious award was the Fred V. Heinkel Award for Excellence, which employees, as well as members of the wider community, may win. In 1995, Sue Jackson of Training won the honor for her widely-praised work against drug abuse. Awards available to nominated employees included claims department recognition of clerical and branch office employees, Shelter Life's supervisor and employees of the year, support staff employees of the year, and the Corporate Wellness Award. Notable in 1994 was the awarding of the Gustav J. Lehr Personal Service Award to all Shelter employees and agents "for their efforts at sandbagging and clean-up work during and after the 1993 floods on the Missouri and Mississippi Rivers."

Table 11.3 Total Agency Force, Selected Years (Year-end figures)

1980	1,218	1988	1,188
1982	1,318	1990	1,227
1984	1,249	1992	1,192
1986	1,158	1994 (Nov. 30)	1,252

Source: Marketing Department Reports to the Board of Directors

Table 11.4 Numbers of Agents by State, Selected Years

	August 31, 1981	December 31, 1985	December 31, 1989	December 31, 1993
AR	155	157	169	171
CO	42	38	52	57
IL	75	69	68	67
IN	51	44	58	56
IA	41	21	28	27
KS	88	85	83	82
KY	110	89	86	74
LA	49	48	66	58
MS	47	36	39	42
E. MO	159	152	163	162
W. MO	196	168	176	176
NE	52	48	53	50
OK	92	92	93	96
TN	82	72	78	83
Total	1,239	1,119	1,210	1,201
MO % of Total	29%	29%	28%	28%
MO & AR % of Total	41%	43%	42%	42%

Source: Marketing Department Reports to the board of directors

Stability of the agency force is the primary message of Tables 11.3 and 11.4. Although Shelter's management has tried various methods since the 1970s to increase the number of agents, including a salaried agents program still active in the mid-1990s, those efforts have not met their goals. With all of their experience in marketing coverages for 50 years, Shelter officials have not discovered any sure formula for identifying successful agents among a group of recruits, or of shepherding them to success in a community. Nor, of course, has any other company. What is certain is that Shelter will continue to sell its policies through exclusive agents, and will not embark on a campaign of agency-growth in which increased numbers are the only goal. Quality agents writing quality business will remain a hallmark of this company's marketing efforts.

Table 11.5 Total Commission and Bonus Paid to Shelter Insurance Agents, Selected Years

	Agents' Commission and Salary	Agents' Bonus	Total
1981	$22,482,485	$3,195,034	$25,677,519
1983	33,266,648	2,782,862	36,049,510
1985	31,331,033	3,182,821	34,513,854
1987	35,439,588	7,465,570	42,905,158
1989	39,876,473	8,036,246	47,912,719
1991	47,029,149	6,239,080	53,268,229
1993	54,862,650	9,044,260	63,906,910
1994	59,779,815	9,872,652	69,652,467

Source: Year-end Financial Statements, Underwriting Expenses, Shelter Mutual

Table 11.6 Average Income Per Agent (Commissions, Bonus, Salaries)

Year	Income
1980	$21,951
1983	37,333
1986	43,467
1989	52,201
1992	56,280
1993	60,829

Source: Marketing Department Reports to the board of directors

When Gus Lehr pointed with pride to employee compensation in 1985, he also praised the company's "excellent compensation package for career agents." In 1984, he pointed out, 50 agents earned over $100,000 in commissions alone, and "a generous bonus program will further enhance these earnings." When he became companies' president and CEO in 1981, compensation was a source of discontent among some agents. Other issues derived from the unsettling changes of 1979-1981. Executive Vice President Ray Jones has suggested that Shelter neglected agent concerns during the final, illness-plagued years of A. D. Sappington's leadership. Gus Lehr, in 1995, noted that the media ascribed unjustified importance to the agents' organization of 1981-1982 that expressed the discontent of a minority of primarily Missouri agents. What is important in the longer historical view is that there were grievances; and that Gus Lehr took decisive steps to hear and address issues, and to enhance agents' ability to succeed as representatives of the Shelter Insurance Companies.

Formed in February, 1981, as the National Association of MFA Insurance Agents — with retired agent Harold Remley, Sr. of Jefferson City as its chief spokesman and organizer — the agents' group immediately came to the attention of company officers. MFA President Eric Thompson learned that "some of our agents were getting together for the purpose of presenting demands" to the insurance company, and he assured Will L. Nelson on February 9 "that he had nothing to do with any such movement." In a letter dated February 11 — copies of which Howard Lang dispatched to MFA Mutual's directors on February 12 — Remley proposed to Missouri agents that "an association should be formed to represent the agents as a unified group in conferring with the company." In a second letter of March 4, Remley reported that "over 200" of the 365 Missouri agents in receipt of the first letter had responded, all but one favorably. Further, agents in five other states "have inquired about our objectives and how they could join with us." On March 20, 1981, the board meeting discussed the fledgling organization and, to quote President Howard Lang, the "unrelated agent questions [that] had precipitated this attempt." In another review of the situation on May 22, Lang reported to directors that neither he nor President Designate Gus Lehr "would meet with any person or persons as representatives of an association." Both the current and future president, however, were eager to discuss pressing issues with individual agents. As Lehr told the annual meeting on April 1, a company which sells through exclusive agents had a special responsibility to be "responsive to the needs of our agents."

His organization was not a labor union, Remley insisted, seeking to make demands of and negotiate with management. Instead, agents wanted to "make sure they have a medium in which they can meet and talk freely" with company officials. With agents ready to talk, and with Lang and Lehr more than willing to listen and respond, what would be the agenda for discussion?

Director Laurence Kullmann, who had informally surveyed agent opinion in Missouri, believed a central issue was agents' desire for a retirement plan such as employees had. Howard Lang recognized the corrosive effect of inflation as a cause of agent discontent, giving substance to the Remley group's statement "that the first item of business should be increased commissions." Clearly, for some Missouri agents, the impending separation of MFA and MFA Mutual was a threat: "we are being asked to commit time, energy . . . and money to help sell a new corporate identity and image." Also included in agents' concerns was a perception that the marketing department used heavy-handed, but unspecified tactics in its relations with agents. Whether the reference was to Home Office pressure to sell more, or more carefully, is unclear.

That newly-installed companies' President Gus Lehr quickly responded to these issues was one additional proof of his leadership. Indeed, mechanisms for company-agency interaction established in 1981 continued to function successfully in 1995. And older means of communication continued under Lehr, including fall agent meetings and the bi-monthly SHIELD magazine. Bruce Meentemeyer was the editor of SHIELD, in which beautiful color photography enhanced well-written articles. Maggie Wood prepared issues of CONTACT, the company's weekly employee newsletter. She published her 400th issue in April, 1987. By late November, 1981 Lehr reported to the board his experience in 55 agent meetings held that autumn, 14 state gatherings (two in Missouri) and 41 open, round-table discussions, characterized by:

Highlighting the fall meetings is a question-answer session. Up to his retirement, Gus Lehr joined Bob Maupin to answer questions from the audience. The meeting originated as a communication tool for agents, but soon was expanded to respond to both agents and employees.

a free exchange of ideas. . . . Agents asked all conceivable insurance questions, made hundreds of excellent suggestions, and left the meetings with a good feeling about the direction, the openness, and the leadership of our Companies.

The meetings, Bill Conboy of marketing confirmed, "had a positive effect on agents' morale."

Before November Lehr took even more decisive action. While A. D. Sappington had met, infrequently and unsuccessfully, with his President's Advisory Committee of Agents, Lehr formed the PACC — President's Agents' Communications Committee. First announced in May, 1981 at the Conference of Champions in Hawaii, the select group of top agents met in Columbia on July 7-8, in Little Rock on December 1-2, and in Denver on March 25-26, 1982. As Lehr commented in 1988: "The PACC works well. It is here to stay." Indeed it was. Presidents Jack Pettit and Bob Maupin have continued to interact with the PACC, consciously perpetuating a Lehr innovation that worked.

Gus Lehr's initial meeting with these representatives revealed without doubt "that commissions are the principal matter of concern to agents." In a letter of July 24, 1981, Lehr announced a 10% increase in total commissions paid by Shelter Mutual, amounting to an additional $2.4 million, and an increase

These six former agents-of-the-year were among the members of the 1982 PACC—Bill Bell, Frank Riekhof, David Jeffs, Tommy Hight, Mike Thompson, and Gerald Brandorff.

President Lehr answers a question.

Tennessee's Tommy Hight's intensity reveals the give-and-take tenor of the PACC meetings.

Dickie Cooper and Bob Riley

in Life Company commissions as well. The National Association of Shelter Insurance Agents continued to express views through an executive committee into 1982 before it faded away. But Harold Remley, Jr., Association president, while urging the election of an agent to Shelter's board of directors, clearly was impressed with President Lehr's success:

We, as agents, feel strongly that Gus Lehr must be the first person named to the Company Board of Directors. In his first six months as President, Gus has demonstrated the forward thinking progressive leadership that our companies need.

Tables 11.5 and 11.6 reveal how Lehr led the companies to a new era in agent compensation.

Table 11.7 Conference of Champions, 1981-1995

	Location	Number of Agents Attending	% of Agents Attending	Agent of the Year
1981	Honolulu	166	13.6	Tommy Hight TN
1982	London	204	16.6	Mike Thompson CO
1983	Munich	237	17.9	John Hosford KS
1984	Paris	201	15.1	Don Mosier KS
1985	Rome	150	12.0	Richard Leleux LA
1986	San Francisco	211	18.9	Larry Henderson, MO
1987	Interlacken	242	20.9	Chuck Wilson MO
1988	London	217	18.5	Ron Harmon MO
1989	Washington D.C.	145	12.2	Bob and Richard Cargiles, AR
1990	Vienna	160	13.2	Weldon Jones MO
1991	Honolulu	131	10.7	Roger Earnest AR
1992	Rome	157	13.5	Robert Roberts AR
1993	Portugal	109	9.1	Ken Joplin MO
1994	Amsterdam	202	16.8	Harvey Hales LA
1995	Geneva			Ron & Brad Wright, Reggie & Shane Ledford MO

Table 11.8 Millionaire Trip, 1981-1995

	Location	Sappington/President's Award & Chairman's Award (1989-)
1981	Caribbean Cruise	Buddy Anderson, MS
1982	Kauai	Buddy Anderson
1983	Barbados	Bill Gardo, MS
1984	St. Thomas	Bill Gardo
1985	Marco Island	Chuck Wilson, MO
1986	Maui	Frank Reikhof, MO
1987	Naples	Frank Reikhof
1988	St. Thomas	Bob and Richard Cargiles, AR
1989	Palm Springs	Bill Gardo Bob Riley, MO
1990	Boca Raton	Roger Summer, MO Ron Harmon, MO
1991	Naples	Bill Gardo Gerald Brandorff & Joe Methe, NE
1992	Turnburry Isle	Gary Smith, AR Bob and Richard Cargiles, AR
1993	Ft. Lauderdale	Bill Gardo Ron Harmon
1994	Palm Beach	Bill Gardo Bob and Richard Cargiles
1995	San Diego	Joe Yamen, IA

Shelter continued successful forms of agent recognition begun by Presidents Silvey and Sappington. Tables 11.7 and 11.8 summarize in numbers and words what were in fact memorable personal and collective experiences: the Conferences of Champions and Millionaire Trips. Shelter gave 30 awards to agents and DSMs at the 1994 Conference in Amsterdam, Holland, the top one being Agent of the Year. Given during the Millionaire Trip each year, the top award for life-insurance production was known for years as the A. D. Sappington Memorial Award. This honor gained the name President's Award in 1995. Also given on the Millionaire Trip was the Chairman's Award, which recognized agencies exhibiting overall excellence. Only past Agents of the Year are eligible for the Chairman's Award, and

Bill Gardo's devotion to life insurance has earned him six A. D. Sappington Awards as top life producer—the first in 1983, the most recent in 1994.

to receive it an agent must have qualified for both incentive trips that year. Bob Riley of Paris, Missouri won the first Chairman's Award in 1989.

Agents like Riley represent the best, by whatever measure, of Shelter's agency force. To select a few members as examples of any group is difficult, for the exercise inevitably leaves aside many worthies. But the benefits of looking at the few to learn about the many are real. What follows is an attempt to define key traits of successful Shelter agents during the company's first 50 years.

Shelter's best agents are careful — even "tough" — underwriters. Frank Reikhof of Higginsville was among the best "front-line underwriters," filtering out bad risks and seeking out quality business. The result: an average loss ratio through the 1970s of better than 40%. Agent Don Mosier of Salina had previous experience as a DSM and Colorado State Sales Manager, which may have made him sensitive to what the marketing department's monthly agent reports revealed. In the fall of 1983, back in his own Kansas agency, one of Don's reports suggested an accident frequency problem which threatened his good loss ratio. "I saw something bad happening," he recalled, "so I requested a risk review of my auto business. It wasn't a popular move, but by this June [1984], my loss ratio was back down in the 30s." Harvey Hales, 1994

At the 1980 Millionaire Trip on Paradise Island, John Ross, Bethany, Missouri and Bob Riley, Paris.

Agent of the Year, hailed from Louisiana, "the third most litigious state in the country — we sue a lot down here." So Hales concentrated on lines other than auto. Agents, he advised, had to understand that agency profitability in the long run came not from volume sales that included poor risks along with good ones. "Profit is . . . determined by the quality and character of policyholders."

Top agents know the products they sell and those of competitors. They read, study, ask questions of Home Office personnel, take notes at agents' meetings. They reflect on their agency experience and learn from it. And they study their territory. Larry Henderson's sales territory in central Missouri included the northern edge of the Lake of the Ozarks, which filled rapidly with weekend vacationers and retired persons who differed in income and insurance needs from native residents. On the lookout for an agency of his own while serving as a Kansas DSM, Henderson "discovered that lake areas had wonderful demographics. I studied any marketing reports that I could get my hands on — the telephone company has the best, you know." By the mid-1980s, Larry had built a good business in an area booming with second home purchasers.

Between 1980, when he earned the Rookie of the Year Award, and 1984, when he won the Sappington Award for life sales, Columbia's Chuck Wilson shifted his emphasis from auto to life sales. Relatively unfamiliar with life policies at first and therefore somewhat lacking in confidence while talking with clients, Chuck found intensive study to be the answer. "I'm comfortable going into presentations because I've learned more about the product and about the art of selling it," Wilson said in 1985. Frank Reikhof spent eight to ten hours preparing for some life insurance presentations, mastering the policy features so that he could anticipate the prospect's questions.

The agent who becomes a role-model to others establishes a "full-line business"; he develops a reputation as "a single agent who can handle all your needs." The words are those of champion life salesman Bill Gardo of Jackson. Agents, like other people, tend to follow the path of least resistance, which means selling auto and property lines. Successful life sales were more difficult, Bill found, because the agent had to educate the client about the features and benefits of policies as well as the need for life protection. But Gardo believed that to fully serve his clients, a Shelter agent had to pursue life insurance prospects as vigorously as those wishing other lines. As a new agent in 1981, Steve Harp of Springdale earned both the Conference trip to London and the Millionaire Trip to Hawaii. The full-circle sales concept motivated his efforts from the start. And it has long motivated Bob Riley:

After receiving his 40-Year Service Award, Richard Kratz, and wife Dorothy, visit with 1994 retiree from Underwriting, Jim Wise and his wife Vivian.

Curtis and Brenda Watts, Jackson, Mississippi accept the 1979 Agent of the Year Award from President Lang.

Bob Maupin arrived at Shelter in 1981 as vice president and general counsel.

*We are fortunate that we are a multi-line agency. We do have a rather large casualty agency. We intend to make sure that every one of our casualty clients has the opportunity to be life and health clients also. We strive for the full-circle selling concept. . . . a multi-line agency has built in prospects.*Riley won Shelter's Full-Circle Sales Award in 1970 and 1971.

There is no need to illustrate another trait evident in award-winning agents: they are hard workers. But more than that, they are goal-setters. Goals give hard work direction and purpose. Starting a scratch agency in Jackson in 1974, Curtis Watts rose rapidly to company-wide prominence in the decade that followed. Surprised to become Agent-of-the-Year Second Runner-up in 1977, Curtis saw that "first place was only two steps away, so I went for it." First Runner-up in 1978, he won Shelter's Agent of the Year Award the following year. Striving for the 1980 award, Frank Reikhof learned what levels of sales in casualty and life previous contenders had achieved, and then determined to exceed them — and he did.

Agents who became a part of Shelter's recorded history were willing to invest in their businesses, in new technologies as well as in traditional sales support. Richard Kratz, Shelter agent since 1954 in Falls City, was one of his community's first insurance agents to advertise on radio and in the newspaper. Remaining competitive in 1988, Kratz used a personal computer to provide premium quotes to customers and to keep track of prospects. "If you don't have a computer," Kratz concluded, "you'll get left in the dust." Don Mosier, Richard Harp of Berryville and Bob Riley were among the pioneering agents who went on-line with the Home Office long before Shelter had heard of the HUON Solution. Veteran St. Charles agent Earl Doerrie poured $1,500 annually into various forms of advertising in 1962. As Bob Riley advised: "A good agency should always do some consistent advertising."

facing page: New agent Ronald McConnel, Greenfield, Missouri and his wife, Mary, visited the Home Office on their 1954 honeymoon. McConnell remains today as the only charter agent still active. He became an agent in October 1946, so matches company anniversaries year by year.

Finally, good agents like Tommy Hight of Columbia, Tennessee realize that they are in "the people business," only one aspect of which is insurance. Insurance provides help in time of need. Serving people includes an active community role, and many Shelter agents share such a role with Tommy. Long-time Greenfield agent Ronnie McConnell was a leader in his church, the local Chamber of

David Mattson, vice president of Shelter Life since 1987.

Don Light, vice president of Claims since 1987.

Robert Magnuson, vice president of Internal Auditing since 1988.

Commerce, and various fraternal organizations. A busy Harvey Hales in Monroe enjoyed his involvements in the Chamber of Commerce, the United Way, Salvation Army, Arthritis Foundation, Ronald McDonald House, and Crime Stoppers. His approach was not for everyone, Hales admitted, but "to those bent in the direction of politics or community service, I say get in there and get involved and make a difference." Agents who seek civic involvement must find satisfaction beyond its indirect rewards for their businesses, Bob Riley advised. "Join because you want to share some of your time with others and your community."

The final pages of this chapter turn to Shelter's officers since 1981. As the company's business became larger and its operations more complex, the number of vice presidents and other officers also grew.

Robert T. (Terry) Cox, vice president and general counsel since 1986.

Bob Minnick, vice president and treasurer since 1990.

McConnell is still winning awards after more than 49 years as an agent. Here, at the 1995 Conference of Champion in Geneva, Switzerland, he accepts the Life Persistency Award from President Maupin.

Bob Reid, vice president of Underwriting since 1995.

Max Dills, vice president of Actuarial since 1987.

Paul Burris, vice president for Shelter Financial Services since 1990.

Lanny Barton, vice president of Communications since 1992.

Table 11.9 Shelter's Officers, 1981-1995

Executive and Administrative Vice Presidents:
Jack L. Pettit, Executive Vice President 1981-1984
Robert W. Maupin, Executive Vice President 1986-1987
James A. Offutt, Executive Vice President 1987-1995
John W. Lenox, Executive Vice President 1987-1995
Raymond E. Jones, Vice President for Administration 1982-1994; Executive Vice President 1994-1995; Secretary of Board 1986-1995
Vice President and Treasurer:
George Kent, 1978 -1990
Bob Minnick, 1990-1995
Vice President Underwriting:
Charles J. Dysart, 1981-1995 (retired as Senior Vice President)
Robert W. Reid, 1995
Vice President Marketing:
William H. Conboy, 1964-1982; also Vice President Industry Affairs, 1982-1984
Mark E. Zimmer, 1982-1995
Vice President Claims:
James L. McTurnan, 1981-1982
John W. Lenox, 1982-1987
Donald E. Light, 1987-1995
Vice President and General Counsel:
Robert W. Maupin, 1981-1986
Robert T. (Terry) Cox, 1986-1995
Vice President Finance:
J. Donald Duello, 1978-1995; Secretary of the Board, 1978-1986; Managing Director Shelter Reinsurance Company, 1986-1995
Vice President Actuarial:
James A. Offutt, 1972-1987
Max T. Dills, 1987-1995
Vice President Communications:
Jean Madden, 1971-1992
Lanny Barton, 1992-1995
Vice President General Services:
Vernon L. Jennings, 1987-1993
Donald Northway, 1993-1995
Vice President Personnel/Human Resources:
Victor (Vic) A. G. Ohman, 1988-89
Robert W. Reid, 1989-1995
Ken Nivens, 1995
Vice President Information Services:
Don Goodwin, 1970-1992 (retired as Senior Vice President)
Don McCubbin, 1992-1995
Vice President and General Manager, Life Company:
William Toler, 1959-1983
David Mattson, 1987-1995
Vice President and General Manager, Shelter Financial Services:
Carroll Raper, 1979-1990
Paul Burris, 1990-1995
Vice President Auditing
Robert W. Magnuson, 1988-1995

Don McCubbin, vice president of Information Services since 1992.

What generalizations arise from a list this long? One obvious development is the emergence of departments and functions missing from earlier Shelter Insurance organizational charts. The multiplication had several causes: the rise of technology created Information Services, for example, and the growth of new companies like Shelter Financial Services called for officers to manage them. In addition, Gus Lehr helped the company conform to general business practice by raising some department heads to officer status. Examples were the leaders of Personnel/Human Resources and General Services. On the other hand, the core operational departments in the 1990s remained the same as they had always been: Underwriting, Claims, and Marketing. The officer list suggests other thoughts. As

Ken Nivens, vice president of Human Resources since 1995.

Donald Northway, vice president of General Services since 1993.

Charles Dysart retired in 1995 as senior vice president after leading Underwriting since 1981.

was true before 1981, the majority of Shelter's officers had small-town Missouri roots — many in traditionally strong territory for the Missouri Farmers Association. Bob Maupin: Carrollton; Ray Jones and George Kent: Chillicothe; Jim Offutt: Mexico; John Lenox: Rolla; Don Light: Mansfield; Bob Reid: Clinton — these are a few examples. While the ties to MFA naturally weakened with time, they did not disappear. Bob Maupin spent half of his career with the farm co-op, and Ray Jones came from a strong MFA family. His parents met while working at MFA's Producers Creamery Company in Chillicothe. Of the officers listed, only seven originated outside Missouri, including Gus Lehr. Several, like Jack Pettit and Terry Cox, moved to Missouri at a young age and attended high school there.

facing page: Vice President and Treasurer George Kent and longtime secretary Mary Jones in 1978.

As for educational background, several trends emerge. With very few exceptions — J. M. Silvey is the outstanding example — Shelter's officers even in the earliest MFA Mutual days were college-educated, and a good proportion had law degrees. Nearly all of the most recent generation of Shelter's officers received college degrees at three institutions: the University of Missouri-Columbia's undergraduate colleges; that university's School of Law; and Central Missouri State

Kent with members of the Accounting Department review the 1977 annual report. Ralph Rohrer, left, has retired, but the others continue in various positions with Shelter — Ron Allen, Steve Boyd, Terry Pauley, and Gary Ford.

Don Duello, vice president of Finance in May, 1980.

University at Warrensburg. And they studied business and law. For example, Don Light and Terry Cox held degrees from MU's Law School; Ray Jones, John Lenox, and Bob Reid earned business degrees from CMSU; and Don Duello and Jim Offutt studied business at Missouri University. Jean Madden earned an M.A. in education at MU. After college, a few Shelter officers briefly pursued careers in education, as Madden taught college English and Lenox taught and coached in high school. Sixteen Shelter officers obtained their first full-time job with the company in the three central departments: Claims (2), Underwriting (10), and Marketing (4). While several in the last category began as agents or DSMs — Ray Jones, John Lenox, and Mark Zimmer — most future officers have spent their careers in the Home Office. And while Jean Madden and Bob Maupin were exceptions, having been brought into the company as vice presidents from other organizations in Columbia, most officers in 1995 had spent their entire careers with Shelter. Promotions came from within the company's ranks.

Those who consider Shelter's history after one-half century might wonder what the company's experience during the next 50 years will be. What, for example, will be said of in 2045 of officers, employees, or agents? The final chapter of this book will attempt some predictions.

Virginia Etheridge, longtime executive secretary to Presidents Sappington and Lehr.

Mark Zimmer succeeded Bill Conboy as vice president of Marketing, to become only the second person to hold that office since the 1964 change in management. He moved up from his post as Tennessee state sales manager, and received the 1982 William H. Conboy Award for excellence in sales management.

facing page: Bob Riley has established a record matched by few, but it was John Buckman who first introduced the company name to Paris, Missouri in the late 1940s.

The East Missouri state office in the St. Louis metro area.

chapter 12

Our Widening Ties 1981-1995

As this history of the Shelter Insurance Companies draws to a close, it will focus on Shelter's roles in industry affairs, government, and community service, and will look forward to what observers of Shelter can expect in its future.

In November, 1983, President Gus Lehr wrote to officers and other managers. "In this troubled time in the insurance industry," he argued that it was more important than ever that they serve not only their company, but also the wider industry. And Lehr urged continued involvement in civic affairs, too. By "sharing your knowledge, skill and experience," Shelter Insurance would continue to strengthen the proud industry of which it was a part, "a free market economy," and healthy community institutions.

Earlier chapters have made clear what President Lehr knew: that Shelter personnel had, since the 1940s, been involved in the work of the industry. And, Lehr followed his own advice. As a lobbyist, he represented the interests of the NAII, as well as Shelter's, before legislators and regulators. His testimony on the independent contractor issue before a subcommittee of the House Committee on Ways and Means in March, 1982 is an example. After Gus Lehr retired as companies' CEO, the 1993 Annual Meeting lauded his industry service in a resolution. Lehr was a member of the Legislative Committee and chairman of the Insurance Law Committee of the Missouri Bar. He chaired the directing bodies of both the Missouri Fair Plan and the Missouri Guaranty Association. He served as state vice president of the American Life Insurance Association, and as the state legislative chairman of the Health Insurance Association of America. And he contributed his expertise and energy as a member of the Association of Life Insurance Council, a member of the Legislative and Steering Committees of NAMIC (National Association of Mutual Insurance Companies), and as a member of the board of governors of NAII. Gus Lehr had set a good example.

As an organization, as well as through its people, Shelter contributed to a stronger industry. In 1990, when NAMIC established an exhibit in its new Home Office to honor past presidents, Shelter made a contribution on behalf of Howard Lang, one of those presidents. As required by law, through its membership in the Missouri Guaranty Association, Shelter had paid out more than $700,000 in the first five months of 1986 to meet the policyholder obligations of six insurance companies that had become insolvent.

Through its NAII membership, Shelter contributed to several industry efforts. In the late 1980s, the quality of "after market parts" — replacement parts for automobiles — became an issue. Two concerns could be met by an independent parts-testing organization: that replacement parts met the standards of auto manufacturers; and that those firms themselves did not establish a monopoly of

Home Office employees stood at curbside to catch a glimpse of President Ronald Reagan during a 1987 visit to Columbia.

The transformation of the corporate logo has been gradual through the years, from the first stand-alone logo to the present Shelter shield. Some changes were subtle, such as the adding of a second outline in 1956, or changing "insured" to "insurance." When the separation from the farmers' association came about, a new design was called for, and was executed in 1980 by George Tenne and Mike Windler of D'Arcy, MacManus & Masius, the companies' advertising agency at the time. To more clearly identify the company name, the wording in the shield was changed in 1992. Countryside is now Shelter General.

replacement parts. Insurance companies which paid for auto repairs had a vital interest in both questions. In 1988, Shelter contributed $60,000 to support the work of the Certified Automotive Parts Association, which NAII helped to create. In 1987, Shelter's directors approved a $15,000 contribution to the Insurance Institute for Highway Safety to help pay the expenses for a series of public service announcements. When the Institute, which received major support from NAII, built a vehicle-safety research facility in Virginia, Shelter paid over $16,000 of the construction costs during the period 1991-1993.

While President Lehr retained an active interest in state and national government as it affected the insurance industry, after 1981 General Counsels Bob Maupin and Terry Cox took primary responsibility for tracking legislation. They received assistance from Mike McMillen, Shelter's public affairs director. As allowed by law, Shelter maintained two political action committees during this era, one to which the company contributed funds, the other to which officers could subscribe. Annually, Shelter hosted a dinner for members of the Missouri Senate. Occasionally, it arranged luncheons or receptions for members of the Missouri congressional delegation, such as Democratic Representative Harold Volkmer and Republican Senator Christopher Bond. As a large taxpayer, Shelter Insurance helped to support the functions of local, state, and federal governments. From 1981 through 1994, Shelter Mutual paid states $89.5 million in premium taxes.

That a conservative, pro-business Congress and president controlled the federal government during most of the 1980s did not guarantee that the insurance industry was safe from legislation it opposed. Nor did the industry's preference for state over federal regulation mean that all state laws received warm acceptance. In 1983, Bob Maupin warned the board of directors of current congressional schemes for taxing insurance companies. In May, 1985, Gus Lehr and Maupin, while in Washington to attend NAII meetings, contacted Missouri's members of Congress about "the taxation of [the] property and casualty insurance industry, and the President's [Ronald Reagan] legislative proposals as they relate to taxation of fringe benefits." The critical issue of the taxable status of independent contractors did receive a satisfactory resolution in 1982. Congress extended indefinitely an earlier limited moratorium which prohibited the Treasury Department's tax agency "from issuing regulations and rulings concerning employment taxes" for most independent contractors, including insurance agents. Maupin termed the decision by Congress "a major victory for the retention of independent contractor status for the company's agents."

Often, in the 1980s and 1990s, the general counsels' reports to the directors reflected a slowing of the impulse to regulate that had been more intense in the late 1960s and 1970s. Bob Maupin commented in 1983: "there has been very little legislation which has an adverse effect on the insurance business on the state level." And in 1986: "no significant legislation has been passed in any state which would affect Shelter's current operations." Satisfying results were not uniformly the case, however. Kentucky legislation required that companies selling health insurance "provide a policy for long-term health care"; a second Kentucky law ordered "rate decreases on auto comprehensive coverage for the installation of anti-theft devices"; and a Colorado measure mandated "90-day notices of rate increases." These illustrate laws which concerned Shelter officials.

But the biggest scare came from California in 1988. Although Shelter did not do business in that state, an initiative — Proposition 103 — passed by California voters that November, threatened to begin a trend that other states might join. Lowell R. Beck, president of NAII, saw the initiative's potential to "seriously

Claims and Information Services personnel scurry to deliver a branch claims office in a box to a catastrophe site. The use of computer technology has allowed a complete information system to be set up in nearly any remote site to help with processing claims resulting from major storms.

cripple, if not destroy, the private insurance industry." Among other provisions, Prop 103 allowed insurance companies to impose rate increases only if seriously threatened by insolvency, and forced a 20% rollback in rates. Through a substantial contribution, Shelter joined the efforts of NAII and other groups to sway California voters to defeat the measure. Following its passage, the California Supreme Court invalidated some of the new law's provisions as unconstitutional, but upheld others. While many consumers did experience understandable frustration with rising insurance rates, along with the general increase in the cost of living, measures like Proposition 103 did not take into account the rising costs of doing business that insurers faced. As Shelter's experience over a half-century of time demonstrates, even the soundest, most responsibly-run casualty and property insurance companies may not make a profit on their insurance operations. Although California's Proposition 103 raised a scare among insurers, rate rollback measures put to popular vote did not spread to Shelter's sales territory.

Since 1981, Shelter Insurance has used the Shelter Foundation as a vehicle for community betterment. Inaugurated with the transfer of nearly $400,000 from the MFA Foundation when Shelter Insurance came into being, the Foundation grew through regular contributions from the companies. By February, 1987, the Foundation had awarded $414,488 in gifts. Its assets on June 30, 1991 totaled $1,575,225. The companies' contributions to it in 1995 totaled $240,000.

This Owensboro, Kentucky branch claims office is indicative of the quality presence the companies have established throughout the territory.

Recipients of Foundation gifts included winners of the Fred V. Heinkel Award for Excellence and the William H. Lang Award, the latter earmarked for an outstanding vocational student at the Missouri School for the Deaf in Fulton. Foundation grants went to public-safety and law-enforcement agencies: the Missouri Highway Patrol Museum and the Missouri Fire Training Institute. Educational institutions received gifts, including Boy's Town of Missouri, the United Negro College Fund, and the Woodhaven Learning Center in Columbia. The Cancer Research Center, also in Columbia, and Lake Ozark General Hospital were among the medical recipients of Shelter Foundation monies. Three building programs received assistance: those of the Salvation Army in Columbia, the Missouri Symphony Society's renovation of the old Missouri Theater building, and the Arrow Rock Lyceum Theater.

As a company rather than through the Foundation, Shelter Insurance continued as one of the strongest supporters of the Columbia Area United Way campaign. Its corporate donation in 1993 was $19,000, for example. Three years earlier Jim Offutt had chaired the community's fund-drive. Shelter contributed to local United Way campaigns in other communities where it based employees. In 1985, the company's United Way gift, plus the $65,000 contribution of Home Office employees, constituted 10% percent of Columbia's United Way funding.

To honor the founders of the West Junior/Shelter partnership, the Lehr-Battle Achievement Award was established. The award is named for Chairman Gus Lehr and principal emeritus Muriel Battle.

Numerous other company and employee community service contributions marked the years 1981 and after. Employees served on boards and committees, raised money for worthy causes, and helped to save lives through contributions to regular Red Cross blood drives in the Home Office. In 1991, the Columbia Chamber of Commerce named Communications Vice President Jean Madden its Outstanding Citizen. Among his service activities Madden had been chairman of the Children's Miracle Network Telethon. During his years with Shelter Bob Maupin had been a commissioner of the Columbia Land Clearance Authority, a board member of the Chamber of Commerce, and a member of the Boone County Board of Jail Visitors.

Since 1981, Shelter, through its foundation, committed to four new programs that deserve mention. One is available to students at the University of Missouri School of Law. It is the Gustav J. Lehr Scholarship Program, established in 1992.

Begun in 1984, the Shelter Insurance Foundation Scholarship Program offered a partnership between the Foundation and participating agents. Agents who joined did so enthusiastically. In its early years, the program made available a $750 college scholarship to one graduating high school senior in an agent's community, with the agent contributing $250 and the Foundation $500. Given without regard to race, religion, national origin, sex, or employee or policyholder status with Shelter, the amount awarded increased to $1,000 in 1989 (agent's share $300). In the spring of 1985, 127 agents took part — about 10% of the agency force — which meant a total expenditure of over $95,000. The award winners attended 72 institutions in 19 states the following fall. In 1990, 233 agents presented $1,000 scholarships.

The Foundation also awarded scholarships to top students in Columbia's West Junior High School, to be used when they began their college work. But that was

Through its Partners In Education relationship with West Junior High School, the companies present scholarships and other awards each year. Company officials join student and staff winners after the 1994 awards assembly.

Corporate Christmas cards are designed each year by art students at West Junior. Here, the 1993 winning artists receive their artwork originals framed. With the students are Bob Maupin and Principal Magie Roberts.

West Junior choral groups entertain guests at Shelter's annual meeting each April.

Shelter sponsored the yearlong statewide tour of this group, the University of Missouri Sesquicentennial Singers in 1989.

only one aspect of a rich partnership that developed, after its beginnings in 1984, between Shelter and West Junior. Cooperation and sharing continued on many levels. West's teachers and students made their presence felt at the Home Office, as musical groups performed during the Christmas tree lighting in December and the annual meeting each April; as art displays brightened the cafeteria; and as faculty and students shadowed Shelter employees on their jobs. Shelter people have made recreational use of West's gymnasium, learned woodworking and other shop skills from industrial arts teachers, and assisted with the celebration of Multi-Cultural Week. Involving both parties and parents, too, was the drug-education program called REACH: Recognizing Everyone and Changing Habits. In 1988, a national Partners in Education seminar in Washington, D.C. recognized the drug education program and other wellness projects implemented by Shelter and West Junior High.

By joining the NAIA's (National Association of Intercollegiate Athletics) Patron Program in 1988, Shelter chose to support a different group of students. As Jean Madden put it: "The NAIA is the last bastion of true student athletics." Students in under-funded athletic programs in smaller colleges used corporate contributions provided through the Patron Program to meet expenses in post-season tournament play. Shelter's support of the NAIA program grew to a contribution of nearly one-half million dollars by 1993-1994. Schools in NAIA districts in ten of Shelter's 13 operating states benefit from the company's participation in this program. Beginning in 1995, Shelter contributed a $1,000 scholarship to the general scholarship fund of an institution in the name of an outstanding student athlete, one in each participating state.

We can safely predict that, in the year 2045, there will be both historians and the Shelter Insurance Companies. When Shelter's historian of that time sits at the computer to pick up the company's story where this book leaves it, with what will that person begin to work? Certainly there will exist an abundance of data, and it will be well-organized on information retrieval systems whose complexity and capacity will dwarf those of the 1990s. Much of this information, including artifacts such as the MFA Mutual fans given out by agents in the 1950s and advertising signs from the early days, will be located in the Shelter Corporate Archive and Museum, by that time over 50 years old and perhaps housed in its own building near Shelter Gardens.

The historian of 2045 will have some fundamental concepts with which to begin. Given that organizations do not quickly change their character, it is not a difficult task to predict the kind of a company that those who celebrate Shelter's first century will know. Shelter will remain a mutual insurance company. The fact that all other companies in the Shelter Group are stock companies has not changed the essential mutual nature of Shelter Insurance. The subsidiaries are wholly owned by the mutual company that is the head of the family. Shelter has proudly retained its identity as a mutual company through the first half-century. And, while the reason for

R. J. and Jo Betty Rosier, next to clock, presented this grandfather clock to the companies in appreciation for Mr. Rosier's many years of association with the board of directors. Flanking them are three who have served as president of the companies, Howard Lang, Gus Lehr, and Bob Maupin. The clock sits in the board room, chiming regular reminders of the man who spent so many years in that same room.

A second Christmas tradition has been added to the lighting of the Shelter Christmas tree in the fountain. Employees enjoy a Christmas Concert by the Missouri Pops Orchestra in the historic Missouri Theatre each December.

An informal recreational program has fielded teams in many sports throughout the years. This 1955 team won second place in the Columbia Looper League.

This team duplicated the 1958 feat as runner-up in the 1967 Looper League tournament.

The interdepartmental basketball champs of 1976.

During the mid-1960s a series of company-agent bowling tournaments brought teams from throughout the operating states to compete for trophies, prize money, and bragging rights.

Golf has become the sport of choice in recent years, with several tournaments each year. The A. D. Sappington Memorial Golf Tournament is an opportunity for agents and employees to play together.

forming a mutual company in 1945 was the similarity of purpose and compatibility of a farm cooperative and a mutual insurance company, as a mutual company Shelter retains advantages in the 1990s. Among them is the fact that no one who works at Shelter or leads the company has an ownership interest in it. The Shelter companies are owned by their policyholders, as they will be in 2045.

Shelter's growth to financial strength will continue. When the year 1995 ends, Shelter Mutual's surplus will be approximately one-half billion dollars. If it has taken 50 years to reach that milestone, it will take less than 25 to attain one billion in surplus. Shelter will continue to be primarily a casualty and property company, with strength in other lines, including life insurance, to maintain the multiple-line concept for the company and its agents. Shelter will grow in the first half of the 21st century and will remain an important regional company, but it will remain a relatively small company compared to the industry giants. But from J. M. Silvey's, Fred Heinkel's, and A. D. Sappington's earliest days as insurance executives, that was the company's goal. Not to be the biggest, but instead "the best of all the rest," as an early slogan put it. Nor will Shelter in the future be able to claim that it has the lowest rates. It has never claimed that, but instead stressed competitive rates plus the best in personal service, from the agent who sells the policy to the claims representative who signs the check after a loss. These fundamentals will remain, and form a part of the history written in 2045.

Those who watch Shelter's development in the next 50 years should not be surprised if geographical expansion occurs. If it does, as of 1996 it will be the first growth in operating territory in 25 years. As it has done since 1971, Shelter Insurance will continue to expand its operations in 13 states. If the companies do grow into new sales territory, their leadership will do so only with careful study. Some of the geographical expansion of the late 1950s, the 1960s, and the early 1970s occurred without that careful preparation, and became a financial drain on the companies. The plans once made to operate in most of the United States were unrealistic and

The success of the many recreational programs is due in large part to Tee Dozier, who has volunteered as coordinator for most of the events for many years.

next two photos: What does an insurance company do with its salvage? In this 1986 case, it donated this 1957 fire truck to the Polk County Fire Protection District to be used as a backup unit. Agent Wes Campell has an interest in good fire protection, so arranged for members of his county's fire department to come to Columbia to accept the truck from company officials.

HOLTS SUMMIT

Some photos simply demand to be published. This one of John Baumgartner, one of the company's first sales managers, is one such photo. At Disneyland during the 1976 Conference of Champions, Johnny B. couldn't resist the urge to pose with one of the seven dwarfs. After retiring, Johnny B. kept in close touch with the company, and has been honored with a golf tournament bearing his name. He died August 5, 1994, but the legacy of Johnny B. lives in this, his favorite photo. He was a very short man with a very tall agenda for success for the agents under his management.

The American Cancer Society's Jail and Bail campaign of 1994 received some special help from Home Office folks, Bruce Meentemeyer, Mark Zimmer, and Larry Fuller. The authentic British taxi belongs to Zimmer.

The Great Flood of 1993 brought out the community spirit at Shelter, as the Home Office staff worked more than 420 hours of sandbagging and cleanup for flood victims. The flood figured in 1994 Shelter Day awards, as Boone County Fire Chief Steve Paulsell received the Heinkel Award for coordinating the massive emergency effort. Employees received as a group the Lehr Award for their efforts.

THE GUSTAV J. LEHR
SERVICE AWARD
Presented to
Shelter Insurance
Employees and Agents
for their remarkable relief effort before, during
and after the 1993 floods – those who served
at the flood site and those who maintained
Shelter's office operations.
Presented
SHELTER DAY
1994

NSTER CO

unnecessary to the growth that has made Shelter a billion dollar business.

Shelter will continue to market insurance coverages through exclusive agents. A top company priority will continue to be creating the best conditions for agent success: attractive policies that sell; generous commissions, bonuses, and incentives; effective training, advertising, claims, and other support systems.

True to its past also, Shelter will treat employees fairly and generously. If salaries and wages were low when the insurance company was tied to MFA, they have not been so since the break with the farm cooperative. Two facts say much about employer-employee relations at Shelter: the company has never laid off an employee in 50 years. And over 60% percent of all employees in 1995 have been with the company for ten years or more. How many American businesses can say that? If, even with growth, the company remains small, the family feeling that grows out of employee workplace interaction and good employer- employee relations will continue.

That empty lot from 1954 has become a complex of offices, parking lots, warehouses, and acres of beautiful landscaping which have made the Shelter Insurance Home Office a landmark at 1817 West Broadway in Columbia, Missouri.

True to its roots also, Shelter Insurance will remain politically active, a leader, especially within Missouri, in representing insurers' interests and a general pro-business, free-market viewpoint. And on issues of special importance, such as the independent-contractor controversy with the Internal Revenue Service, Shelter's voice will be heard in Washington. It is noteworthy that five of Shelter's seven presidents have been lawyers. Perhaps this trait, too, grew out of the company's early roots in MFA, where both William Hirth (who studied law) and Fred Heinkel (who did not) were powers to be reckoned with in national farm politics and in Missouri's political life. Probably the field of law will not provide all the company's top leaders in the second 50 years; but if it does, no one should be surprised.

Shelter's civic consciousness will not diminish in the future. From J. M. Silvey's days to the present, Shelter has been an active "good corporate citizen" in the home city and beyond, in support of education, medicine, culture, and social service. Its contribution to community betterment will continue to include aesthetics, as the grounds and buildings in Columbia and at state offices and many branch offices will attest.

The historian of the mid-21st century will have a longer story to tell than this one is, but hardly a more interesting one, whatever happens in the decades to come. If this account assists that historian, as well as some Shelter employees, agents, policyholders, and others to understand the historical evolution of the Shelter Insurance Companies from 1945 to 1995, its purpose will have been met.

left: Among winners of the Heinkel Award for excellence in a wide variety of areas was Mikhail Gorbachev for his work in ending the Cold War while leader of the Soviet Union. The presentation was made during Gorbachev's speech at the Churchill Memorial in Fulton, Missouri. Here he is shown thanking the audience in front of portions of the Berlin Wall which have become a sculpture at the memorial.

This panel emphasizes the corporate slogan at a 1970 agents' meeting.

index

T

U

V

W

This 1970s television commercial featured a young actor who became a popular star in the TV series, CHEERS. Ted Danson portrays a fast-talking car salesman in the spot.

notes